T0271526

NOW
WHAT?

CAROL VORDERMAN

NOW WHAT?

On a **Mission** to **Fix** Broken **Britain**

HEADLINE

First published in 2024 by HEADLINE PUBLISHING GROUP

1

Cataloguing in Publication Data is available from the British Library

Hardback ISBN 978 1 0354 2124 4

Typeset in Dante by CC Book Production

Printed and bound in Great Britain by Clays Ltd, Elcograf S.p.A.

Headline's policy is to use papers that are natural, renewable and recyclable products and
made from wood grown in sustainable forests. The logging and manufacturing processes
are expected to conform to the environmental regulations of the country of origin.

HEADLINE PUBLISHING GROUP
An Hachette UK Company
Carmelite House
50 Victoria Embankment
London EC4Y 0DZ

www.headline.co.uk
www.hachette.co.uk

For everyone who believes in a brighter future . . .
let's get the party started!

'It's easier to fool people than to convince them that they have been fooled.'

– Attributed to Mark Twain

CONTENTS

PREFACE

It's happened. It's done.

The general election has given us both a new Labour government with a landslide victory and a loud farewell to the Tories, and what a moment in history it was.

I don't know about you, but for days after the general election I was feeling an exhaustion which went deep into my bones. I think the whole country might have been suffering from some form of collective trauma after 14 years of Tories. Why?

Well, to repurpose a phrase from Winston Churchill, to describe this time: 'Never in the field of political conflict, has so much damage been done to so many, by so few.'

But now, together, we have repaid the Conservative government handsomely in the ballot box and it's time to smile and briefly breathe out. Utterly spent with their lies and corruption, completely in contempt of how they've treated us all, we voted to eviscerate them and the Tories were all but wiped out. They've gone off to lick their wounds with the lowest number of parliamentary seats in their history, losing 244 MPs since 2019, ending up with just 121, a comparative murky shadow of their former selves. And I'm proud to have been an active part of a movement giving tactical voting advice to millions, which nudged many seats towards the final result.

Back to the day itself: 4 July 2024, which may go down in our modern history as our new Independence Day.

Here are some raw numbers which show the change since 2019:

Party	Number of seats	Percentage of votes
Labour	412 seats (up 209)	33.7
Conservatives	121 seats (down 244)	23.7
Liberal Democrats	72 seats (up 61)	12.2
Scottish National Party	9 seats (down 39)	2.5
Sinn Fein	7 seats (no change)	0.7
Independents	6 seats (up 6)	2.0
Reform UK	5 seats (up 5)	14.3
DUP	5 seats (down 3)	0.6
Green	4 seats (up 3)	6.7
Plaid Cymru	4 seats (no change)	0.7
Others	5 seats (up 2)	2.9

When the exit poll was released just after 10pm on the night of the election, a Labour victory was more or less expected, but nevertheless it was still strange to see the evidence there in red and blue. The relief was palpable. As the results came in, the 'big beasts', including Jacob Rees-Mogg, Grant Shapps and Liz Truss (previously with a colossal majority of 26,195 in 2019), lost their previously 'safe seats' and were sent packing with tactical voting and a spirit of 'we've had enough'.

The results also, rightly, kicked off various discussions, about our voting system (how Reform UK Party Ltd – yes, it's a company, but we'll refer to them as just Reform throughout – garnered 4 million votes but only five seats); mistrust in politicians (the turnout was notably low); and how detached Westminster is from the rest of the country (can't argue with that). The Lib Dems made their leader Ed Davey smile widely as the party had its best result in their history, bringing home 72 MPs. All the bungee jumping, paddle boarding and water sliding during the campaign had evidently paid off. More of which later.

I don't know what you did through the night of 4 July, but at times I cried happy tears knowing that we had finally had our chance to treat the Conservatives as they deserved.

I also cried for those long months when they locked us in our homes while they partied, for those who couldn't say goodbye to the people they loved the most, for those who couldn't hold hands at the funeral of their husband, father, mother, son or daughter, while at Downing Street, those in the corridors of power drank so much they puked down the walls – the very night before the Queen sat alone at Prince Philip's funeral.

I cried for how they lied to us, while granting billions of pounds' worth of PPE and test and trace contracts to their associates and donors, who made obscene profits. And then they lied about it some more and 'lost' the WhatsApp messages needed by the Covid inquiry.

NOW WHAT?

I cried for the NHS frontline staff who died and for those who today still suffer the effects of the Covid years, who were left unprotected by government, for whom we clapped on a Thursday night and who were then treated by the Tories like some kind of First World War cannon fodder.

I cried for 14 years of austerity, for many children going to school unable to learn properly because of hunger. I cried for parents working two or three jobs but still dependent on food banks to put dinner on the table. I cried for the elderly forced to choose between heating and eating, winter after winter. And I cried for the vulnerable kids whose support services and day care centres have been closed by councils starved of funding. All while the richest became obscenely richer and the UK became one of the most unequal countries in Europe.

I cried for the division the Tories created, for the lies their friends in the media perpetuated, for the bullying of those who have dared to tell the truth about them, and for the collapse of our national conversation into abuse and gaslighting.

Finally, I cried with utter relief for an opportunity to take a short breath as our new hopeful era begins.

It's far from over. And we have to remain aware of how it could all change back again so easily. Labour wasn't voted in with a huge mandate of goodwill; half of those who voted for them were merely voting against the Conservatives. Labour has a lot of work to do to earn our trust and make us believe in our political leaders again. They've started well (at the time of writing), but in less than five years there will be another general election and the choice may be between Labour and a far-right option. Please don't think the battle is over. We have to change our politics and the system in which it operates.

But for now we must also believe that 'people power' has worked. Back in late 2022, when some of us said that together we could destroy the government at the next election, by showing the evidence of the lies and deals which had been taking place, many scoffed. They said, 'They'll always get away with it', 'Nothing will change'.

But look at what the decent people in this country have achieved since then.

Look at what happened on 4 July 2024.

WE ONLY WENT AND DID IT.

WE BLOODY WELL WON.

Carol Vorderman, July 2024

POLITICS: THE THREE VOWELS AND FIVE CONSONANTS WHICH CONTROL OUR WORLD

I've packed this book with fact, emotion and fun, ending with a Plan for Change for the future. But I thought it might be good to start with a few charming mentions of yours truly from the last couple of years, just for a laugh:

> 'Carol Vorderman's hatred of Tories has turned her into a raging snob.'
>
> – *Daily Telegraph*

'You have a sh*t lonely life. No one cares about your views. You're mad.'

 – Tory Cabinet minister Johnny Mercer on X

'A person who obviously has bitterness, arrogance and envy in her heart. There's no amount of plastic surgery or Botox that will cure that.'

 – Marco Longhi, Tory MP

'Single-use plastic. What she should do is act her age, get the bus pass out and go and enjoy life.'

 – Former Tory Deputy Chairman Lee Anderson MP,
 now Reform

'Here's a *Countdown* Conundrum – what's turned nice Carol Vorderman into a ranting, embittered Twitter troll?'

 – Amanda Platell, *Daily Mail*

Then there was the evening in 2023 when I met a wonderful woman who has been working for the Labour party in the Houses of Parliament for many years (I won't give away exactly where she worked but it was located near a Conservative office of some kind). She came up with a huge smile and said, 'We hear your name every day; the Tories can't stand you.'

'Brilliant,' I said. 'I know I'm doing something right then.'

'Yes,' she said, 'we hear the Tories shouting about you. Can't help but laugh – we hear a certain phrase A LOT.'

'What phrase?' I asked her, already chuckling.

'It's what we hear them shout more or less every time you post on Twitter: "THAT F**KING CAROL VORDERMAN!"'

I burst out laughing. Very proud of that. I might get a badge made up with those four great words on it, and wear it with pride!

It's true these Tories have been a bit shirty with me sometimes, when all I've been doing is pointing out a little evidence of their bad behaviour.

As Corporal Jones said in *Dad's Army*: 'They don't like it up 'em.'

SO WHAT'S IN THIS BOOK?

Before we get going, let me just tell you what's in this book.

This is a book for everyone who knows that something very wrong has been happening in the public sphere for the last 14 years, for people who have seen and lived with the cruelty that has been inflicted on millions.

Yes, we have a new government now. And hopefully it'll be a damn sight more decent and compassionate, and more competent than the one we endured under the Conservatives. But the real political issues that allowed the last government to mismanage and deceive us for so long run deep. Not only that, we have to be extremely aware that in 2029, or sooner, we will have another general election, and possibly another government, which could be the same or worse for the nation than the one which has just left. We've found our voice once, and I hope to show you how to continue to find yours, if you haven't done so already.

In fact, what this book aims to do is to give you the strength to question matters. Politicians aren't our masters. They aren't 'better' than us. They're just humans and, as we all know, humans vary widely.

So this is a book for people who may not normally think about politics.

A book for those who have been made to feel as though politics isn't for them.

A book for good, kind people who want society to be fairer, and who want to feel safe and cared for once again.

I'll show you how you *can* make a difference.

Like Dorothy, the Tin Man, the Lion and the Scarecrow, together we can trot down the Yellow Brick Road to Westminster and pull back the curtain on the artifice of politics to reveal what turns out to be simply a bunch of people with the privilege of a microphone (i.e. particularly the friendly Tory media over the last 14 years), just like the Wizard of Oz scaring the people of the Emerald City with his booming voice when really he isn't a wizard at all.

But we can, and did, expose the Tories. We need to remember that.

I really want this book to inspire you to want to know more.

I want it to inspire you to ask the simple questions, and to not feel afraid to ask them.

I want you to feel the righteous anger of someone who's been lied to constantly, and doesn't want that to happen again.

Above all, I want to persuade you that politics really is something which affects every part of your life and you can use your voice to change things.

I'm going to share my diary from the last 20 months with you, which covers the time when I've become more involved in politics, particularly online. There are some funny stories and some which will possibly make you cross. I hope it'll make you laugh out loud in places too.

I've also included some special explainer sections, dotted throughout. These cover the basics of how Westminster works, for those of you who don't follow the ins and outs of politics (i.e. the vast majority who are busy getting on with their own lives). So I'll tell you how the House of Commons and the House of Lords currently operate, how the Tories changed the election rules, and similar topics too because, believe me, I've been learning a lot alongside you.

At the end of the book, you'll find some key things which I believe need changing to even things up for all of us, clean up politics and challenge what is effectively a two-party system. Some are bold ideas and others less so. I'm calling this my 'Plan for Change'. Listen to me, eh? It sounds posh but I've called it a 'Plan for Change' because it's a list of things I'm willing to fight for as we move forward.

Thank you for joining me here, and if you've joined me on social media, thank you too. I know that together we can change things and have done so already; I know that we can come out of this into an even better place than we were before; and I know that there are so many in the usually silent majority in this country who are prepared to speak up and be a part of a new beginning.

You might not be persuaded by some of my arguments, but come along with me for the ride and see what you think by the end of the book. I promise it will be fun.

But first, you might be asking yourself a critically important question . . .

WHAT HAS POLITICS GOT TO DO WITH ME?

Well, quite a lot really. Whether you like it or not, it affects every single thing in life from the moment you wake up in the morning until you crawl into bed at night. It even affected you before you were born.

I have heard and seen so many people leading up to the general election, say, 'Nah, politics isn't for me'; 'Well, it's all those politicians just arguing with each other and lying'; 'They only care about themselves, nothing to do with me'. Even the low turnout at the election indicated the same.

I know why someone might say that; I totally understand, and I wouldn't blame you if you do think like this, not for a second. But I also KNOW that many in the political class have deliberately manipulated you to think that way by talking about politics in a particular manner, because it serves them to do so, and by and large many of their media pals go along with it.

It's been like a club to which we were not invited. The Tories would say, 'we want more people involved in politics', but I can't think what most of them have done to make you believe it. The majority don't mean it at all. They only seemed to want more of their own people in the gang.

OK, so even the Tories are not *all* like that. But one of the rotten things about the past 14 years was the way too many people with a certain background floated to the top.

The well-trodden road of politicians who go to private school, then to Oxford University to read politics, philosophy and economics, and then straight into Westminster to work as a special adviser – a SPAD – is one of the key fault lines that has developed in the system. The privileged few who want to keep it all for the privileged few.

I've got some thoughts about that later in this book – oh boy, have I got some thoughts about that! – but for now, let me answer this question:

'OK, Carol, if you're so bloody clever, what HAS politics got to do with me?'

Well, let's have a look at your life in chronological order. From cradle to grave (and beyond that with inheritance tax), I'll show just a teeny tiny part of how political decisions affect you and your family. I'll give you some specific examples from my own personal experience and look at how it works in the wider political landscape.

Buckle up and come with me on our political rollercoaster!

Before you're born

YOU: When your mother is pregnant with you, where she lives will decide the level of maternity care she gets, the advice available and how good your survival chances are when you're born.

ME: In 1992, my daughter was born very suddenly and two months prematurely. The time between the start of my initial 'tummy ache' and her popping out was about three hours . . . I was rushed in the back of a car to the local hospital where they had a special care baby unit (SCBU). Thank God. She was there for a month before they let her leave with us. Those were probably the most anxious weeks of my life.

That hospital where she was born has since been knocked down and a new one built, but it doesn't have a maternity unit. If Katie had been born years later, I'd have had to travel a much greater distance to the next nearest hospital. Would she even have lived? I don't know. I just know I'm grateful that the small hospital was there.

POLITICS: We interact with the NHS in literally our first moments of life, and it's there with us till the day we die. The decisions made in Westminster regarding its funding have real-world impacts on us from the very instant of birth. A report in 2023 by the baby loss charities Sands and Tommy's found hundreds of babies are dying unnecessarily each year because overstretched maternity services are delivering substandard care, particularly to those who are poor and/or not white. For example, in 2020, there were 4.3 stillbirths for every 1,000 births in the most deprived parts of the UK compared with 2.6 in the least deprived areas. Around 500 tiny babies would have survived if stillbirth rates in deprived areas were the same as in wealthy areas. Black babies are still more than twice as likely to be stillborn as white babies. It's heartbreaking and it doesn't have to be this way.[1]

It's politics that can make a difference to a scandal like this.

Early life

YOU: Did both of your parents work? If not, how was their income affected? Who looked after you? Could they afford childcare? What's your memory of those early years? Were you a child growing up in a single parent family? If so, did your father pay child maintenance? Were either of your parents abusive to each other?

ME: I grew up in poverty. My mum was a single parent after my father had an affair. She had three children to bring up in the 1960s, she had five part-time jobs and she was exhausted. There was no system to force my father to pay proper maintenance back then and very few handouts. We lived from day to day and cherished everything.

POLITICS: Various laws have been passed in recent years that affect how much money parents of young children have, including the two-child benefit cap introduced by the Tories in 2017, which has had a huge effect on larger families. Just imagine you're in a couple where both of you have worked all of your lives and you have three kids. Then one of you gets sick or, God forbid, passes away. There's only a safety net for two of your children. Presumably the third has to survive on fresh air and the kindness of strangers.

The idea that people in poverty are feckless and lazy is one that has been frequently peddled by politicians over the years. There's something far deeper going wrong when almost 300,000 families with children are living in poverty despite their parents (either single parents or a couple) being in full-time work.[2]

Decisions made in Westminster also affect what support you get for childcare costs, child payments for divorced families, carer allowances and so much more.

Where you live

YOU: Can you afford to live where you grew up, near to family and friends? Or where would be convenient for work? Are you – or your kids – struggling to save up enough for a deposit because house prices are sky high? Do you feel ripped off and insecure in rented accommodation? Are you thinking about downsizing but worried about any tax you might have to pay? Would you like to get out of the area where you live because you're worried about crime?

ME: My mum and I had to live in temporary accommodation at times, and our family of four lived in a rented flat when I was growing up. We were lucky: there were plenty of places to rent back then and a lot of social housing. That's no longer the case. On average, young people now can't afford to buy a home until they're 35. THIRTY-FIVE.

POLITICS: The failure to build enough new houses over decades means prices are now colossal, and more and more families are being forced to fork out for hugely expensive privately rented properties or join the scramble for social housing. Nationally, 142,000 homeless children are being housed in accommodation such as commercial hotels, converted offices and hostels, an all-time high, after rents and no-fault evictions soared across the country.[3]

Primary and secondary school

YOU: Which school did you go to and which ones do your children or grandchildren go to now? Was it a private school or maybe a religious school? How many children were in your class? Did your school have playing fields? Could you get swimming lessons? Was your building in a good state of repair? Did you have good maths lessons or music lessons? Were you on free school meals? How did you travel to school?

ME: I was brought up as a Catholic girl and went to a little local school. In North Wales, there were only a few Catholic schools, so we were bussed in every day, which I loved. Our schools were nice and the teachers were excellent and kind. I was a free school meals kid.

POLITICS: Think about the RAAC scandal, with many children having to learn in crumbling units with no heating, wearing gloves and coats to keep themselves warm. Think of Rishi Sunak almost halving the schools' rebuilding budget when he was Chancellor.[4] Think of there being five Tory Secretaries of State for Education in just one year. No continuity because they didn't seem to care about the kids.

Then there's the question of whether Ofsted is fit for purpose; the continuing shortage of teachers; the undervaluing of the profession which has led to strikes, and so on. Facilities have been closed down. Over 10,000 school playing fields have been sold off. Who owns the land now? Where does any profit go?

The answers to all of these questions lie in politics. All of it is about your children. Who you vote for gives you the answers.

Further education

YOU: Is it worth taking on debt to go to university? Is an apprenticeship better? What percentage of students now go to university? Are bright students from low-income families getting a fair chance? How much are lecturers paid? Is what universities provide good enough for students, and does it lead to employment?

ME: I went to university in the 1970s on a full maintenance grant. Tuition fees weren't even thought of back then. All of that was paid for and I also received money to cover living and food. I left university without debt, as we all did back then. Fewer of us went, only about 5 per cent in the 1970s, with a much higher proportion of those from private school than we see today.

POLITICS: It's thought to be only a matter of time until the first universities go bankrupt. And half of all university vice chancellors say their institutions are running at a loss in 2024.[5] What happens to the students if they go belly up? And why have they been allowed to continue for so long taking vast amounts of cash from families? Meanwhile, the value of outstanding student loans currently stands at more than £206 billion, with students who began their course in 2022/23 to average £45,600 debt by the time they graduate. Goodness knows how much of this will ever be repaid. It's politicians who will attempt to find the answer. That's why we have to choose them wisely.[6]

Your job

YOU: Does working mean you earn a salary that's sufficient to support your family? Are there enough 'good jobs' near where you live or is your best hope casual work on a zero-hours contract? Will you get parental leave and pay if you have kids? Could your boss just fire your entire team then try to rehire you for half the money?

Have you got any rights about which hours you work and what happens if you become sick?

ME: I've worked as a staff member, as an engineer, been self-employed for decades and, as a bit of an entrepreneur, have had a couple of companies and been an employer over the years too. I know how many rules and regulations there are – and how difficult it can be when they constantly change. And I see how challenging it is for the young people who I work alongside in the TV industry. It used to be people were automatically employed in staff positions, but now lots of them are on short-term contracts or freelance, which makes life much more insecure.

POLITICS: Tony Blair's Labour government introduced the national minimum wage, the 48-hour working week, 28 days' paid holiday, parental leave and greater protection from unfair dismissal. So politics can change things for working people. But this year (2024), three-quarters of the record 1.1 million people on zero-hours contracts in the UK are in severely insecure work with a lack of rights and protections.

How safe and secure you feel

YOU: Do you worry about walking home? Are you scared when your kids go out because of the threat of knife crime? Does it make you fume when you hear how the police may not even turn up if your house gets burgled or your car gets stolen? What about the rise in shoplifting – doesn't anyone care any more?

ME: My sense of personal safety as a woman has always been high; that might be through naivety but perhaps because I grew up in a different time. The stories we read of people being mugged in the street for watches or handbags wasn't 'a thing' back in the 1970s/80s. I'm not saying it never happened and this was a golden age, but it just wasn't something we heard about. Now the Met website has advice on how to protect yourself in the street. Look confident. Cover jewellery. Don't use your mobile phone as it's more likely to be snatched. I'm particularly horrified by the stories I hear about spiking – either in drinks or by other means. I've had so many calls to my LBC radio show about this. It's a crime that's exploding, with both men and women as victims, and we aren't talking about it enough.

POLITICS: Crime is an area where politics can make a real difference – by making new laws, giving police new or different powers and changing sentencing rules. In 2024, prisons in the UK were declared to be full, literally. Entirely the fault of the Tories, who hadn't invested in them over the years. The consequences have been numerous, including releasing prisoners on bail to relieve overcrowding and delays in cases getting to court. Police cells were repurposed to serve as prison accommodation. When prisoners were released on an emergency basis during Covid in Scotland, 40 per cent had reoffended within six months.

The Office for National Statistics showed knife crime was up by

5 per cent in the year to September 2023, with a 'notable' increase in robberies involving a knife. In the run-up to the election, Labour said dealing with violent crime would be a priority – whether it is or not remains to be seen.

The cost of living

YOU: Have there been times in the last few years when you've not wanted to open a bill or the email from the energy company? Do you sometimes feel things just go up and up and up – and no one in power does much to stop it? I mean, how can the water bosses keep charging us more when they're spewing sh*t into our rivers and giving billions of pounds to their shareholders and hefty bonuses to themselves? Why does no one protect us from that? And what about companies that put up the bills when there's nothing you can do to get out of the contract – that can't be right, can it?

ME: When I was young, my expectation and that of my mates who were also growing up on a council estate was that many of us would get married and have a council house – and lots of them did (before the houses started getting sold off under Margaret Thatcher). We assumed that some of us would be able to afford our own home. Even when mortgage rates were high, houses were cheaper, so the amount you actually needed to borrow was markedly less.

Mum and I bought a three-bed semi in Headingley in Leeds together when I was just 21, before I started working at Yorkshire

TV on *Countdown*. Our combined income was probably about £10,000 a year and we could borrow twice that for a mortgage – and that was enough for our beautiful little house with a nice garden. We had no money to decorate it, and we were given curtains which didn't fit so we had to peg them together every night to close them, which made us laugh. Interest rates were high, but the bills were manageable. We didn't live a grand life, but it was a happy one – utilities like water were nationalised and so we weren't facing massive bills for private companies to cream off a profit.

POLITICS: It feels to me that it was in the 1980s when everything changed, due to Thatcher's politics. It was then, with the ascendance of the free market economy, that profit became the be all and end all. Harry Enfield's 'Loadsamoney' character was indicative of the time. And it has just got worse, so the bulk of people are now paying the price for the greed of a small minority. Our politics has allowed it, with the super-rich continuing to buy influence.

The cost of living crisis was primarily caused by inflation at home and around the world; bad political decisions by Conservative prime ministers; and the aftershocks of Covid and Russia's invasion of Ukraine. And, of course, here, there was the little matter of Brexit. Politics was at the heart of all these issues. But the impact was felt by real people, particularly those with low incomes.

By May 2024, the number of adults struggling to pay their bills and debts had soared to nearly 11 million, according to the Financial Conduct Authority.[7] The Office for National Statistics surveys in 2022 found 77 per cent of UK adults reported feeling worried about the rising cost of living.[8] Half said they had cut back on energy. In the same year, the Food Foundation think tank found 1 million adults went a whole day without eating during the month they studied.[9]

Even now, with inflation having fallen, prices, of course, remain higher than they were pre Covid. The Bank of England inflation calculator tells us that goods and services costing £10 in 2021 would now cost around £12.

If you feel you're worse off, then it's real, and it's all politics.[10]

Looking after ageing parents

YOU: They say that how we look after our older people is a mark of a good – or bad – society. People are living longer but sometimes the care homes they're sent to seem to have fewer staff. And they cost a fortune. Will your parents' life savings be spent paying for that care? Will they have to sell their home? What if they don't have a home to sell? What if they have to be separated because there isn't enough accommodation? Or the home is miles away from the rest of the family? And how can you be sure they'll get the proper care when they're there . . .?

ME: I employed my mum from when I was 25 and she lived with us for over 30 years, so mine is an unusual story. But I felt responsible for Mum until the day she died. I see how hard it is for people now. It used to be that people were able to live closer to where they grew up so could care for parents as they got older. Now people often have to go further afield for work or commute so much more. By July 2024, the average cost of care homes is around £60,000 a year, with the cost of nursing homes even higher.[11]

POLITICS: Age UK says 2.6 million people in England alone who are over 50 are unable to get care, with hundreds of thousands stuck on waiting lists.[12] The shortage of carers is putting a strain on care and nursing homes. Political parties have been talking about the importance of a proper social care plan for years, but so far it has remained just that – talk. Since the election, the Liberal Democrats say that they are now going to concentrate on carer policies, which is a good sign at least. Politics could, and certainly should, fix this.

And so it goes on. Even your death is affected by politics. If you want to have an assisted death – something Dame Esther Rantzen has recently been campaigning for – it is politicians who will decide whether you will or won't be able to. The cost of living crisis will affect your funeral, as it does everything else. (And even beyond death, you will be liable for taxes – except for the super-rich, many of whom will have set up offshore trust funds to benefit their children without the need to pay tax. It's called 'inheritance tax planning'.)

So politics has EVERYTHING to do with you. Probably three-quarters of all decisions you make, if not more than that, will involve politics. So much of what you see or touch or buy or sell is affected by taxes and politics.

So you have to ask yourself some questions.

Do you want a world that's fairer for you and your family?

Do you want a country where we look after the vulnerable?

Do you want to live in a society where you feel hope for the future?

If you care about any of the answers to these questions, then you already care about politics.

WHERE MY POLITICS COMES FROM

We are all built in some way by what we live through, particularly as children. It moulds us. Our backgrounds shape who we are, our understanding of others and their circumstances.

So before we get going, I need to tell you a bit of relevant stuff to explain who I am a little bit better than some clickbait media headlines may have done in the past. (I'll try not to bore you to death, I promise.)

I'm a woman in my mid-sixties, post-menopause. I'm not part of the Westminster Bubble and I don't live anywhere near London. I laugh too loudly, I'm very stubborn, I loathe bullies, I'm bloody good at parties and I don't give a flying f**k what people I don't respect think about me.

Older people will tell you that it's in these years you find your inner strength. For me, an older woman gets her power when she truly doesn't care what others think of her any more; she becomes a woman who is comfortable in her behaviour, her mind and her reasons for raising the roof.

David Bowie said something wonderful about ageing: *'Ageing is an extraordinary process whereby you become the person you always should have been.'*

How true.

As a child, I was helped out of poverty by many kind people giving me a chance, if I was prepared to put in the effort. So I put in the effort. And I know only too well that the opportunities given to me only came thanks to the grown-ups who had fought hard for those chances in the years before, the people who had been determined to change things, not just for themselves, but for others too. The ones who stood proudly against the privileged establishment to fight for rights, freedoms and equality for the rest of us.

I was born in December 1960, part of a generation lucky to have the advantage of the early years of the NHS. Just 12 years earlier, Britain had become the first country in the Western world to offer free medical care to the whole of its population.

The NHS began on 5 July 1948, and five years later my wonderful older brother Anton was born with the severest form of cleft lip and palate. He had 24 operations in his younger life; he suffered a lot but he would not be here now without the NHS.

I was also rushed to hospital as a toddler in 1962 with twisted bowels. The NHS was there and it saved me.

So in answer to the question, what did politics have to do with me and my brother as babies . . . Well, politics literally saved our lives.

These are just two of tens of millions of similar stories. We each have examples from our own lives. And it was good and strong politics after the end of the Second World War which made that biggest change happen.

Allow me to go on a little detour here to tell you about Aneurin 'Nye' Bevan MP, a proud Welshman, who was the Labour government's minister for health in the 1940s under Prime Minister Clement Attlee (names you may have heard of). He's known as the 'father of the NHS'; he was the man who forced through the beginnings of the welfare state, and thank God for him.

Born in 1897 in Tredegar, South Wales, Bevan was one of ten children, five of whom died before adulthood. He left school when he was 14 to work in the local coal mine. He was dismissed a few years later as the bosses considered him a troublemaker due to his support for the new unions. But it was this troublemaker who led the campaign for a universal health service that is free at the point of care. It was a pivotal moment for Britain.

I want to go into a little of our political history here and there throughout this book to show how politicians aren't just people on the television or in the newspapers, they are people who have the power to create or destroy huge aspects of how we live.

Nye Bevan, a man born into poverty in the 1800s, is still affecting all of our lives today. That's how powerful an impact a great politician can have.

I remind myself of the respect I hold for the great politicians because it couldn't be more important right now to remember that politics is capable of achieving good – even while we also understand that, at the opposite end of the spectrum, there are those who will fight and cheat to take all good things away from us for their own greed and selfishness.

It's the history of those who came before that brings us to the point we are at now, which is one where a significant turn in our future has been made once again. That is what I believe.

So what's my own history, which has led me to what I believe today?

Well, you can tell the story of a life in many different ways, and we each have our own script written in our heads. For me, my story is one of a happy childhood with a strange mix of adventure and stability. Though it could be written otherwise, as I had an absent father who had an affair with another woman when my mother was pregnant with me.

My father was born in Amsterdam in 1920, the fifth of seven children born to Marius and Maria Vorderman. His mother died when he was just five years old. In the Second World War he had fought with the Dutch Resistance in a town called Tegelen, risking his life every day.

Part of his work involved being what's known as a 'radio man', which was instantly punishable by death if the Nazis had found him. During the Nazi occupation of the Netherlands, radio broadcasts reported on the war developments and called on the Dutch population not to cooperate with the occupying forces. Sometimes, the broadcasts included encrypted messages meant for the Resistance. In May 1943, the Dutch were ordered to hand in their radios. There were many who did not obey. With the curtains drawn and the radio low, they still listened to those messages from abroad.

NOW WHAT?

When I filmed my edition of *Who Do You Think You Are?*, I learned that my father was chased out of hiding a few times by the Nazis, but they couldn't catch him. However, late into the war, as the Allies were advancing, he and his fellow Resistance cell members were forced to flee from their cover working in a small hotel. Many were killed that night as they tried to get away. My father stepped on a landmine on the banks of the River Maas, the searchlights came on and the Nazis shot dead a number of his friends, though my father was dragged to safety by the others.

After the war, he joined the Dutch Army and was stationed in Bodelwyddan in North Wales, where he met my mother. This quiet little Welsh farm girl married this brave, handsome soul in Breda in Holland in 1947. Eventually, they returned to Wales and set up a business in Prestatyn called Tony's – a cycle, pram and toy shop – and it did well, I believe, back in the 1950s. They had my older brother and sister and then, at some point, they moved to Bedford.

I was born in Bedford in 1960. My parents split up when I was two weeks old, when my father admitted he'd been having an affair while Mum was pregnant with me. Mum took her three children back to her hometown of Prestatyn, on the coast in North Wales, where she could be surrounded by the love of her family.

I grew up in poverty. We were dirt poor with an absent father who refused to ever see me as a child. I didn't meet him until I was 42.

Mum, my brother Anton, and my sister Trixie and I lived in a cold ground-floor flat, four of us in one bedroom (including my wonderful cousin Pamela who moved in with us), my brother in the box room and one bath of hot water a week to share between all of us on a Sunday night. Mum had five part-time jobs to keep us fed. It nearly killed her. All I ever had to give her was my school report because I knew it made her happy. I did really well in school so she would smile.

My mum was poor and exhausted, with no chance of 'making it in life' – except there were good people around her and us. Very good people who gave us chances.

Mum rented the whole house from her uncle Will for £1 a week and let out the upstairs flat for 10 shillings (50p) a week. We had all sorts of interesting people living up there. One night, the young female tenant had a visit from Roger, her boyfriend, who was carrying an axe. He destroyed a lot of furniture that night (he didn't touch her, thankfully, but there was a lot of screaming). He is still known in our family as 'Roger the Axeman'.

My first ten years were lively, that's for sure.

Christmas presents were scarce, other than those that came from the jumble sale. All my clothes were hand-me-downs from a lovely girl who lived in the next street.

During the school holidays, I stayed with my cousins Sian and Robert on their small dairy farm a few miles away and got to help to milk the cows every night, play cards and assist with the hay baling. I'm sure I wasn't a help at all, but my aunty Dilys (Mum's sister) did her bit in that way to make life easier for Mum and all of us. It helped so much.

She wasn't the only one who helped our family. At the bottom of our little garden behind the flat there was a low hedge, and on the other side was the garden of a small grocery shop called Hillcrest. Every Saturday in the late afternoon, my brother and I would sit in the window and watch the hedge like our lives depended on it, because, if they could, the ladies who ran the shop would leave the leftover cream cakes they couldn't sell (and which wouldn't stay fresh until Monday) on the lid of a cardboard box on top of the hedge. Then they'd walk away so that Mum never felt any shame in taking them. That's how it was then. Good people helped. Good people still help now: think of food banks and warm banks and volunteers. There are so many good people in this country and we have to protect them.

Those years in poverty have never left me. And I'm glad of that.

I was a clever little girl, always very keen on numbers, which is probably the least surprising thing I'll write in this book. Ha.

The little Catholic primary school I went to in Rhyl was called Ysgol Mair. It was a happy place and I was 'put up a year' when I was four because I was fast (very fast) with sums and numbers.

My headmaster was called Mr Jemmett. The school was full of poor kids, many of us on free school meals, but he didn't care about that. He knew we were equal to others in spite of our financial situation, and he did all he could to make sure we did as well as possible, no excuses. Mr Jemmett did that with a smile and plenty of love. He loved us in the best way a person can and I will never forget him. Wider society expected kids like us to 'stay in our lane'; Mr Jemmett made us into doctors, accountants, lawyers, TV people . . . there was even one who went on to run one of the biggest media companies in the world. Mr Jemmett made us believe that we were equal to everybody else.

The fundamentals of my politics came from him, I think.

I stayed a year ahead, either top or second in the class (I'd get very annoyed with myself if I failed to get 100 per cent in maths, by the way) and then when I was ten, I hopped over the fence to the Catholic comprehensive school, Blessed Edward Jones High School.

My maths teacher in secondary school was a Welsh Nationalist, as they were called back in the 1970s. Mr Palmer Parry was the best maths teacher in the history of maths teaching in the history of the world (he was that good). He was strict and funny, and he would make us line up in the corridor before lessons while he walked past us in his polished steel toe-capped boots, then open the door to the maths room and laugh while we scurried in.

He made us work hard, but by hell he explained things well. I think every one of us in his O level class got a grade A (the highest grade available at that time). He was superb, magnificent.

Mr Parry's politics were fervent: he loved Wales and he loved the Welsh language. By the 1970s, Welsh as a first language had been reduced from half of the population to around one in five. This political process began in schools after the introduction of the 'Welsh Not' – a horrendous system introduced in the nineteenth century to stop children speaking their native tongue. The Not was usually a piece of wood with the word 'NOT' written on it, with the end of a rope tacked onto either side. When a child spoke Welsh in class, they would have to wear the Not, then when the next child spoke Welsh, the Not would be passed to them. Whichever child was wearing it at the end of the day was punished, I'm told. This awful practice persisted well into the twentieth century. Welsh is a language with an emotional history.

Back to Mr Parry. By the 1970s, all the road signs in Wales were written in English. Mr Parry was once up in front of the magistrates as he'd been caught spraying out the English road signs in green paint in protest – it's one of the things the Welsh nationalists did to reclaim our language in the 1970s, and it worked. I visited him and his wife this year and asked, 'Is it true that you used to spray the signs out at night?' and his wife answered with a smile, 'Oh no, we did it in the daytime too.' Love that.

He was passionate about his country and his language, and millions will be grateful to him and his wife and their many friends for their protesting. The Welsh Nationalist movement was centred around Caernarfon and Bangor, not too far from Rhyl, where I went to school. This book is about politics and part of my politics came from Mr Parry too. A sense of belonging and speaking out is important. And a belief that together with others, we really can force change to happen.

In 1970 my mum remarried. I was nine. My stepfather was a hilarious, loud, hard-working Italian. Gabriel Rizzi became my 'dad' and I truly adored him. He had been an Italian prisoner of war, captured by the Allies in North Africa, then brought to work on a farm in Wales. His first language was Italian, his second language was Welsh and his third was English – which made life interesting, to say the least.

He swore every third word and laughed like a drain and slapped my leg or the table when he was making a point. When I was a teenager, he threatened that if I ever got a boyfriend he 'would shoot the bass-tad'. He didn't have a gun, obviously, but he'd roar laughing and so did I whenever he said it. It was our humour and I truly loved him. You know how you feel about someone when if you think of them your face just smiles. Mine turns into an instant beam when I think of him.

By this time, things were better financially. Gabriel was a great 'dad' but I'm not sure how suitable he was for my lovely mum as a husband. Mum left him many times, dragging me off from a nice house with a warm-bedroom to some cold B&B or the circus (yes, Billy Smart's Circus put us up for a while in Leicester) or a flat somewhere. It was how life was, transient to a degree. It shapes you and you never forget it. I know that instability casts a dark shadow over everything you think about, and it can put a lid on hope and ambition as you dare not dream. And that's where two elements of my politics came from too.

One of them was a desire for some sense of stability.

The other was an admiration for forgiveness.

If the Welsh population could forgive my Italian stepfather for fighting against us in the Second World War, then they were a kind people. Forgiveness is always possible.

I've only thought of it recently, but my father and my stepfather, both from other lands, fought on opposite sides in the Second World War and yet both were fully accepted in the UK, both were happy and fulfilled here, and isn't that wonderful?

NOW WHAT?

Once I had done well in my O levels at age 15, I had to think about what I wanted to do. How could I change my life?

I'd spent a lot of my growing-up on building sites, as my 'dad' was a builder; on farms with my mum's relations, who were mostly either tenant farmers or had small dairy farms; and thinking about engines and going to stock car races and rallying. I loved it all. But my burning ambition was to be an astronaut (this was the era of the moon landings, after all) or a fighter pilot.

Obviously, being an astronaut was a bit of a non-starter – fat chance, being both a woman and a Brit. But I thought a fighter pilot might be possible. I'd never actually been in an aeroplane or knew anyone in the Royal Air Force (girls weren't allowed to join the Air Cadets back then), but I knew I wanted to fly. I worked out that because no woman had ever been a fighter pilot in the UK, I had to be better than anyone before. Laughable, perhaps, but being laughed at has only ever spurred me on.

So I applied to read the most suitable subject for a pilot – engineering – and at the best university I could think of – Cambridge.

I'd never been there or – you guessed it – knew anyone who'd been there, but, hey ho, off went the application. My chances were more or less zero. A 17-year-old girl from a comprehensive school in North Wales? I don't think any girl from a North Wales comp had gone to Cambridge before. If you know differently, then please let me know – stats weren't easily available back then, so I'm repeating here what I was told by my headmaster.

Well, you have to have a go, don't you? My college, Sidney Sussex College, was a beacon of support for state school kids like me. And here I found another hero: Mr Donald Green, my senior tutor and admissions tutor.

At that time, very few colleges had become what they call 'mixed' and had started to accept a small number of female students along with the boys in the previously all-male colleges. So, get in there, Vorders! Jeez. I applied and was interviewed by Mr Green, who was a life-changer for so many students. He wrote his own rulebook, and thank God he did. Of course, now Oxbridge welcomes girls and boys equally, and quite right too. But at the time, Mr Green was a pioneer in his attitude. Society was changing but it was still geared to keeping poor kids (especially girls) down.

In that single year as admissions tutor for my wonderful college, he accepted three girls from 'northern state schools' (I'm including North Wales in that description). That might seem a tiny number nowadays, but at the time, it was revolutionary. All of us have done all right. There's me, then my roommate the amazing Sue Thomas (now Gibson) from Blackburn who became a young female professor of chemistry at Imperial College London and has won international prizes for her work, and Ann Mather from Stockport, who moved to America and went on to become a director and/or chair of Pixar, Google, Bumble, Netflix and countless other tech companies.

Mr Donald Green helped so many of us. He was funny and strict and truly loved by his students.

Cambridge students back then were mainly from private schools (not all posh, but many were) and I learned a lot from being around them about life and class, snobbery and arrogance. I also learned that kids with posh voices were no better than anyone else; they were just born with the advantage of wealth, a private-school education, their parents' contacts and, for some (NOT for all by any means), a bizarre and unearned sense of entitlement which their particular top end private schools had bred into them. May I just remind you of David Cameron, Boris Johnson, George Osborne, Jacob Rees-Mogg and others of recent times. I knew I never wanted to be one of them, EVER.

I turned up at Cambridge, age just 17, in my Welsh boyfriend's fast car, wearing thigh-length leather boots and wanting to get into life there as soon as I could. I loved it, especially wearing my boots to lectures in the engineering department (the boots were difficult to cycle in, but hey, it was the 1970s and Abba were riding high). I graduated with an Honours degree in Engineering in 1981, age 20, and a few weeks later my mum left my Italian stepfather (they'd been together on and off for ten years by then). She ended up, in her fifties, living in one room in a student house in Windsor.

I got a job working as a 'graduate trainee' for Christian Salvesen and lived in digs that year, keeping all I had in my broken-down old rust bucket of a Datsun. I would drive from wherever I was working to stay with her one night a week and sleep on her floor. I knew I had to do something to get her, and both of us, out of that life. My boyfriend, whom I'd met while working underground as a junior engineer, was from Yorkshire and by going up to see him in Leeds a fair few times, I knew that Mum and I could afford a house there. Mum was a brilliant secretary so she applied for jobs (there were a lot available back then), I found us a house to buy and we moved there in the summer of 1982, happy to be reunited once again. How life can spin on a sixpence.

I only got onto television because my mother wrote a letter to Yorkshire Television, who said that they wanted to find a person to do the 'numbers game' on *Countdown*, in 1982, a year after I graduated. I always had an immense ability with mental arithmetic. Mum wrote the letter to the producer and forged my signature. That's how desperate I was to be on television – in other words, I wasn't desperate at all and never have been.

Anyway, I'm telling you this bit of background so you will perhaps understand what has always been within me, my memories of the people who had the courage to stick up for me and others back then, and those who acted in the opposite way.

I started voting in 1979. I've voted for all colours of parties over the years. I have never belonged to a political party; it's doubtful I ever will. Their policies and leaders and heart change significantly as the decades roll by, so it's always good to stay current.

I've lived all over the UK (my first 30 years in North Wales and Leeds); I love to belly laugh; I'll stick up for myself; and I've worked underground as an engineer with 2,000 men. I've made a lot of money by being on the telly, and I've also been sacked by a number of TV channels for not toeing the party line. I have set up two educational companies with around 30 employees each, written many bestselling books, worked with both the Labour and Tory parties on education and child safety matters, taught around half a million primary school children their maths for free for many months during the first lockdown through my online maths school and given bursaries for many years to kids from my kind of background to help them at a couple of universities.

The fundamentals of the key influences on my politics come from where I'm from and how I lived and won't change. And it may be exactly the same for you, and your children, and all of those you know and love.

What are your key beliefs?

Mine are these:

Work hard. Everything worth having needs effort, no matter what it is.

Help others without expecting anything in return.

Laugh a lot.

Know that being posh absolutely does not make you better or brighter.

Know that we have a responsibility to help those who need help.

Enjoy people.

Fight.

Try new things with good intention.

Be fair.

Own your sh*t. My best friend (who rose through the ranks of the RAF to wing commander) told me this and I stick by it. It's freeing. Owning your sh*t and not making excuses is the finest piece of advice I can give you.

Judge a person not by what they say they'll do, but what they actually do.

Don't fall for the fibs, in politics or in your private life.

If someone shows you they're a wrong 'un, believe them.

And above all, don't allow yourself to be silenced.

That last one needs a bit more explanation. Let me tell you about what happens when you start to try to voice your opinion about politics, if you're not someone who is already in the Westminster Bubble.

HOW SOME TRY TO MAKE YOU THINK YOUR OPINION DOESN'T COUNT

Here's a little quote from Benjamin Franklin you might have heard before:

> *'Tell me and I forget.*
> *Teach me and I remember.*
> *Involve me and I learn.'*

Politicians like to tell us things. They talk 'at' us all the time. When they tell us their opinions, they wrap them up in 'political speak' that we might not really understand unless we follow politics on a daily basis, and few working people have time to do that. So we forget them, get bored by them, think they're not relevant to us.

It's the difference between a good teacher (see the second line of the Benjamin Franklin quote) and someone who just talks at you to show how clever they are. A good teacher understands the level of your learning and knows their subject so well that they can explain it to you on that level. A bad teacher is just trying to impress you with THEIR knowledge, which makes you feel inadequate. We've all been through school and know the difference.

Well, it's exactly the same in politics.

For instance, the Tory government over the last 14 years has had the highest turnover of secretaries of state in modern history. Let's be fair, the highest turnover of prime ministers too! And every time one of them took the position of defence secretary or education secretary or whatever, they came out and pretended they knew all there was to know, when they patently didn't.

It's a case of 'believe me because I'm better than you'. Well, they haven't been better than us – they've often been much worse. The sense of entitlement over the Tory years has been staggering. And sometimes, but not as often, that applies to politicians in other parties too.

The last thing a number in Westminster, particularly Tories, want to do is truly involve us. That way, of course, we would learn.

You'll see in my 'diary' to come what happens if you really get involved in a cause and you don't agree with their policies, or you ask them an awkward question – they and their ridiculous outriders come for you with all guns blazing. They will try to belittle you, attempt to humiliate you and make *ad hominem* attacks, like the ones with which I opened this book. For someone living a normal life, it's the way they try to keep you in your box.

The thing is, politicians are just normal, fallible people, but many in the last 14 years have had puffed-up opinions of what they do and have been protected by a powerful and friendly mainly right-wing media. Many front-page headlines have been absurd. But with the application of a little logic, the whole illusion opens up for all of us to see.

Remember, you have every right to ask the question and to expect an honest answer.

One of the classic techniques is to talk about subjects using words and phrases that will not be comprehensible unless you already have a deep knowledge of the subject. If you don't understand, you would be forgiven for thinking that you must be stupid, and that they are better or superior or more intelligent than you.

But you aren't stupid. And they aren't better. It's a technique to put you in your place. I believe it has been deliberately done to confuse.

Bad politicians will use the law against you (I know and I'll show you). They use their wealth against you. They use their powerful contacts against you. To take on a battle is difficult: it gets nasty, it becomes relentless, and they rely on that. They have relied on people giving up under pressure.

But the thing is, when you know you've got so many others on your side, then you can carry on. And together we've done just that. Social media has brought many of us together by bypassing the usual routes of access to information and connecting us with like-minded people.

The most inspiring thing of all in the last couple of years has been to watch how people have gone from being completely despondent to feeling a sense of power. In that time, I've worked with some incredible people and organisations whose sole motivation is for the good of all. Seeing the evidence, giving people data – these things give us power. It does the third of those things on Benjamin Franklin's list: it INVOLVES us. We got involved, the voters spoke out and the Tory government is history.

We have turned from a country on its knees thinking we can't do anything to change matters, to showing them we can bring about the change we demand.

Now we just need to be on high alert that the new lot don't let us down!

NARCISSISM AND POLITICS

'You will never get the truth out of a narcissist. The closest you will ever come is a story that either makes them the victim or the hero, but never the villain.'

Shannon L. Alder

I'd like to take a moment to tell you a little bit about narcissists, as the relationship between narcissism and politics is something I mention a few times throughout this book, and it will go some way to explain what we all have lived through since 2010, including austerity, Brexit and the Covid years. I'm smiling as I write it, simply because this is going to trigger all the narcissists.

Wait for the columns in the newspapers, the predictable ones, which will say, 'Carol is a narcissist'. They'll make me chuckle.

But this is a serious subject because narcissists are bullies and there are many in all walks of life, including possibly your own.

We've all met bullies. We've met them in the playground. We've met them in the classroom. We've met them at work. You might have met them in your own family or found yourself in a relationship with one.

The thing about narcissists is that they have a pattern, and once you recognise the pattern, their power starts to crumble.

Sadly, I believe a fair few people in and around politics over the last 14 years are narcissists. Westminster seems to attract them.

Let's look at the evidence.

In 2018, an independent review by Dame Laura Cox found evidence of 'widespread' bullying, harassment and sexual harassment in Westminster, with some MPs behaving in appalling ways to junior staff.[13] Since then, other high-profile figures, ranging from the former Commons Speaker John Bercow to former Cabinet ministers Gavin Williamson and Dominic Raab, have all been accused of toxic behaviour. In another recent parliamentary inquiry into bullying – the third in five years, which tells you something – a quarter of staff said that they had experienced or witnessed bullying.[14] It's an outrageous figure, far more than you would expect to see in most workplaces.

Sunak said he would bring 'integrity, professionalism and accountability' to Parliament when he became the prime minister. As we all know, none of that happened.

Scientific research says that around 5 per cent of a population will display narcissistic behaviour. That's about one in 20 people.

I believe that this type of person is often drawn to politics, so the percentage of narcissists in Parliament would be higher than in the general population. It would explain so much.

These political bullies are the same nasty ones you knew at school, with the same techniques, more or less the same words, and definitely the same intentions – to big themselves up by making you cower. It's always about their need for power, in the playground or in politics. I loathe bullies.

I'll show you how we have been under their control for a very long time, and how they've used the system to destroy parts of the fabric of our society for their own benefit.

The 'DARVO' tactic

Psychologists have determined that narcissists use a tactic known as DARVO to manipulate others. DARVO stands for:

> **D**eny
> **A**ttack
> **R**everse the role of
> **V**ictim and
> **O**ffender

Over the course of this book, I'm going to give you a few examples in politics of when this tactic has been used, but this is something to watch out for in your private life too. Narcissists ruin lives; their kicks come from controlling others. DARVO is their way to avoid taking any responsibility for what they've done and to put the blame onto their victims. It allows them to control the narrative and to avoid any accountability for their behaviour. But once we know about it, we can call them out.

So let's run through DARVO and how it appears. Let's use as our example the insulting, disgraceful Partygate affair, where over a hundred police fines were issued, including to two prime ministers, Boris Johnson and Rishi Sunak.

The parties happened. Everyone there knew they happened. This is what they did when the word began to get out.

Deny: first they lied, lied, lied about it all.

Attack: Johnson said reports were 'deranged' and 'patently absurd'.

Reverse the role of **V**ictim and **O**ffender: Johnson and his staff were the offenders, but in 2023, Johnson claimed he was a victim of a Partygate and Brexit 'witch-hunt'. It's a very common technique.

This is just one instance of DARVO in action in politics. The list is, unfortunately, endless.

So watch out for this in the behaviour of those who lead us. So far, Sir Keir Starmer and his government don't seem to have displayed the same techniques, and certainly not to the same degree, but all this may change over time and as we head towards a future general election. And here's another thing to watch out for either in politics or in your private life . . .

The Circle of Acceptable Behaviour

There's something else you should know about narcissists, which goes some way to explaining what we've had to put up with politically over the last decade or so.

When I was in the *I'm a Celebrity* camp in South Africa with a number of famous faces, we would sit around and chat about anything from pizzas to politics.

I had come up with this theory of what I call the 'Circle of Acceptable Behaviour' a long time before and I explained it very briefly. I was surprised at the intensity of attention everyone paid to it.

The response when it was broadcast was extraordinary, with thousands of people saying, 'Finally, I understand how it happened to me' and 'Now it all makes sense'.

This Circle of Acceptable Behaviour shows how control and gaslighting incrementally escalate to become a new normal in a life with a narcissist. It doesn't just happen with partners, it happens within families, at work with bullies and on a national level too. It has definitely happened in politics over the last 14 years. Once you understand it and know to look for it, you will be warned early, and then it's up to you to call it out early where you can.

So here it is. I can only apologise if it triggers some bad memories for you. That is not the intention.

You can find 'controllers' everywhere, sadly: at work, maybe in your own family, among friends, partners, husbands or wives (many men suffer this kind of abuse too). Controllers have their own pattern of behaviour which is very different to that of a 'normal', reasonable person.

If you are a 'normal' person, it's likely you may not recognise the pattern until it's too late. In addition, society's rules have been established by controllers to protect controllers. Nobody wants to think badly of others. We don't like to question, on the whole. *Be polite; don't cause a fuss; gosh, don't say that; nobody's all bad* – these are all common phrases which protect bullies and shift the blame onto you. And this is the catch: even the most vile person you can imagine isn't always bad. They will be nice to someone somewhere along the line, usually to those who they aren't controlling. But remember those actions don't make them 'nice' or 'good': it's merely part of their 'charm'.

Before we start, let me ask you a question.

Think of all the people you've vaguely known or known well in your life: kids and people at school, family, extended family, people at work, customers, clients, people you know at the gym or the pub – all of them altogether.

Now answer this. What percentage of them would you say are nasty, or troublesome, or pick on people, or are unpleasant to be around? (I'm not talking about full-blown narcissists, by the way – just difficult, controlling people.)

I've asked hundreds of people this question, and the answer is never less than 10 per cent (one in 10 people), although research suggests the percentage of full-blown narcissists in a population is nearer 5 per cent (one in 20 people, which is still very high). The answers I'm given to this question normally range from 10 per cent up to 30 per cent, depending on that person's history.

Those are bad odds. Particularly if you are never taught how to deal with them and, let's be fair, where and when are you taught this?

For a happy and strong life, you have to know how to deal with them and be able mentally to face up to it.

Controllers have a burning desire for power; it gives them a kick, a buzz, it makes them feel good about themselves. Controlling is a game to them – a game they play so that only they can win.

It's difficult if you're a nice, good person to imagine why they would want to do that, and that is one of the reasons why they continue to get away with it. We want to believe that everyone is nice. They aren't. And that is step one, accepting that not everyone is nice, that bullies abound. It isn't a pleasant thought so we want to push it to the backs of our minds, but that won't help you when you next encounter a bully, or if you are in a coercive relationship with one right now. Strength comes with wisdom.

The first step, then, is to accept that controllers and bullies exist.

The second step is to understand how they work. Let me show you now.

Let's draw a circle, YOUR Circle of Acceptable Behaviour.

Inside this circle is your 'happy state'. This is the lovely circle in which everything is fine. You're happy. Your life is good, you aren't made to feel ashamed, or nervous, or uncomfortable. You wake up with a smile, enjoying the feeling that even if life isn't perfect (when is it?), you don't feel threatened. Fundamentally, you feel SAFE.

If somebody does something that makes you feel uncomfortable, scared, humiliated or nervous, their action sits *outside* of that circle, your Circle of Acceptable Behaviour.

We all know that almost animal-like, intuitive feeling of being threatened. There's a sense of discomfort in the pit of your stomach. You feel nervous or worried, and your brain starts spinning. Perhaps it happened in school, perhaps it happened at work, perhaps it happened with an ex, or perhaps it is happening now.

A controller will always operate within your Circle of Acceptable Behaviour to start with, so all is nice and rosy. Think about when politicians are trying to win your vote. The charm is real. The policies offering you what they think will win your vote come tumbling out.

Once the Conservative government took power in a coalition with the Liberal Democrats in 2010, they brought in 'austerity'. At that point, in effect they operated outside of our Circle of Acceptable Behaviour.

Now, there is nothing you can do in our democracy other than complain. You have little power. They can do exactly what they want, and nothing you can say or do will alter that until the next election.

So the Circle of Acceptable Behaviour gets bigger. Now a narcissist will operate within the bigger circle. It feels much less comfortable now for the person being controlled. The narcissist enjoys this, so they do more things within that bigger circle and you can do nothing about it. Your resistance is lowered. In your private life, you don't want another argument as bad as the last one.

That sense that nothing will change, the sense of helplessness which we all felt in recent years – so many of us have felt it. Every scandal deepened the sense that they could get away with anything, which was almost true. Lies and scandals were happening in plain sight.

The circle kept growing until gaslighting began.

In your private life that might mean the following phrases shouted at you.

'Oh, not that again,' they say, if you raise something they've done to harm you. 'You're mental, you're always kicking off.' 'You're crazy.'

Why am I telling you all this? Obviously, this is something that can happen to you in your private life. But I believe this is also exactly what has happened to the British public, on a much wider scale, over the last 14 years.

Our Circle of Acceptable Behaviour was pushed to the limits with each successive lie that the Tory politicians in power spun for us.

The behaviour of the people in charge of this country has been so appalling in recent times, so outrageous, that we became desensitised to it. We started to forget what was normal; what good, honourable politicians look like. With each lie, we became more resigned, felt more powerless.

This stops now. I hope that with our new government we can start to shrink the circle again so that we have a clearer sense of what is acceptable and what is not.

But we must be on guard to prevent that circle from ever increasing once more. There is a strong danger that it might.

And if anything I've said above speaks to you on a personal level, then please ask for help now. You are not alone.

Here are some words from a psychiatrist about former US president Donald Trump:

> *'Pathological narcissists can lose touch with reality in subtle ways that become extremely dangerous over time. When they can't let go of their need to be admired or recognized, they have to bend or invent a reality in which they remain special despite all messages to the contrary.'*
>
> – Bandy X Lee, *The Dangerous Case of Donald Trump: 27 Psychiatrists and Mental Health Experts Assess a President*

SO WHY THIS BOOK AND WHY NOW?

In late 2022, I started openly fighting the appalling Tory government with facts and data, looking into the morally corrupt and questionable contracts they signed with donors and associates, including via the multibillion-pound VIP PPE lane, which fast-tracked companies often with little or no experience of supplying personal protective equipment and in many cases resulted in the NHS receiving essential supplies that could not be used.

It's been an endless, exhausting and, in many ways, heartbreaking time.

I'd never known this country in such a state, with so little help and hope offered to those who need it.

NOW WHAT?

At 63 years old, I've witnessed a lot, and I'm now fortunate enough to be in a position where I am free to speak my mind. And frankly, I'm fuming about the blatant corruption of the system and the abuse doled out by the entitled to those who they regarded as beneath them. I felt I needed to speak out and to do what I could to amplify the voices of others who also wanted to be part of the change.

I've been trolled, abused, put on the naughty step at work, sacked by the BBC after refusing to give in to their new rules to force me to stop speaking truth to power on social media, but I wouldn't stop, and I won't stop.

Why? Because of a belief that what all of us have been doing is right, which comes from the knowledge – from what many tens of thousands of people have told me – that what we are saying *has been* helping. And most of all, I won't stop because I won't miss an opportunity to give a voice to so many who have been told that they have no voice. It's about all of us. I just happen to be someone who has been given a platform because I've been on the telly. It doesn't make me any better or superior or more triumphant than anyone else. I know that in every cell of my being. I've taught that to my kids and I can't bear snobs who think that they are above others.

My position has allowed me to call out the injustice I've witnessed. By myself and others showing the evidence and the data concerning the previous Tory government, the tide turned from frustration to rightful anger. We can see it clearly now and I'm proud to have been a very small part of that change. Obviously I hope that the new Labour government will behave in a proper manner. We all hope for that. They've inherited a terrible economy and numerous problems. My concern is that if they don't manage to make a real difference in people's lives, and it's a tall order, then at the next general election – which will happen in the blink of an eye – we may be looking at a far-right movement with more power, and there will be no turning back.

I'll cover all this in my diary later. But first, I'll take you back to 2022. By this time, there were bits and pieces of news (particularly if you went looking for it) about what had really been going on in Boris Johnson's government behind closed doors.

It was tough to learn progressively more about the lies, and then to be lied to again and again. It gave a sense of powerlessness. Like you, I found the fact that Partygate could have happened at all so utterly unthinkable, but as we came to know, it was all true.

So many were suffering long-term illness, the loss of members of their families. While frontline NHS workers were lied to and told to get to work with little or no PPE. The lies which had begun to be exposed were shocking.

I was lucky. I didn't lose anyone in those years. Mum had died a few years beforehand, which in one sense I was grateful for, as she would have been terrified by it all. My family was safe and I am eternally grateful for that.

Something happened at that time, though, to strengthen my resolve, which I haven't spoken about before. In early 2022, I was dealing with two 'stalkers'. What's that got to do with politics directly? Not a lot. But it was one of the key things that made me even more determined to hold bullies to account.

At first, the experience totally knocked the stuffing out of me.

It was unnerving and threatening and nasty. For a short time, I hit rock bottom, but I knew I had to find a way of dealing with them. I had a choice between going to the police in the hope they would investigate or getting lawyers involved. In 2020, during Covid, the police had been great in helping me deal with harassment from a pair of paparazzi photographers at my home, but this time, I felt that going to a lawyer would be a better option. Was I right? I don't know, but it's what I did. In the end, both 'stalkers' signed what were effectively 'civil restraining orders'. They are not allowed near my house or to make contact and all the restrictions you would expect.

It was shocking and overwhelming at first but once I'd dealt with it, the whole experience changed me. I went from feeling shaken and diminished by the threat to feeling stronger than ever. I was born a fighter and that spirit – which I'd lost for a while – came back. With bells on. I'm not very good at fighting for myself. I do it when I have to, but I'm a nightmare to a bully if I'm fighting for someone else.

You see, if *I* couldn't deal with it and had been pushed to the edge, as a woman with a loving family, supportive friends and enough money in the bank to get a good lawyer, then how the hell could a young woman without any financial resources or the safety of a family get through something like that? Those women and others need protecting.

So 2022 was the year I found my strongest political voice.

By the end of 2022, things were looking politically grim. In addition to the waves of revelations about parties at Downing Street during the lockdowns and the cronyism of the government PPE contracts, among several other scandals, we had the catastrophe of Liz Truss's 49-day premiership, and the lasting damage she managed to inflict on our economy and the lives of millions.

The more I saw, the more outraged I became. It was shocking how low and how quickly this country had sunk under successive Tory governments. I thought at the time, *I've been so lucky to have grown up in this country and had the opportunities I've had, and I'll be damned if I'll sit back while this gang of political hooligans destroys it all.*

So I flicked a switch and began to amplify stories, facts and data on social media. Often, they were stories which brilliant journalists (many of whom have since become allies and friends) had been investigating but hadn't necessarily come to mainstream media attention.

Social media can be immensely powerful and I started to use it to its fullest, but of course, as it began to make some noise, there were those who just wanted me to keep my mouth firmly shut.

Predictably, in the last year or so, I've been trolled, abused and threatened on a more or less daily basis online. All those quotes at the top of this introduction are real. I guess the Tories hoped the abuse would make me wobble and keep quiet, but it had the opposite effect. I found it became my oxygen. I looked at the people attacking me and knew I must be doing something right.

The more the bullies came for me, the stronger I felt. I think it related back to the 'stalking' episode, although not in a conscious way.

The more I fought, the more good people kept saying, 'Don't give up – you are speaking for us.' If you were one of those people online or who stopped me for a chat anywhere in recent times, thank you – it made a difference, and we have all been in this fight together.

It hit my career too, when I was sacked from my radio show on BBC Wales.

In the showbiz world I inhabit, there is an unwritten 'female celebrity rulebook' (which I'll explain more about in a moment), which says things like: 'don't upset the bosses', 'don't upset the newspapers', 'look nice', 'do nice things' and – crucially – 'don't get involved in politics'.

To get started on this road I had to decide to rip up that rulebook. I thought, *Throw at me what you can, I'm not stopping*. Did I stray out of my lane? I bloody drove a coach and horses in the opposite direction. And sure enough, they came after me.

In truth, I am just an old bird with an iPhone – at first with a lot to lose and, if I'm truly honest, absolutely nothing to gain, but with a burning feeling within that I had to do something, no matter how small.

The thing is, once I got started, and once I scratched the surface, I found (with the help of and through the brilliant journalism of a rare breed of people – honest and without fear – who you'll be reading about shortly) a trail of endless conflicts of interest and contracts representing an awful lot of OUR money being given to Tory donors, and I have come to the conclusion that the last Tory government has been the most corrupt, lying government in my lifetime.

In this book, I'm going to show you the blatant hypocrisy of those who governed us over the last 14 years and how certain people, not just the Tories, have made our antiquated and pretty useless political system work for them and not for us. I'll also be shining a light on the fights, the bullying, the resignations and the backroom deals – and a whole lot more about what goes on behind the scenes.

But we have to believe that things don't have to be this way. They can be better. I hope this book will show you *how* things can be better – and how *your* voice can be heard, alongside thousands of others, to make the changes we deserve. Above all things, I know that together we're stronger.

Even now, with a new Labour government, which has such power it can push through an immense amount of legislation, it's important that we still keep holding them to account.

Millions of us loaned our votes to Labour, the Liberal Democrats and other parties to tactically vote out the Tories, and with that voice we can keep going.

But, I hear you ask, *why* should we keep going?

Isn't the job over now?

I keep asking myself this and I hope you keep asking that question too, because I've learned so much in these last two years about how people have been told to think. As a result of being lied to and abused – yes, abused – by the most disgraceful government in modern times, too many people have become disillusioned and cynical. Responses have so often been 'nothing will change', 'they'll always get away with it', 'don't bother, it's how life is'. But it doesn't have to be that way.

Over the last 20 months, many people who previously felt they had no voice have found their voice and they've spoken. It's been the most wonderful thing to witness.

There's a collective sense of: 'We aren't taking your sh*t any more.' And that sense persists past the election.

So, having found our voices, it's important we don't lose them again. The job is far from over. The previous government has left us with a political system that has been degraded and broken. We know that the path ahead for the new government will be long and hard. It's essential that we hold the incoming politicians to account, in just the same way as we did with the outgoing ones.

If we want to see change, we need to be part of that change ourselves.

MY FIRST
POLITICAL TWEET

Before I tell you about my first political tweet on 23 November 2022, I need to give you a bit of background about its subject, the Scottish businesswoman and Conservative peer Michelle Mone. In particular, I need to explain her role in the scandal of how the last government gave contracts to its cronies during the Covid-19 pandemic to supply personal protective equipment (PPE) for the NHS, raking in vast profits in the process.

So, where to begin?

The obscenity of the government's PPE 'VIP lane' became obvious towards the end of 2020. By then, the National Audit Office had reported that early in the pandemic, the government had set up a 'high priority lane' to process contract leads from 'government officials, ministers' offices, MPs, members of the House of Lords, senior NHS staff and other health professionals'. And that any company recommended through this VIP lane was ten times more likely to get a government contract to supply PPE than companies funnelled through other paths.[15] That, in my mind, and probably yours, is how corruption works, I guess!

We now know – after the endless pursuit by a number of journalists and organisations – that all of those firms awarded contracts through the 'high priority lane' were referred by Conservative MPs, advisers and Lords (none from any other political party), and billions of pounds of our money went to companies, often without any PPE experience, with links to the Conservative party. Many of those linked to the companies were Tory donors, or even Tory councillors. The profligacy of the previous government and its refusal to this day to accept any responsibility for the £9.9 billion of PPE which they ordered but which was unfit for use by the NHS (some not through the VIP lane) is, in my opinion, the worst corruption scandal of our time.[16] For some of these companies to consider blatant profiteering[17] – as I would call it – during a pandemic says all you need to know about them. But the creation of the VIP lane is just one instance of the pattern of behaviour of the relentlessly appalling previous Tory government, members of which still believe they have done nothing wrong.

One such VIP lane company was PPE Medpro, a firm set up in May 2020 with links to the Isle of Man. The company received two government contracts – the first for £81 million of PPE masks and the second for £122 million of gowns, a total of £203 million.

In December 2020, the *Guardian* newspaper ran one of the

first stories about Michelle Mone's possible links to PPE Medpro, written by the brilliant journalists Russell Scott, David Conn and David Pegg.[18] It revealed that Michelle Mone had referred a non-existent company, PPE Medpro, to the government on 7 May 2020 as a potential PPE supplier. PPE Medpro wasn't even registered as a company in the Isle of Man until 11 May 2020 and in the UK on 12 May 2020. If ever there was intent to profiteer this was as blatant as it could be.

The directors of the company were based in the offices of Michelle Mone's second husband, Doug Barrowman, under the roof of the Knox Group (his business HQ) on the Isle of Man. Two of the three directors of PPE Medpro, including Anthony Page, also worked for Barrowman. This might seem like quite a coincidence, when you consider that neither Michelle Mone nor Doug Barrowman 'had any role or function in the company, or in the process by which the contracts were awarded' – at least, according to one of their lawyers who spoke to the *Guardian* at the time. Three years later, in December 2023, these denials were revealed to be a lie.

In November 2021, a year after the first questions were asked, more details emerged after a freedom of information (FOI) request from the Good Law Project. GLP is a crowdfunded organisation of lawyers and activists who do incredible work. The Tories often try to denounce them, which is, as far as I'm concerned, a great recommendation in itself.

The evidence supporting the link between Mone and PPE Medpro started to build as GLP discovered that, contrary to all that had been said before, it was Michelle Mone who had recommended this brand new company to the VIP lane, through Michael Gove and her fellow Tory peer Lord Agnew.

At this point, Mone, having been caught out, carried on lying to – and through – her lawyers, who wrote: 'Having taken the very simple, solitary and brief step of referring PPE Medpro as a potential supplier to the office of Lord Agnew, our client did not do anything further in respect of PPE Medpro.' Also: 'Baroness Mone did not declare any interest [in the Lords' Register of Interests] as she did not benefit financially and was not connected to PPE Medpro in any capacity.'

In spite of endless lawyers' letters denying Mone's involvement in an attempt to shut the story down, things began to hot up, thanks to the sterling investigative work at the *Guardian*, the *Financial Times* and the Good Law Project. They weren't backing down, and thank God for them.

Early in 2022, the *Guardian* once again reported on Mone and Barrowman's involvement with PPE Medpro. In turn, Mone's lawyers claimed that the *Guardian*'s report was 'grounded entirely on supposition and speculation and not based on accuracy'. Hmmm.

But all was not well in Tory Story Land: a mythical place where a Tory could say and do anything they like without being questioned. In March 2022, it was revealed that the NHS had rejected the £122 million of gowns provided by PPE Medpro as they had not been fit for purpose.

Weeks later, booommm. The National Crime Agency (NCA) raided many of Mone and Barrowman's homes and offices, as it said it was now analysing 'suspected criminal offences'. Well I never, or as my mum used to say, 'Well, I'll go to the foot of our stairs.' I'm sure the collar of your detective rain mac is now turned up at a jaunty angle.

Just as the trail to the truth was beginning to make headway, it all seemed to stop, as Mone was issuing multiple lawyers' letters threatening to sue newspapers. These so-called 'SLAPP notices' can be pretty frightening – more of which later.

But then on 23 November 2022, the *Guardian* dropped a bomb-shell.[19] Someone had leaked documents produced by the bank HSBC which showed that approximately £65 million of 'profit' from PPE Medpro had been paid to Doug Barrowman through a series of offshore accounts, which often credited and debited large amounts within minutes. From there, via a complex web of trans-fers, around £29 million had been deposited in a secret offshore trust called Keristal Trust, of which Mone and her children were the beneficiaries.

Enormous sums of money – amounts of money from which dynasties can be founded – all on the back of PPE deemed unfit for use by the NHS, acquired through a morally bankrupt govern-ment process, handing over taxpayers' cash. Not only that, it was also reported that Barrowman had had three-way contact with the Cabinet Office, a supply chain partner called Loudwater Trade and Finance, and PPE Medpro, while all the time denying through law-yers that he or Mone had anything to do with it. If this is proven, then it will mean that the government knew all along that the couple were involved.

It was on that day in November 2022, after reading the article, that my rage with the Tory government boiled over. Bugger the unwritten rule that 'celebrities should stay quiet'. This was an obscenity. So, in spite of warnings from others that Michelle Mone might sue me or that it wasn't 'my place', I decided I wanted to say something publicly about it. As I've said before, I am just an old bird with an iPhone, but what happened from here made me realise that we all must find our voice in one way or another.

What made me want to speak out on this particular scandal? Well, here we go with a bit of a story.

I not only want to tell you how I briefly got to know Michelle Mone, but I also want to show you how, with a wrong 'un – and it seems that both Mone and Barrowman could be considered in that way – there is always a pattern.

I knew Michelle Mone for a short period of time over ten years ago and let's just say, leopards never change their spots. The reason I dropped her as a 'friend' was the scale of her lying. She was, in my opinion, a con woman. I'll explain.

The traits of any con artist and his or her habits are pretty predictable. They lie, obviously, and they gain recognition by associating themselves with people or organisations that have credibility.

I was introduced to Michelle Mone by the BBC in 2009. I was part of a team on the Comic Relief show *Celebrity Apprentice Does Comic Relief*. In the boys' team were Alan Carr, Jonathan Ross, Jack Dee, Gok Wan and Gerald Ratner, and in the girls' team, it was me, Fiona Phillips, Patsy Palmer, Ruby Wax and this person I'd not really heard of before, called Michelle Mone.

The BBC introduced her to us all as a hugely successful female entrepreneur, founder of a lingerie company called Ultimo, which again I wasn't really familiar with. But there were suggestions that the success of Ultimo was not as rosy as her marketing pitch would have you believe – later reports by the *Guardian* and *Business Matters* among others suggested there was a fair amount of smoke and mirrors.[20] It was claimed the company was worth over £40 million; that valuation has been questioned. It is not clear who was right, but the claims had given her credibility (you'll begin to see the pattern), as this number had gone into what is known as 'the cuttings' in the media, meaning it was repeated endlessly in the press as if it was the truth. In that way, reputations can be made and lost. And this really was before the advent of the power of social media.

By then, Mone had already hit the headlines for various attention-seeking manoeuvres, such as her claim that Julia Roberts, playing *Erin Brockovich* in the movie by the same title, had worn an Ultimo push-up bra (a business associate of Mone's later claimed that *Erin Brockovich* was wrapped up before Ultimo was even launched). In 2004, after a marketing campaign featuring Rod Stewart's then girl-friend Penny Lancaster (now wife and she's a wonderful woman) came to an end, her next signing was his ex-wife Rachel Hunter, presumably as a publicity stunt.[21] Rod Stewart has described Mone as 'devious and conniving'.

Later, after she and I had parted ways – no big row, I just shuf-fled off stage left – Mone had a number of negative brushes with publicity. MJM International (the Ultimo parent company) made large losses and after it was sold it eventually went bust (!); Mone's diet pills brand Trim Secrets closed; two former employees took the company to tribunal, one for having his office bugged (he was awarded compensation), with the other, Hugh McGinley, settling out of court.[22]

Then there was her EQUI cryptocurrency company, which amounted to nothing and closed owing its agents money, despite Mone's ludicrous claims on X, where she said: 'I never thought I could go from being on [sic] of the best technical lingerie designers in the World, No.1 woman entrepreneur to one of the biggest experts in Cryptocurrency & Blockchain #believe.'[23] She told the *Financial Times* (in a brilliant piece by journalist Jemima Kelly) that she and Barrowman were staking their 'incredible reputations' on this launch and that there was 'no way [they were] going to do anything untowards [sic] to let these people down'.[24]

EQUI (not to be confused with other companies) raised less than 10 per cent of its target in the first month. There followed a lot of marketing puff about the firm being 'a mega exciting new global strategy'; meanwhile, the 'bounty hunters' (online sales people, generally from poorer countries, who receive payment in cryptocurrency for promoting the brand) say they did not receive what they were promised. The *FT* reported that when these 'bounty hunters' complained, EQUI threatened them with lawyers or even the police if they 'bad-mouthed' the company; another message sent the same day said, 'You are all so stupid'. EQUI declined to comment on the messages to the *FT*, though it claimed it had paid the money owed to a third party who would distribute it to the bounty hunters.

There is always a pattern.

And then there were the bizarre stories: when Mone bought a house in Glasgow, she made a video for a magazine in which she claimed that Albert Einstein had lived in the house. Einstein, as you've probably guessed, never lived in Glasgow. A minor, relatively inconsequential example perhaps, but one that shows the pattern of outlandish statements and nobody questioning it. (Until the journalists at the *National* did in 2023, a decade after she had made the claim.[25]) Following the well-worn script, Mone threatened to sue them . . . and then didn't. Mone's lawyers claimed the developers had told her that, though it was an odd thing for her to repeat unquestioningly if so.

And then there is the strange case of the reported £50,000+ settlement of a libel claim from a man of Indian heritage, Richard Lynton-Jones, in 2021. Following a tragic yachting accident,[26] Lynton-Jones claimed that Mone had sent him racist messages, including, 'Your [sic] a low life, a waste of a mans [sic] white skin so don't give us your lies. Your [sic] a total disgrace.' He also claimed that Mone had said of Mr Lynton-Jones's partner that she was a 'mental loony' and 'nut case bird'. Mone repeatedly denied she is a racist and her lawyers questioned the authenticity of the messages. After the settlement, Mone's lawyers announced, 'Both parties have settled their differences on a no fault or damages basis in relation to the alleged racist claim and the matter is now concluded.'

Back we go to 2009 and Comic Relief, and who were we to argue with what the BBC told us about her being a successful entrepreneur, and what they believed to be true? So the BBC, one of the most trusted institutions in Britain, innocently gave Mone credibility. She was also working with the Prince's Trust – again, a credible organisation.

After the Comic Relief show, lots of us exchanged phone numbers, though I didn't hear much from Michelle, other than a request for Alan Carr and I to go to a charity gig in London with her. A year or so later I took a contract to host *Loose Women* on ITV. I should explain that I live in Bristol, so when I work at the ITV Studios in London, I need to stay in a hotel. So I started to stay more regularly at the Dorchester Hotel on Park Lane. Very nice. I'm a lucky woman and I felt safe there. I got to know a lot of the staff very well – one of them remains a close friend.

At this time, Michelle was staying there as well and we started to hang out a bit. When you're a single woman staying away from home, it's comforting to have people you can easily ring and say, 'Shall we meet downstairs and have a drink or a cup of tea?' rather than sitting in your room every night. And that was how, quite simply, the 'friendship' started up. We went out together, often with other friends, when we were both in the hotel and not working.

Over the course of the year, when I was staying at the hotel on and off, Michelle would sometimes say things that made me think twice. And a little trigger would flip in my head. Nothing major, just a question mark here and there.

Nowadays, that sort of action from someone I didn't know too well would be a red flag, but back then, my life was stupidly busy. I had two young children in school, one with special educational needs. I was a single parent; my elderly mum lived with me and wasn't well; I was running my online maths school company in Bristol with a lot of employees, and I was presenting a show in a city where I didn't live. Plenty of other things were going on in my life. London was just a part of it.

Michelle was then married to Michael Mone, who seemed like a nice bloke when I met him. Within months, she started to rent a flat in Mayfair, around the corner from the Dorchester Hotel, and she kept telling people that I was staying there. I can remember staying there one night. I might even have stayed there for up to three nights, at the very most.

Michelle would say, 'Oh yes, we've named a bedroom after Carol,' which was an odd thing to say, but I treated it like a joke.

The first clang sounded, however, when she did an interview and photoshoot with a celebrity magazine. In this article, she told the journalist that she'd bought the flat for £2 million. But that's not what she'd told me.

And it was at that point that I thought: *I don't like this, I'm backing out.* Which I did. I started to rent a flat in London with my then partner, and I saw her less and less.

But there was a point when I wanted nothing more to do with her. There was never an argument (not my style), nor a big bust up (no pun intended), just me disappearing into the shadows. That was in 2012. In that year, she and her husband split up, and after that I would get a text from her every now and then but I didn't keep in contact.

In 2015, David Cameron put Michelle Mone into the House

of Lords. A strange decision, hugely unpopular with the Scottish Tories: one declared that Mone was 'a public relations creation, a personal brand rather than a serious businesswoman' and another said that if David Cameron had asked their opinion 'he'd have been told she's a nightmare'.[27]

When I heard this news, I admit that it did concern me. And the reason why is that now somebody who I regarded as a con artist was in a position to influence legislation. I had a feeling it might amount to something happening, but obviously had no appreciation of what that might be.

Now, before I tweeted about Michelle, I thought about two things.

The first was libel, as journalist friends had told me she was sending lawyers' letters out like confetti, and the second was about crossing the 'celebrity line', jumping the reputational shark. Let's talk about libel first – and SLAPPs.

How the rich own the 'truth'

Libel is a funny thing. Well, it isn't funny at all. It's a very serious piece of law which, as I've learned, generally belongs to the rich. Tom Burgis, a superb and brave investigative journalist, discusses the subject in his recent book *Cuckooland: Where the Rich Own the Truth*. He has often been threatened with libel suits but continues in his pursuit of the facts. A good man to follow.

So how does a libel/defamation claim work here in the UK?

Briefly (and please don't accept this as a legal definition for anything which you may be involved in), it's a game of poker.

One party – the claimant – decides that their reputation has been damaged by something which has been published by the defendant. A tweet is classed as a publication by the way; 'publication' doesn't just refer to newspaper articles or books. The claimant may give the defendant the chance to put what they regard as their defamatory piece right and may or may not ask for an apology and a sum of money.

If the claimant then issues a claim (a particular piece of legal form and letter), then from that point, the claimant is liable for the defendant's legal costs unless the whole thing goes to court and the claimant wins. There are opportunities for the court to throw out a poor claim and in the UK only around a dozen cases get to court in a year.

Often, if the claimant wins, the court will award damages of up to around £100,000 (although it can go higher), but the big bill is the legal costs, as the losing defendant will then have to pay both parties' legal bills. Now you're talking about a potential cost of over £500,000 or higher.

So unless you have a spare half a million pounds, if somebody comes after you, you are more likely to cave in and make good your so-called 'error of judgement' than risk your house. And don't forget that one of the most chilling effects of our libel laws is that the burden of proof is on the defendant, so it's up to the person who publishes the allegedly defamatory remarks to *prove* they are true (or that they have another defence), not for the subject of the comments to prove they're *not* true.

So that, ladies and gentlemen, is how the rich own the truth as the law stands right now.

I also mentioned SLAPPs earlier. These are 'strategic lawsuits against public participation', which as the former Labour MP for Caerphilly Wayne David explains, are 'legal threats brought to intimidate and financially and psychologically exhaust journalists, campaigners and anyone who would criticise or expose corruption'. Not surprisingly, Michelle Mone and Doug Barrowman have issued many of these over the years. Slapped with a SLAPP and you're forced to sit up and take notice.

Given her litigious nature, it seemed only the brave were willing to publish the details about Michelle Mone.

I also had a second issue.

In my world, as a so-called 'celebrity', whatever that means, I had other things to consider. You see, there are unwritten 'rules' about what a celebrity should and shouldn't do. Here's my attempt to tell you what they have been and what they are now. Feel free to laugh, such is the ridiculous nature of 'celebrity' world.

The unwritten Celebrity Rulebook

I've been on the telly since 1982, which to me seems like yesterday but is actually a very, very long time ago. In all of that time, it has seemed totally normal to me to be known by most people I bump into. I suppose it's quite odd really, but that's been my life and I enjoy chatting to people.

When you are in the public eye, there seems to be a bit of a rulebook to keep your career on the straight and narrow. I jokingly call it the Celebrity Rulebook. It's unwritten – no one has really ever put it into words, until now – but here are the secrets, just between you and me of course.

Fundamentally, before social media really got going in the mid-2010s, everything you saw about a famous person had to pass through the filter of newspaper editors and TV bosses – they aren't baddies, by the way, many are pretty wonderful people – but in terms of what a well-known woman (different rules for a man, obviously) could/should say, the rules basically used to go like this:

1. Be nice to all newspaper journalists and especially to those women who write 'columns'.

2. Make sure you have good publicity so that people can see how nice you are, what a good mother you are, that you look OK in photographs. Say the right things so you aren't seen as being too loud or too stupid or too smart or living outside of society's 'rules'. (I struggled with all of these, incidentally . . .)

3. Don't say anything bad about any journalists, even if they say bad things about you.

4. Don't name any names, even if you know they've done wrong.

5. Keep in 'your lane'.

6. Don't get involved in anything political unless it's to show how nice you are.
7. Be witty.
8. Be pretty.
9. Be especially nice to the *Daily Mail* (whose opinion used to hold great sway in TV companies, though far, far less nowadays).

Yep, that just about covers it . . . And in that way, you were very much beholden to the whims of columnists and editors. They were powerful people. Most of my TV life was run under these rules; I did pretty well, to be honest, and have had a lot of friends in the press over the years. Still do.

After social media began, most notably in the last five to ten years, the rules have changed dramatically – and by and large they are better for it. Yes, the newspapers remain quite powerful, but absolutely nothing like they were before. They are far less trusted by the public (the *Sun* and the *Daily Mail* are two of the least trusted newspapers in the UK[28]) and most under-forties get their news from social media. The newspapers have become more fixed in their political agenda, moving further to the right on the whole – which is sad but not surprising when they're largely owned by billionaires who may tend to pay little UK tax. They don't like the influence of social media, and the freedoms it gives us, but there we are. I do.

These are the Celebrity Rules as they stand in 2024:

1. A celeb has the power to reply immediately to a 'story' and to everyone. It's an open forum. Post on X or Insta or TikTok and the world knows your side of the story.
2. People of all persuasions can say what they like to you and about you. Some of that is good, some of that is bad.
3. Newspapers (their sales have diminished rapidly over 15 years) report on what you say and also on what others say about you. That can be good, that can be not so good.
4. Online versions of newspapers have reporters whose job it is to scour social media and report on what celebrities have said. That is not a criticism from me, by the way. It's just life.
5. Social media is a very powerful player indeed. It costs nothing, more or less, and it's immediate. It can be very friendly and extremely informative, and it's powerful. I've made so many strong bonds of friendship online with people who feel the same way as I do politically.
6. You have to be careful where you get your source data from so that you don't spread untruths. I try to stick with trusted sources.

It's a whole new set of rules, and ones which I, and others, have used over the last year in order to demonstrate, with facts and data and evidence, how corruption and cronyism has taken place, how laws have been changed, how people have been given seats in the House of Lords when they shouldn't have, and so much more.

So, back to Michelle Mone

My journalist friends said, 'She'll sue you.' I said, 'She won't sue me. I know things' (from ten years or more before, not about the PPE). I thought about the libel issue, I thought about the Celebrity Rulebook and peeing off my bosses, I thought about all of the things I know about Michelle and then I thought – *feck it.*

On 23 November 2022, I sent this tweet, linking the *Guardian* article on Mone that had appeared that day, written by David Conn:[29]

Carol Vorderman ✔ @carolvorders   1hr ...

'Lady' Mone broke Lords' code & was seemingly involved in fraud while nurses & doctors slaved all hours to save people in the 1st lockdown. She denied any involvement but her husband got £65m profit & she £29m. If so, slam them in jail where they belong

O   t⏎   ♡   ◻   ⬆

The papers went wild, some with a predictable 'Vorderman in bitch-fest' style of headline. Of course, a man saying another man has done wrong is never labelled in that way – he's brave or courageous, whereas when a woman calls out the wrongdoing of another woman it's a whole different story. But there we are.

The fallout was immediate, but from then on I felt free of the constraints of the press. I have never felt freer. To genuinely not give a flying crap what the *Daily Mail* writes about me has been one of the biggest releases of all. You can tell a lot about a person by the company they keep, so to be screeched about by some screechy Tory paper on a screechy day – well, I must be doing something mighty fine!

In the course of the following days, after the *Guardian* article, Labour called for Mone to step down, the Tories did bugger all (as ever) . . . but on 6 December 2022, Mone took 'leave of absence' from the House of Lords 'in order to clear her name of the allegations that have been unjustly levelled against her'.

Of course she did . . . the liar.

THE DIARY

To tell the story as it happened from this point on, I'll be sharing parts of my diary with you. I've been very active every day online since my first political tweet in November 2022, but here I've pulled out some pieces I think might interest you. There's a lot more online, believe me; we'd probably need five volumes to get through all the Tory misbehaviour.

Welcome to a mad world of highs and lows, shocking discoveries, belly laughs and raucous rows.

18 DECEMBER 2022

I'm already staggered by the amount of information online, which is demonstrating a plethora of conflicts of interest on the part of Conservative politicians. There's so much to be discovered simply by scratching the surface and knowing where to look that sometimes it's overwhelming.

Just in this first month of tweeting politically, I've had both incredible support from thousands of people on and offline (thank you so much for that) and, on the other side, I've run a wild gamut of abuse from right-wingers who, with one glance at their online profile, seem to support Putin, misogynists and bullies. If I've triggered them, then it means I must be doing something right, so I'm sure as hell going to carry on.

I'm also beginning to find others online who think as I do, that this country needs not just a change of government from the abysmal one we have at the moment, but a change in the system itself.

I get thousands of replies to tweets a day and have been trying to read as many as possible. At first, the comments were very despondent – 'there's nothing we can do', 'they'll always get away with it' – but I can feel a change in our collective mood now. We can make a genuine difference if we raise our voices and call out wrongdoing, whether it's government corruption or good old-fashioned misogyny and bullying.

One small example of this occurred today. This morning, in the *Sun* newspaper, Jeremy Clarkson wrote this about Meghan Markle:

I hate her. Not like I hate Nicola Sturgeon or Rose West. I hate her on a cellular level. At night, I'm unable to sleep as I lie there, grinding my teeth and dreaming of the day when she is made to parade naked through the streets of every town in Britain, while

the crowds chant 'Shame!' and throw lumps of excrement at her.
Everyone who's my age thinks the same way.

Now, I've known Jeremy for many years; telly is a small world, he's a 'character', his schtick is to amuse through insults, sometimes self-deprecating. He has a brilliant command of language. This piece, however, was on another level. A general point, not specific to Jeremy, is that for decades, women (me included) have had to 'take the joke' when no joke was intended, by some, the intention is merely humiliation. It's how bullies and narcissists work, by the way. You'll have seen it happen to others in many small ways or had it happen to you. The bully knows what they're doing, you know what they're doing, and everybody stands by saying nothing as they 'don't want to cause a fuss'. Well, bugger that. From now on, I'm going to 'cause a fuss'.

Many of us tweeted in response. This morning I wrote:

Carol Vorderman ✔ @carolvorders   1hr ...

NO Jeremy Clarkson. Not on any level, in any circumstance, is it OK to write this stuff about any woman. And absolutely NO to 'everyone who's my age thinks the same'. No no no. We absolutely do NOT think the same. Listen to the noise Jeremy. The crowds are chanting 'shame on YOU'.

　　　○　　　⟲　　　♡　　　🔖　　　⬆

The tweet was viewed 16 million times with 117,000 likes. It was reported in the press. Other people also joined in the chorus of disapproval. Even Jeremy's daughter Emily put up a post on Instagram to reprimand her father, saying: 'I stand against everything that my dad wrote about Meghan Markle.' A lesson in how you can love someone but still be able to call out their bad behaviour when you think it's wrong.

Staying quiet meant nothing would happen. By many of us calling it out, action had to be taken.

As night follows day, the so-called 'free speech merchants' (for 'free speech' read 'free to insult and abuse all who disagree' with them) and the misogynists came for us online. The very same people who would say about a woman 'she was asking for it', I would guess. The two are linked. It's what society says is acceptable. Clarkson claimed it was a 'joke' – all the usual excuses. Just apologise, Jezza, and move on. We all get it wrong sometimes. Sometimes you just have to own your sh*t.

19 DECEMBER 2022

It's been a couple of weeks of intense and bad publicity for the Tories, culminating with Michelle Mone taking 'leave of absence' from the House of Lords. Today, it may have become apparent why she took that decision.

It's been reported that the Department of Health and Social Care is taking PPE Medpro to court over the £122 million of unusable PPE which it provided after it was awarded the second contract through the VIP lane.

Mone's leave of absence means she will also no longer be bound by parliamentary rules to declare any directorships, shareholdings and non-financial interests. Quite handy in the circumstances.

Note that the Lords' Commissioners for Standards are already investigating the Baroness over multiple 'potential breaches' of the Lords' Code of Conduct. Well, I never.

The Labour party, quite rightly, is not giving up. Angela Rayner, who's been a key figure in Labour's pursuit of the PPE wastage said, 'After nearly a year of hiding behind a mediation process with a company linked to one of their own peers, Conservative ministers have finally been shamed into action to recover taxpayers' money after damning revelations, public outcry and Labour pressure. Time will now tell if the shoddy contracts they drew up are sufficiently robust to retrieve the public money they carelessly handed over.'

To add insult to injury, it's also been reported that Barrowman and Mone may have been on a spending spree since PPE Medpro received the money, including the purchase of a private jet for £7.5 million a matter of months after PPE Medpro had received over £203 million from the government. Coincidence – or blatant profiteering and two fingers up to the public?

20 DECEMBER 2022

The fallout from Jeremy's nasty comment about Meghan Markle continues. Today I put out another tweet:

Carol Vorderman ✔ @carolvorders   1hr ...

The Clarkson Effect.

I've received a lot of abuse obvs, but it's like watching the last death throes of a dinosaur age. Sad souls who are angry at new thought, at equality, at kindness. BUT this chapter has also brought the calm, normally silent people together. We fight on 🖤

Tory MP and chair of the Select Committee for Women and Equalities Caroline Nokes has sent a letter to the editor of the *Sun*, saying the article was 'role modelling . . . to young men and boys that they can verbally attack women without any consequence'. The letter is countersigned by many MPs from all political parties.

23 DECEMBER 2022

The *Sun* and the Independent Press Standards Organisation (IPSO – the self-regulating press body) have received more than 25,000 complaints about Clarkson's now infamous column. Today, the *Sun* apologised to Meghan Markle and they've taken down the column from their website.[30]

What I'm pointing out here is that collectively we have the power to change things. This might seem small, and it's 'just' about a newspaper column, but what we deemed acceptable in the 1970s (which actually wasn't remotely acceptable but women just had to put up with it) isn't now because people have come together to change those rules in society. And through government, politics can do the same.

As we go into the New Year, I am hopeful that the same can happen again.

4 JANUARY 2023

Less than three months ago, Rishi Sunak put on his serious face, stretched his limbs and, in his best private-school debating voice, spoke some profound words at his lectern outside Number 10 Downing Street. Here was our third prime minister in three months, following the Liar-in-Chief Boris Johnson and the Lettuce Liz Truss; here was an unelected man speaking after the economy had gone into freefall and mortgages are through the proverbial roof, the cost of living is causing pain for millions, the gap in inequality is growing and the super-rich are getting ever richer.

This is what he said:

'The government I lead will not leave the next generation, your children and grandchildren, with a debt to settle that we were too weak to pay ourselves. I will unite our country, not with words, but with action. I will work day in and day out to deliver for you. This government will have integrity, professionalism and accountability at every level. Trust is earned. And I will earn yours.'

How's that going?

Pretty badly, I would say, with a total lack of integrity, utter ineptitude and zero accountability at every level.

Today, he gave his five pledges for the year ahead, which he claimed we could hold him to. Jeez. Here they are, in full:

- We will halve inflation this year to ease the cost of living and give people financial security.
- We will grow the economy, creating better-paid jobs and opportunity right across the country.
- We will make sure our national debt is falling so that we can secure the future of public services.
- NHS waiting lists will fall and people will get the care they need more quickly.
- We will pass new laws to stop small boats, making sure that if you come to this country illegally, you are detained and swiftly removed.

He then went on to list a few more goals: 'A stronger NHS. Better schools. Safer streets. Control of our borders. Protecting our environment. Supporting our armed forces. Levelling up and building an economy that embraces the opportunities of Brexit, where businesses invest, innovate and create jobs.'

Well, a new year lies ahead. Let's see how he gets on, shall we? Welcome to Tory World 2023.

EXPLAINER: THE HOUSE OF COMMONS

Before we get too far into the diary, let's get the basics out of the way so we can get going.

If you know it already, brilliant. If you don't, then some of this might be useful.

The aim here is to clarify and take the 'political language' out of politics.

The most important decision-makers in the 'Palace of Westminster' (the official name for the Houses of Parliament) are in the **government**. The government, as opposed to a political party and all of its MPs, is a small group which consists of the prime minister, his/her Cabinet members, including secretaries of state, and also junior ministers who may or may not sit in the Cabinet. They are supported by independent, non-political civil servants who work in government departments.

Then there is **Parliament**, made up of the King, the House of

Lords and the House of Commons. Their job it is to examine and challenge the work of the government. No new laws can be made or taxes raised without Parliament's agreement.

The **sovereign**, King Charles III right now, or his officials, give royal assent to any new laws. That's the moment that bills become law. He opens Parliament and also 'dissolves' Parliament at the request of the prime minister when a general election is called. As it stands, the maximum term of a government is five years, but a prime minister can call an election at any time, as we've seen in recent years. They are called 'snap elections'. Lots of words and shenanigans, but basically, that's what happens.

Just over half of Parliament sits in the House of Lords (see the Explainer on page 175). These members have mostly been appointed for life. I've written a separate piece on how we must have complete reform of the House of Lords soon (see my Plan for Change, page 340).

The House of Commons is made up of 650 members of Parliament (MPs). MPs, as we know, have all been elected by the public in a general election or by-election. Their job, theoretically, is to take part in government votes and debates and represent the concerns of their constituents. They are generally members of political parties, though it's perfectly possible to be an independent MP.

What is the Cabinet?

The Cabinet is the senior decision-making body in government, made up of the prime minister and around 20–25 top government ministers, typically the heads of the government departments (the secretaries of state). They meet once a week in the Cabinet room in 10 Downing Street whenever Parliament is sitting.

Their role is to propose and implement new laws and policies, advise the PM and deal with any crises that are affecting the country.

The official 'opposition' is the party with the second largest number of MPs in the House of Commons. The official opposition has people who 'shadow' those in the ruling Cabinet, so the Chancellor and the Shadow Chancellor, the Secretary of State for Defence and the Shadow Secretary of State for Defence, and so on. So the 'Shadow Cabinet' is made up of senior members of the main opposition party – essentially acting as the Cabinet's opposite numbers.

Speaker of the House of Commons

You've probably heard of the Speaker, most recently Sir Lindsay Hoyle, an MP who was formerly with the Labour party. Their main role is to represent the House at ceremonial occasions and to maintain order during parliamentary debates.

They are meant to be entirely impartial – in fact, they are

expected to resign from their party when they are appointed (via a secret ballot of MPs), though they still remain a serving MP. But they do have limited powers of discretion – the Speaker can decide who to call to speak in debates and they can also exercise their judgement when it comes to things like whether to allow an urgent question or emergency debate.

Occasionally, this appearance of careful impartiality goes wrong – this memorably happened to Sir Lindsay Hoyle in February 2024, when his handling of the SNP's Gaza motion caused fury as it appeared to favour Sir Keir Starmer. Hoyle was in the news again the following month, when he failed to call on Diane Abbott at PMQs after front pages led with a story about Tory party donor Frank Hester having made racist comments about her.

As a general rule, the Speaker should try to avoid becoming the story themselves.

I remember the incredible Betty Boothroyd, a former stage dancer with the Tiller Girls in the 1940s, who became the first and still the only woman Speaker in UK history from 1992 to 2000. Born and brought up in Yorkshire, she was legendary and took no nonsense from MPs from any party in the House.

Frontbenchers and backbenchers

The government's Cabinet and the Shadow Cabinet ministers occupy the front of their respective benches in the House of Commons – hence the name 'frontbenchers'. The others are the regular MPs who are known as 'backbenchers'. Traditionally, as we view it on our TV screens, the governing party will sit on the left of the Speaker, with the Speaker in the middle and the opposition to the right.

How laws are made

Let's go through the various stages of how a proposal and a policy, can be brought into law.

1. First, the proposed law, known as a bill, is drafted. It can be brought by the government or individual MPs.
2. The bill is introduced for its 'first reading' in either the Commons or the Lords. It's essentially just a presentation at this stage.
3. On the second reading, the bill is debated then a vote is taken. If the bill passes, it goes on to the next stage.
4. The committee stage is when the bill is examined in detail by a special committee of MPs or Lords, and amended if necessary.
5. Now the committee reports back. More debate and amendment.
6. Then it goes on to the third reading. Another vote!
7. If the bill started in the Commons it then goes on to the Lords (and vice versa). Now the other House goes through the whole process of scrutiny again.

8. Finally, once both Houses have agreed the text with all its amendments, it goes to the monarch for royal assent. At which point, the bill becomes law.

How are votes carried out in the Commons?

Every item on the agenda for MPs to consider in the Commons is framed in terms of a question. First, there's a debate, then the question is 'put' to the MPs by the Speaker (or whoever's chairing), at which point they shout 'aye' or 'no'. If one side is louder than the other, then the Speaker will declare that the ayes or the noes 'have it', i.e. one side has won. I know, it sounds bizarre in this day and age, but that's what happens.

If it's not clear who has won, then the Speaker will call for a more formal 'division'. At this point, the MPs will physically walk down one of two corridors on either side of the main Commons chamber – the 'aye' or 'no' lobby. So the House literally divides. MPs have ten minutes to get there if they are not already in the chamber of the House of Commons, after which the doors are locked. 'Tellers' (usually whips, see below) count the votes.

Yes, it's all very archaic, and everyone has to be in London to vote – despite the rules changing during Covid, it's gone back to how it was before and there is no longer a way for MPs to vote remotely. If they can't make it, MPs generally rely on an informal 'pairing' system, by which whips find MPs on both sides who are unable to vote and pair them up, so their votes are effectively cancelled out. But this can fail – for example, in 2019, when the Tory chief whip Julian Smith asked one of his MPs to break a pairing pact with a Lib Dem MP who was on maternity leave in a crucial Brexit vote. Hmmm.

What are 'the whips' and what do they do?

Whips are MPs and peers who are appointed to ensure their party colleagues toe the line when it comes to their leader's agenda or policy. There are currently 24 whips in government – 16 in the House of Commons and 8 in the House of Lords. They act as the link between the front and back benches, with information communicated in both directions – a role that's been likened to a 'cross between a management lackey and a union shop steward'.

Whips also play a key role in organising parliamentary business – they have been described as the 'stage managers' of the Commons.

There are different levels of whipping. For example, a one-line whip means that MPs are requested but not required to attend the vote, whereas a three-line whip means that MPs' attendance is essential. (Very occasionally, a 'free vote' is held, in which MPs are free to express an independent opinion.)

Whips will use whatever means at their disposal – fair or foul – to persuade MPs to vote a certain way. Famously, Tory MPs were bullied and manhandled into backing Liz Truss on a vote on fracking in 2022, according to several witnesses. It's been claimed that whips also keep a 'black book' in which they record information about MPs' bad behaviour in their private lives, which can then be used as leverage when necessary.

Disobeying the whip on a regular basis can have a serious effect on an MP's career development. And if it's a very important vote, they face 'losing the whip', which means that they would have to sit as an independent MP.

It's hard to disagree with Manchester Mayor Andy Burnham, who said in 2022: 'When we vote in our MPs, we like to think we are sending people to Westminster to be fearless advocates for our places, independent checks and balances on the executive. The truth is, they are often no more than a rubber stamp for the views of [the] Establishment.' Many previous MPs absolutely agree with this view.

What is a Select Committee?

Another important feature of parliamentary life is Select Committees. These are groups of MPs or Lords (or both) from across all parties – backbenchers only – who have been charged by Parliament to investigate a specific issue. It's one of the main ways that Parliament can hold government to account. They can conduct inquiries, publish reports and demand that departmental ministers appear before them to explain their actions. So you have a Select Committee for Women and Equalities, Select Committee for Defence, and so on.

They are fascinating to watch in action as occasionally you do see the wheels come off – for example, Amber Rudd was forced to resign as Home Secretary in 2018 after inadvertently misleading the Home Affairs Select Committee over the Windrush scandal.

And of course, let us not forget Boris Johnson's memorable appearance at the Privileges Committee in 2022, when he was called to explain whether he had lied to Parliament over the Partygate scandal.

It's not just politicians who are called in front of Select Committees. Everyone from public sector officials to whistleblowing members of the public can be asked to appear. In May 2022, for example, the CEO of P&O Ferries, Peter Hebblethwaite, was hauled before the Business Select Committee to justify the company's decision to sack 800 of its workers, and faced a mauling. (The first question: 'Are you in this mess because you don't know what you're doing or are you just a shameless criminal?')

Like I said, they can make for interesting viewing!

It's possible to attend a Select Committee in person as a member of the public. All free of charge. Go onto the parliament.uk website to find details. I'd strongly recommend it as an afternoon out.

What is the Liaison Committee?

Finally, there's also another type of committee you might have heard of. Three times a year, the prime minister will be subjected to a 90-minute grilling by members of the Liaison Committee. This is, in effect, a super-committee made up of all the chairs of the House of Commons' Select Committees – there are 32 of them in total plus the chair of the Joint Committee on Human Rights.

Normally, the Liaison Committee decides on a limited number (three or four) of topical issues on which to question the prime minister at each session; otherwise, with 33 people in the driving seat, it could very quickly get out of hand.

And that is how it all works. There's a lot more but this gives you a flavour of the basic structure of Westminster.

21 JANUARY 2023

Ooohhh.

This morning, the *Sunday Times*, with the brilliant journalists Gabriel Pogrund and Harry Yorke, splashed with another barely believable story about Boris Johnson, the BBC chairman and a loan guarantee. I say 'barely believable' – by now we'd believe anything about Boris Johnson, other than what the charlatan says about himself.

So, what's the new story?

The *Sunday Times* has printed that the BBC chairman Richard Sharp, who was appointed by Boris Johnson in February 2021, has probably broken the rules of his own appointment.

Obviously, those who run the BBC hold a precious national

institution in their care. They are meant to govern with fairness and without political influence. The BBC has the most trusted brand of news in Britain and as such should be seen to be beyond reproach, but the *Sunday Times* tells a murky tale of finance, donations, political bias and how the most privileged in British society look after each other.

According to the newspaper, just weeks before Sharp was handed his BBC job in 2021, he had helped to facilitate a guarantee of an £800,000 personal loan for Johnson from a Canadian businessman called Sam Blyth (who, rather weirdly, is distantly related to Johnson). If Sharp had failed to declare this arrangement, then he would have broken the rules of his appointment and may have to resign.

So who is Richard Sharp?

A hugely wealthy banker (rumoured to be worth circa £200 million-plus) whose father was in the House of Lords, Sharp grew up in privilege in London. After private school and Oxford University (it's a pattern), a young Sharp went into banking, eventually rising to the giddy and lucrative heights of head of principal investment business in Europe at Goldman Sachs.

He has many ties to the Conservatives and has donated over £400,000 to the party. He was an adviser to Boris Johnson when Johnson was mayor of London. And in 2013, Sharp was handpicked by George Osborne, then Tory Chancellor, as a powerful member of the Bank of England's Financial Policy Committee.

In addition, Richard Sharp was a board member of the Centre for Policy Studies, a right-wing think tank based in Tufton Street in Westminster, where most of Britain's right-leaning lobby groups reside. The Centre for Policy Studies was established by Margaret Thatcher. It's fundamentally about a 'free market economy' (very much the Liz Truss philosophy – and look how grateful we've all been for those policies) and has expressed an ideology to get rid of the BBC licence fee. It claims that privatisation has been marvellous for everyone (yep, these souls really do believe it) and issues endless papers written by the usual suspects. I shan't be looking for an invitation to a drinks party there anytime soon.

Back to Richard Sharp.

Sharp was Rishi Sunak's boss when Sunak was a junior banker at Goldman Sachs (what a small world!) and then Sunak brought Sharp into the Treasury as an adviser during the Covid year of 2020 when Sunak was Chancellor.

It's a heady merry-go-round of a small number of people who have influence on government policies and how money is spent.

And so to the BBC. The BBC chair is ultimately appointed by the prime minister and the Secretary of State for Culture, Media and Sport (a bizarre form of selection and obviously and wholly open to political bias by definition) – BUT they must first receive advice from a panel of four people who, according to the rules, must run a 'fair and open' competition.

More surprises. One of the four people on the panel who advised on Sharp's appointment was Catherine Baxendale, who was shortlisted to be a Tory candidate MP in 2017. She also donated £50,000 to the Tory party when David Cameron was PM. Another was Blondel Cluff, wife of the North Sea oil tycoon Algy Cluff. Algy Cluff had owned the *Spectator* magazine and was chairman when Boris

Johnson was editor. Blondel Cluff has described Boris Johnson's leadership as 'inspirational and unifying'.[31]

Righto. Totally independent.

And here is the crux of the issue in the *Sunday Times*. Richard Sharp did not bring his history of helping to facilitate a personal loan guarantor for Boris Johnson to the attention of this appointments panel. This means that Boris Johnson may have breached the code of conduct (again) and that Sharp should have declared this involvement.

So what happens next? I've got a funny feeling a lot of gritty detail might just be Sharp's undoing.

23 JANUARY 2023

I was on the ITV *This Morning* sofa talking about the way I choose to live my private life at the moment (nothing to do with politics this time). Fundamentally, I'm in my sixties, been married and divorced, have ace, funny and loyal friends and a great family life, I'm financially independent and I don't want a full-time partner, so instead I have what I call 'special friends'. I have known one of them for over a decade and they're all single, as am I. Seems fair enough and lots of women do the same, and/or want the same, especially when you're an independent soul, which I am very happily.

Anyway, for some reason or other it's of interest, which makes me laugh.

But something else made me wide-eyed: when I had finished the live broadcast and went to look at my phone, I had an 'admiring' message from none other than Michael Gove! Shocker. I can't repeat it here, but I thought knowing about it would make you laugh out loud. Heck!

27 JANUARY 2023

Today, I again had to get myself off to London to do the 'press review' on the ITV *This Morning* sofa. It's an enjoyable thing to do. There's a lovely team of people who always make me feel so welcome (thanks, gang); I get dressed up for the telly (I'm usually to be found in leggings and my scruffs), wobble around on heels for an hour, read the newspapers, think of some strong opinions and off I go. Nice.

The front pages and TV have been full of the news from the Public Accounts Committee, which examines the value for money of government projects. The link to Michelle Mone and PPE Medpro being sued for £122 million of unusable PPE was an obvious story which I couldn't allow to go unnoticed.

There have been an increasing number of reports about the couple buying multimillion-pound properties, a private jet, a yacht and lavish holidays abroad through various companies or trusts. Mone and her husband have also been issuing lawyers' letters and threatening to sue journalists who write about the PPE scandal.

So on the sofa today, I decided to tell a bit of the Michelle Mone story, so I said: 'Michelle Mone, I knew many years ago – and then I dropped her like a stone as soon as I realised what kind of person she was.' Then I turned dramatically to camera (which I thought was a bit of TV gold, to be honest) and dared her to 'SUE ME, MICHELLE'. It went a bit viral.

Within hours, the *Daily Mail* had done its usual job and said a 'source close to [Baroness Mone] today hit back against Vorderman, branding her "publicity hungry" and calling the comments "outrageous". What are the reasons – a hunger for publicity, or maybe her coming to the end of her TV career?'

Predictable. Remember DARVO and the Narcissist?

Deny

Attack

Reverse the Role of

Victim and

Offender

There were some stupid and easily disprovable claims. This new pile of nonsense involved her obsession with claiming I'd lived with her for two years, when in reality I had spent at the very most three nights in her flat (and I don't even think it was that many). I'm laughing as I'm boring myself now with saying it again! Sorry, wake up in the back!

I drove back home to Bristol and by the time I'd gone online to catch up with my emails after a long day, the claims had already been put up on the *Daily Mail* website. The *Daily Mail* had sent an email to my press man to check the story earlier in the day, but I'd been driving for hours and obviously hadn't picked up his call.

There is one thing I've learned over time, and that is that you have to stand up for yourself where you can, and it's easy to do so when a big story is provably wrong.

So, it was time to ring one of the bosses at the Mail Online to ask them firmly to take the nonsense down within half an hour or I would, without question, take them to court. In fairness, they took it down within minutes. Thank you, *Daily Mail*. Much as we don't agree on many things, and I'm a strong opponent of so much of your politics, when an organisation acts properly you have to credit it.

(NOTE: By the way, Michelle Mone didn't sue me . . . funny that!)

28 JANUARY 2023

Well, what a week it's been. Conservative chairman Nadhim Zahawi and his 'careless' tax avoidance of nearly £5 million. Former Tory Health Secretary Sajid Javid calling for GP appointments and A&E visits to be charged (i.e. partial privatisation) – despite the fact that his previous links to a bank that promotes private healthcare are well known. And much more happening with Richard Sharp in the world of the BBC.

The fallout of the story of potentially improper behaviour by

BBC chairman Richard Sharp not informing the appointments panel of his involvement in Boris Johnson's financial affairs has been leading the news. Slowly but surely, the tangled web unfurls.

SNP MP John Nicholson, a prominent member of the Culture Select Committee, which had interviewed Sharp before his appointment, was on fire in the House of Commons on Monday. 'We grilled him about his £400,000 gift to the Conservative party. However, he did not disclose his role in getting the man appointing him a huge loan . . . Even by the grubby standards of this government, it's all a bit banana republic, is it not?'

Tories: No, no, no, it was an 'incredibly robust process'.

Liar-in-Chief Johnson described any claims of improper behaviour as 'a load of complete nonsense'. He continued: 'Let me just tell you, Richard Sharp is a good and wise man, but he knows absolutely nothing about my personal finances – I can tell you that for 100 per cent ding dang sure.'

Aha, he's brought in the old '100 per cent DING DANG SURE' defence. Then it's probably a given that he's lying like a child whose face is covered in chocolate swearing blind they never went near the Galaxy. I'm ding dang sure of it.

Sharp's close ally Prime Minister Rishi Sunak also defended Sharp, saying the appointment process was 'rigorous' and 'transparent', although being a little Fishy Rishi he added, 'But I didn't appoint him.'

I know I've only been looking into Tory financial affairs here and there for a short while, but I already feel like I'm drowning in the ever-spewing effluent of Thames Water. In fact, it feels like a dam is about to burst. It's exhausting sometimes but I'm fuming about the BBC – OUR BBC – being influenced in such an obvious way by the Conservative party. I've worked for the BBC on and off for nearly 40 years and the organisation, although not perfect, is a precious gift.

Anyway, back to Johnson, Sharp and Sam Blyth, and the loan guarantee of £800,000.

Why did Johnson need the money?

Towards the end of 2020, he was in financial trouble as he was going through his second divorce. He needed multiple payments for multiple children and had to pay back £112,549 for the cost of the ridiculous refurbishment of the flat in 11 Downing Street (the PM's flat is at 11 and not 10 Downing Street). Yep, £112,549 for a bit of decoration! That's half the price of an average house. Jeez, how entitled Old Etonians live, eh?

Bear in mind this was during 2020, the first year of Covid, so his Tory government was also busy siphoning money into the VIP PPE lane for contracts for their associates, while enjoying the heady danger (Tory view) or the insulting disgrace (our view) of Partygate.

Enter a new player onto the stage: William Shawcross.

Shawcross, an old Etonian who'd been to Oxford (naturally), was appointed by Boris Johnson as the commissioner for public appointments. This week, Shawcross has announced he will be leading an independent investigation into the Richard Sharp affair.

But hang on, the *Daily Mirror* has found that William Shawcross's daughter, the exceptionally wealthy Eleanor Shawcross (married to Lord Wolfson), is working for Rishi Sunak at Number 10 as his head of policy. Not only that, she also donated £20,000 to Sunak's leadership campaign last year.

You get the picture.

With all of this and Nadhim Zahawi imploding, it's going to be a helluva week ahead.

EXPLAINER: WHAT IS THE WESTMINSTER BUBBLE AND WHAT IS THE PROBLEM WITH IT?

You'll hear me using the term 'the Westminster Bubble' quite a lot in these pages. It's a shorthand phrase for the insular and often detached 'village' that so many politicians, journalists and lobbyists operate within around Parliament.

Essentially, when we're talking about Conservative circles particularly, it's what happens when a group of people have been brought up in the same environment, go to the same schools and/ or universities, study the same subjects, then gravitate towards the same sector after they graduate. Most of the people involved in the previous Tory government, who you would find around Westminster, came into politics through this route. In this way, they also often decide the agenda, how we talk about politics and how you hear about politics.

So what's the first step on the path to Westminster if you're a fledgling political (particularly Conservative) wannabe? Well, attending an eye-wateringly expensive, top private school is a useful place to start.

According to analysis published in October 2022, when Rishi Sunak first came to power, 61 per cent of his Cabinet attended fee-paying schools – compared to a national average of just 7 per cent. Good odds, and we know how the Tories love good odds!

Rishi Sunak himself attended Winchester College – one of the very top private schools in England (fees for its boarders currently stand at £49,152 per year). Eton College is another public school which has spawned a huge number of senior politicians – in fact, Britain's very first prime minister, Robert Walpole, attended there in 1690. Eton boasts 20 former PMs in total, including David Cameron and Boris Johnson – which in itself is enough to make you want to ban anyone who went to Eton from running the country in future. Its fees currently stand at £49,998 per year, but it's the privilege, contacts and automatic access to the heart of the establishment it delivers to its students which is where its 'value' lies in the Kingdom of Inequality we live in.

These Old Etonians, of course, have for many years decided what our money is spent on with little understanding of how most of us in the country live. And more importantly, they have set the rules about tax and wealth which govern and encourage the inequality between the super-rich and the rest of us.

What next?

Well, if you really want to increase your chances of becoming a top politician, then you'll study philosophy, politics and economics (PPE) at Oxford – as did Rishi Sunak, David Cameron, Liz Truss, Jeremy Hunt, Matt Hancock, former transport secretary Mark Harper, former education secretary Damian Hinds, former social care secretary Helen Whately, former Chancellor Philip Hammond . . . I could go on, but you get the picture. That's just the Tory Oxford PPE graduates, too – there are also plenty of Labour politicians who similarly followed this degree path (but may not have had the private school element). And that's before you get on to the enormous numbers of political journalists and broadcasters, lobbyists and assorted political hangers-on who also studied the same degree at the same institution.

Is it any wonder that when so many politically involved people come from the same background and mix in the same circles, that sometimes voters feel that Westminster is out of touch with their needs?

On yet an even more exclusive level, in recent Tory years, many (male) members of the Westminster Bubble were once in the Oxford Bullingdon Club, notorious for what's been described as its 'champagne-swilling, restaurant-trashing, "pleb"-taunting elitism'.[32] Disgusting antics over the years included the hiring of sex workers to perform sex acts at the club's lavish dinners, the complete trashing of restaurants and some members dressing up as Nazis. Past 'Bullers' include Boris Johnson, David Cameron and George Osborne – the Chancellor known for his austerity measures that brought so much harm to the 'plebs' his fellow club members used to mock.

For almost all of the 14 years of Tory rule, we've been governed by a section of society for whom virtually no part of their lives crosses over with those they are meant to represent. This isn't personal against them (although I might make a few notable exceptions), but if all you've ever known is privilege and power, and people who reflect your own privileged opinions back at you, your views are going to become more insular. And this extends to when you finally make it to Westminster, and you're surrounded by other people who have come straight from their Oxford PPE degree into the Houses of Parliament as special advisers (SPADs) with very little experience of real life along the way.

As any insider will tell you, Westminster is a uniquely heightened, heady, peculiar environment. Scurrying around the corridors of power is a group of people who live and breathe politics, obsessing over the latest political headlines and focusing on policies that are significant within their own circles but not necessarily the same as the issues that are important to our wider world.

It is this problem we've witnessed time and time again over the past years, where politicians seem so utterly disconnected from the real world.

A YouGov poll in 2024 showed that nearly three-quarters of voters believe politicians don't care what people like them think – this has risen from 51 per cent in 2019 to 73 per cent now.

And now 67 per cent of voters feel politicians in Westminster ignore the issues they care about. This sense of detachment can be seen in the low turnout of just 59.9 per cent in the general election in July, the second lowest voter turnout since 1918.

But are things now about to change? After all, not everyone in Westminster came into politics through this route. The new Deputy Prime Minister Angela Rayner went to her local comprehensive school in Stockport and left school age 16, while pregnant, with no qualifications. Her first job was working in the care sector. A great example of how you can rise to the top with enough grit and hard work. Keir Starmer also came from a relatively modest background, going to the local grammar school (which became a fee-paying school while he was there, although as he and others had already begun their education they did not have to pay fees in those transitional years), then studying law at Leeds University, the first of his family to go to university.

Out of 25 people in Starmer's Cabinet, only one (transport secretary Louise Haigh) went to private school and one went to a grammar school (Starmer)[33] – a much closer reflection of the national average.

So there are signs that the Westminster Bubble is bursting – that perhaps in future, politicians will come from a wider variety of backgrounds, with a greater life experience upon which to draw. I hope so, or the lurch to more extreme politics will undoubtedly grow as a rebellion against the Westminster Bubble from people who feel 'left behind'.

29 JANUARY 2023

So here we are, just weeks into Rishi Sunak's premiership and he has already hit a great big ice sculpture in the shape of Nadhim Zahawi. When Rishi Sunak resigned as Chancellor in all the Conservative parasitic tumult about Boris Johnson, Zahawi – an old friend of Johnson – took on the role.

It seems like years ago, such are the shenanigans of the Conservatives, but it was only on 5 July 2022 that Zahawi became Chancellor.

Just two days later, and with stories about his own tax affairs now swirling, Zahawi withdrew his support for Johnson and called for him to resign. It was Zahawi's first move to try to become the Conservative party leader, showing yet again how this bunch of politicians think more about themselves than they do the country or the electorate.

After Johnson was eventually kicked out by his own team, Zahawi put himself forward but was eliminated from the leadership ballot after the first round. Still maintaining his job as Chancellor of the Exchequer, he then threw his weight behind the delusional Liz Truss.

In spite of his support, Truss downgraded him to the job of Chancellor of the Duchy of Lancaster on 6 September, when, to our cost, she appointed her very good friend Kwasi Kwarteng (another Old Etonian) as her new Chancellor. It's sometimes hard to keep up with the Tory game of musical chairs, especially at the moment, but we'll do our best.

So who is Nadhim Zahawi and what had he done?

Thereby hangs a tale.

Zahawi was born into a politically powerful Kurdish family; a grandfather of his had been the governor of the Bank of Iraq. In fact, such was his grandfather's importance, his signature appeared on banknotes at the time. His family decided to leave Iraq for the UK during Saddam Hussein's rise to power, but they maintained a strong connection to the country.

Zahawi has merged business with politics throughout his adult life. He began to work with the Tory Lord Jeffrey Archer in the 1990s and the two worked closely together before Archer was sentenced to four years in jail for perjury in 2001.

In 2000, Zahawi and his friend Stephen Shakespeare set up YouGov, the polling company, which they sold many years later. Zahawi is said to have made more than £20 million profit through this sale, but the complex web of an offshore firm, share allocations and tax avoidance associated with this profit has come back to trip him up this month, as this story will show.

Zahawi became an MP in 2010 and since then, he has not been without controversy. In 2013, it emerged that he had claimed £5,822 in expenses, charged to us as taxpayers, for heating the stables for his horses. As with most politicians, he claimed he was 'mortified' by the error.

He has also maintained a number of extra jobs while being an MP. In 2015, he became the chief strategy officer at the Gulf Keystone company, which ran one of the biggest oil fields in Kurdistan. They paid Zahawi £29,643 per month. He left that role in 2017 after earning at least £1.3 million, including a large leaving bonus.

The issue of MPs' second/third/fourth/fifth jobs is unquestionably another area which needs urgent reform. A member of Parliament can claim a full salary of over £90,000 and taxpayer-funded expenses of up to £250,000, while supplementing this job with work outside of Westminster, which often throws up the question of conflicts of interest. Don't get me started (see the Plan for Change on page 313).

In 2017, the *Guardian* discovered that the Zahawi family's Gibraltar-based trust Balshore Investments had invested money in a new company called Crowd2Fund. Zahawi did not declare it on his register of interests (he denies that he needed to). Crowd2Fund was founded by Chris Hancock, the brother of Matt Hancock, who had been a minister working in the government department responsible for setting up the regulatory framework for crowdfunding. You see the connection? Zahawi and Matt Hancock had also written a book together entitled *Masters of Nothing*. Zahawi's parents (through Balshore Investments) were listed as 'persons of significant control' of Crowd2Fund by Companies House.

I'm writing all of this extra information here so that you can see how opaque our system of government and the dealings of some of those within it are.

In 2020, as a minister in the Department for Business and Trade, Nadhim Zahawi intervened to become a critical governmental link with David Cameron in the Greensill Scandal, where Cameron's lobbying during Covid led to the government-owned British Business Bank guaranteeing loans of more than £400 million before Greensill went bust. One of the recipients, GFG Metals, owned by Sanjeev Gupta, who was in contact with both Cameron and Zahawi, was put under investigation by the Serious Fraud Office for suspected fraud, fraudulent trading and money laundering in relation to the financing and conduct of the companies in the group, including their financing arrangements with Greensill Capital UK. The cases surrounding this are still ongoing as I write.

When *Financial Times* journalists tried to obtain correspondence between Zahawi and Gupta, they were told that 'there was no longer an electronic record of the communication stored on the device used by Nadhim Zahawi, which was his personal mobile phone.' Wow.

You'll find that this is a common occurrence for Conservative ministers. It's strange; we are forced to put our trust in politicians to deal with hundreds of billions of pounds of our tax payments, and yet they seem utterly incapable of being able to run their own mobile phones and emails.

How odd!

Anyway, let's go back to July last year and the story of HMRC, Zahawi, the company Balshore Investments, his father and a healthy dose of tax avoidance thrown in for good measure.

I'd read a little about the story earlier in the year but became much more familiar with it in December. Surfing around looking for good people to follow on X (formerly known as Twitter, which makes me laugh when newsreaders have to say it – it's going to take years to get used to saying X!), I came across a fascinating tax expert called Dan Neidle.

Dan had been head of tax at one of the world's biggest law firms and had retired early, but being a super-bright, investigative person he hadn't stopped work. He set up an organisation called Tax Policy Associates, where he uses his time and his contacts to investigate the tax affairs of various politicians and others if he feels there might be something afoot which he could clarify.

Being a numbers geek, I liked reading his in-depth analyses. The devil, as they say, is in the detail.

I noticed that Dan had been tweeting about Nadhim Zahawi's lawyers, who had threatened to sue him for libel after he had posted this on X on 14 October 2022:

> **Dan Neidle** ✓ @DanNeidle   1hr ...
>
> Can't believe Liz Truss is seriously considering appointing as Chancellor someone who reportedly was investigated by the NCA in the past and is all-but-certain to be the subject of a current investigation by HMRC.
>
> ♡   ⇄   ♡   🔖   ⬆

Zahawi's lawyers immediately demanded that Dan delete his tweet, which he refused to do.

This story makes me laugh in one way too: Dan Neidle had been a senior partner at a huge London law firm, he has lots of friends who are lawyers and, therefore, many who could advise him. Zahawi's lawyers seemed foolish when Dan referred them to the Solicitors Regulatory Authority for abusing libel law in order to shut down debate.

Note to others: be careful who you threaten!

I made contact with Dan to find out more. Here's the story so far, taking us up to the present day.

April 2021: HMRC begins its investigation into the tax affairs of Zahawi based upon the sale of shares by Balshore Investments in

YouGov – the polling company which Zahawi had co-founded and which was owned by Zahawi's parents. Balshore was registered in Gibraltar, which advertises itself as a low-tax solution. It was later found that, as a minister, Zahawi should have declared this investigation to comply with the ministerial code of conduct. He did not do so.

5 July 2022: Zahawi was appointed as Chancellor by Boris Johnson and had still not declared the investigation by HMRC, one of the bodies which he was then controlling, as Chancellor.

9 July 2022: The *Independent* newspaper, which Zahawi was also threatening to sue, reported that Zahawi was under investigation by HMRC, and had been subject to tax investigations by the Serious Fraud Office and the National Crime Agency (the Serious Fraud Office investigation was passed to HMRC; the NCA inquiry did not find any evidence of wrongdoing).[34]

Zahawi then brazenly said on Sky News when he was being interviewed by Kay Burley, 'I was clearly being smeared. I was being told the Serious Fraud Office, the National Crime Agency, the HMRC are looking into me. I'm not aware of this. I've always declared my taxes; I paid my taxes in the UK.'

August 2022: Unknown to journalists at the time, Zahawi reached an agreement with HMRC to pay back an estimated £3.7 million in unpaid tax plus a 30 per cent fine of £1.1 million and interest, giving a total bill of circa £5 million. And all of that because he 'forgot' to mention £27 million profit on the sale of shares in YouGov. It's amazing the effect a foggy memory can have on a politician!

But the critical question is, how can the Chancellor of the Exchequer, Zahawi, do a 'deal' with HMRC *which he is in charge of* and expect us to think that it's fair? It stinks, absolutely stinks. Conflicts of interest are off the scale in this instance, surely.

October 2022: After Truss had made him Chancellor of the Duchy of Lancaster and then been kicked out, meaning we were on to our third prime minister in as many months, Rishi Sunak appointed Zahawi as the chairman of the Conservative party.

At this point, Dan Neidle was still investigating the story and bringing his in-depth analysis to bear. The story might have disappeared but for his doggedness and that of certain journalists who wouldn't let go.

14 January 2023: The *Sun on Sunday* had the scoop – the first time any paper had declared the fact that Zahawi had indeed agreed to pay HMRC millions of pounds.

A spokesman for the Conservative party chairman went into strong bluster mode (gusting tornado force bluster, I would say, if there is a scale of such a thing), saying that Zahawi's taxes were 'properly declared. He has never had to instruct any lawyers to deal with HMRC on his behalf.' Which was a nifty little trick, don't you think? The question wasn't: 'Did he instruct lawyers?' Nobody cares about that. The question was: 'Has he been under investigation by HMRC and had to settle a bill and fine for many millions of pounds?' When politicians don't answer the question directly, it's definitely time for more investigating.

18 January: At Prime Minister's Questions, Rishi Sunak defended his chairman, saying, 'He has already addressed this matter in full and there's nothing more that I can add.' Number 10 contributed that they have full confidence in him. They would change their tune pretty soon. The question is, do we believe what the prime minister says or is it just the Tory party fudging matters yet again? Either way, what followed was a rapid fall from grace.

20 January: The *Guardian* gave the killer blow, running a story that Nadhim Zahawi had been fined heavily by HMRC and had to pay an estimated £4.8 million in total. Now there were calls for him to be sacked – but still, Sunak, just weeks in as prime minister, wouldn't give in.

At this point, Zahawi finally admitted his denial back in July was wrong, but he claimed in a weasly manner (you'll find this is a pattern in this book) that HMRC decided that his tax errors were 'careless and not deliberate'.

I'll tell you what careless is. Careless is not putting the lid on the kettle properly and it boils over. Careless is ordering a coffee but you've left your money at home. Careless is letting your Oyster card slip out of your pocket while you're on a bus. It is NOT getting entangled in a complex system of tax avoidance via a company based offshore in Gibraltar, shuffling share ownership around and claiming that you owed millions of pounds less in tax than you actually did.

In Westminster the pressure began to build on him.

I was on the ITV *This Morning* sofa again on 20 January, this time explaining simply the choice of Sunak's wife to register as a non-dom for tax purposes (until the press discovered it) to save herself an estimated £20 million in tax since Sunak had become an MP. Then we moved on to Nadhim Zahawi. I make no apology for my passion; I remain fuming about the injustice and the lies. I wanted to use the usually cosy sofa to introduce the Conservative corruption to a new audience and to explain it as someone who remains outside the Westminster Bubble.

23 January: Sunak instructed his ethics adviser Sir Laurie Magnus (an old Etonian) to prepare a report. Note that Johnson changed the system so that the 'ethics adviser' cannot operate independently and must now be instructed to investigate rather than independently decide to do so, making something of a mockery of the entire principle of ethics independence. During his banking career, Sir Laurie Magnus had worked with the disgraced Robert Maxwell, the media mogul who fraudulently looted £460 million from the Mirror Group's pension fund leaving many to live in poverty, and whose daughter Ghislaine Maxwell is currently in jail in America for sex-trafficking offences linked to her close relationship with Jeffrey Epstein. Even though Magnus had been commissioned, Zahawi remained as Tory party chairman and was not asked to step aside during the investigation.

26 January: The Radio 2 Jeremy Vine Show asked if I would come on air to discuss Zahawi while a tax lawyer would also be on the line, possibly defending Zahawi's position. Of course, I said yes.

I rang Dan Neidle to make a plan beforehand. The interview itself was an interesting and passionate debate with me sitting in a remote office (I was filming that day) talking to Jeremy Vine through a Zoom call, while my phone was propped up against my laptop with Dan Neidle on WhatsApp as he listened to his radio, so he could make sure I had any relevant pieces of info while I was on air. Cute. I didn't need to ask Dan in the end, but the point is that we need good people to work together, to get accurate information out there and to keep up the pressure.

Today, 29 January: Sir Laurie Magnus had been busy. He's now handed in his report and as a result, this morning, Rishi Sunak has sacked Zahawi as chair of the Conservative party over a 'serious breach' of the ministerial code. Here was my take on it on X:

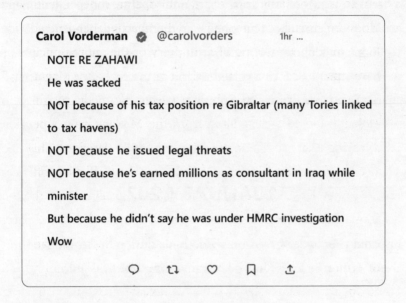

Carol Vorderman ✔ @carolvorders   1hr …
NOTE RE ZAHAWI
He was sacked
NOT because of his tax position re Gibraltar (many Tories linked to tax havens)
NOT because he issued legal threats
NOT because he's earned millions as consultant in Iraq while minister
But because he didn't say he was under HMRC investigation
Wow

Such is the state of Tory politics today.

Of course, Nadhim Zahawi remains as an MP and continues his business activities.

The pattern is the same. Think of Michelle Mone and others: the rich can use legal threats and often do to try to quieten investigations by journalists.

I can't wait for the day when we have proper accountability and checks on all members of Parliament, when lying at this level doesn't just mean you're pushed to one side. It means you're pushed out entirely, and for good.

After the disastrous ineptitude of Liz Truss, inflation through the roof, families suffering, the immense selfishness and corruption of the VIP PPE lane, the discovery of Rishi Sunak's wife's non-dom tax status, the treatment of NHS frontline staff and excuse after excuse, it has become absolutely apparent that this Conservative government just does not care about anyone or anything other than themselves.

People talk about a 'rotten borough', but as far as I can discover, we have morphed into a rotten nation at the mercy of a bunch of charlatans. How can we make things better?

31 JANUARY 2023

I posted this tweet based on something a friend of mine told me about Tories he knew had been canvassing out in London:

This tweet went viral, over 3 million views and 61,000 likes.

Tories denied the basis of what I was saying was true. But it was.

Right-wingers came at me because they were scared that signs of a revolution were being witnessed.

All of us who thought we had no voice – well, we have a voice, and well done to those people slamming doors. We're on our way.

2 FEBRUARY 2023

My agent has just had a call from BBC Radio Wales about my tweeting. Hmmm.

While I wait to hear what's been said, I'll tell you what's been going on over the last few weeks.

After a bit of digging, I've been plugging away talking about the connections between Tory donor/BBC chairman Richard Sharp, William Shawcross, the independent investigator, and Robbie Gibb, whom Sharp appointed to the BBC board in May 2021.

A key Tory party player, Robbie Gibb was Theresa May's former head of communications at Number 10. His brother Nick Gibb has been Tory schools' minister for many years. Robbie was also a founding executive of the right-wing broadcaster GB News.

Emily Maitlis, in her MacTaggart lecture at the Edinburgh TV Festival in August 2022, described Robbie Gibb as an 'active agent of the Conservative party', shaping the BBC's news output by acting 'as the arbiter of BBC impartiality'.

Robbie Gibb led a takeover of the *Jewish Chronicle* newspaper in April 2020 and guess who was also part of the bid? Well I never, it was William Shawcross.[35]

All of this enrages me. So on X, I've been calling for the resignation of Richard Sharp, William Shawcross and Robbie Gibb. I added to my tweets, for those who feel the same as I do, a link to the BBC complaints office! Ahem. Well, I like to be of help!

I think there have been thousands of complaints to the BBC, judging by what I'm hearing online. And a damn good job too.

A few days ago, on 30 January, Shawcross finally 'recused' himself from the so-called independent investigation into Richard Sharp as he'd just remembered he's met Richard Sharp a few times. Funny that!

Shawcross has now appointed a Kings Counsel, Adam Heppinstall, to conduct the inquiry into Sharp. Good.

So we go back to today's phone call from BBC Radio Wales. Bearing in mind that I've just been calling for the resignations of two of the most powerful people in the BBC publicly on X, and giving the link to the BBC complaints office, I think they might not be too happy with me. Well, in for a penny . . .

I've been working at BBC Radio Wales on a lovely music and showbiz chat show on a Saturday lunchtime for about four years. The show does well and I always have a great laugh with my 'radio wifey' Nathan Sussex, and before Nathan with Owain Wyn Evans, who, excitingly, has now got his own show on Radio 2. I love my boys. Anyway, apparently my radio ratings are good and

I'm definitely part of the Radio Wales family, but there's been a complaint about my social media, as it's more of a campaign than an expression of opinion.

Too right it is. It's a campaign to protect the BBC from undue direct influence from a Tory government. But how odd that this has suddenly happened after I raised an issue about Robbie Gibb. Could the two be directly connected?

I know now that the end of my BBC radio show will come, it's just a matter of time.

Luckily, I consider myself at the age of 62 on the last stretch of my career (42 years on telly/radio so far, which is a good innings) so I'm prepared for the inevitable.

However, many of those who work with the BBC who aren't in a financial position, or the age that I am, will be bound by the fear (and it is a fear) of speaking out. Many wouldn't want to speak out anyway, many may not be bothered, but there will be many who do care. That I can guarantee. And when the might of BBC management falls upon you, and you're a freelancer in our industry, it's a scary position to be in.

Anyway, for now, I'm still employed there *and* winding up Robbie Gibb and that's fine by me.

5 FEBRUARY 2023

There have been times I have to admit when, on top of my normal job, I've found researching and posting about the political sewage of the Tory party has been exhausting. So every now and then it's really heartwarming to get a little support from journalists, particularly when it comes from someone I admire.

Carole Cadwalladr is an exceptionally courageous investigative journalist who has bravely challenged those who were involved in Vote Leave and right-wing politics. So when I saw her article in the *Guardian*, written as a letter to me from one Welsh comprehensive girl (Carole) to another (me), it touched me greatly.

Her piece also held a warning. Titled 'Dear Carol Vorderman: I salute your courage, but the wolves are gathering', it went on to say: 'I know what it's like to try to speak truth to power. The trolls will come after you, like they did for me. But stand firm! You've given us all hope.'

Thank you, Carole. The whole article meant the world to me. Yes, the wolves are gathering, but to hell with them.

7 FEBRUARY 2023

The Commons Select Committee for Digital, Culture, Media and Sport has wasted no time in calling BBC chairman Richard Sharp in for questioning. I'm looking forward to the events today as some on the committee will take no prisoners. You can always catch these committee meetings online – and remember you can even turn up to them if you're stuck on a rainy day in London!

To recap, Sharp (friend of Johnson and Sunak) allegedly helped to facilitate a loan guarantee of £800,000 from Canadian businessman Sam Blyth for Boris Johnson just weeks before Sharp was appointed as BBC chairman and didn't declare it to the appointments panel, which he was required to do.

Watching the telly and here they go.

Oh dear.

First of all, Sam Blyth has been a friend of Sharp's for over 40 years (Blyth has a chequered business history, according to Canadian newspapers). At a dinner, they talked about Johnson's financial issues. Blyth said he wanted to help.

Sharp first thought he'd like to apply to become BBC chairman in 2020 when friends said it would be a good idea, so he submitted his application.

Blyth rang Sharp about the loan guarantee. Sharp had a meeting with Johnson about the loan and told him he was going to go to the Cabinet Office to talk to Simon Case, the Cabinet Secretary, about it – but why did Sharp have to do that?

Simon Case wrote a memo to Boris Johnson on 22 December 2020 telling him to stop speaking to Richard Sharp about his 'personal financial matters'. Two weeks later, Sharp, Boris Johnson's preferred candidate, was announced as the BBC's new chair. Sharp is now saying he has no knowledge of Johnson's financial affairs and that he has never given Johnson financial advice.

In comes SNP MP John Nicholson . . . Here comes trouble.

'Why didn't you tell this committee before your appointment that you helped to facilitate an £800,000 loan for the man who then gave you this plum appointment?'

Good question, John. Getting to the very heart of the matter.

Sharp: 'I introduced Mr Blyth to Mr Case. I did not introduce Mr Blyth to Mr Johnson . . . I did not facilitate a loan.'

John Nicholson: 'Nevertheless, you knew what the score was and you didn't tell us about it. Let me remind you of what you signed up to on your BBC application: "You cannot be considered if you fail to declare any conflict of interest." And clearly this was a conflict of interest.'

So the Partygate prime minister appoints Sharp (with no prior experience in broadcasting) two weeks after Sharp approaches the Cabinet Office about a loan guarantee from one of his friends. Then Sharp doesn't think this is a conflict of interest because he wasn't the guarantor, just the man who made the introduction. They really do have a different sense of what constitutes a 'conflict of interest', these posh boys, don't they?

Then we hear that a chop suey dinner party at Chequers, the prime minister's residence in the country, took place between Sharp, Blyth and Johnson the following May after Richard Sharp became BBC chairman.

Nicholson: 'You previously applied for a job on the BBC board?'

Sharp: 'They had a different structure at that time. I applied to be a non-executive on the management board.'

Nicholson: 'And you didn't get the job.'

Sharp: 'I didn't actually get an interview at that time.'

Nicholson goes in for the kill: 'What do you think the difference was between your failed application then and your application now, following the huge facility [i.e. loan] that you helped the prime minister with?'

Sharp: 'I did not help the prime minister with a huge facility.'

It's like watching Mrs Merton's classic line to Debbie McGee: 'What first attracted you to the multimillionaire Paul Daniels?' (Debbie McGee is a nice lady, by the way.)

Nicholson: 'Have you any idea how angry BBC staff are with you? I have a huge mailbag from BBC staff. One of the many things they're angry with you about is that as you are not a journalist, you inexplicably chose to sit on the selection panel of the BBC head of news position.'

Whoa. A hugely unusual move by a BBC chairman. The full implication is that this Tory donor and close ally of Boris Johnson has tried to directly influence who the BBC chooses as head of news – a critically important role in terms of upholding impartiality at our national broadcaster.

Nicholson: 'It is not appropriate . . . It leaves the impression of so much of the establishment that it's pals appointing pals donating money to pals.'

Well, that was worth a watch . . .

12 FEBRUARY 2023

Duh duh duh . . . the Select Committee report is out already and it's bad . . . whoa, it's *bad*. In fact, it's damning.

It says that with regard to BBC chairman Richard Sharp, the omissions 'constitute a breach of the standards expected of individuals' applying for prominent public appointments.

The Select Committee hearing, the Heppinstall inquiry, thousands of complaints from the public to the BBC – but Sharp looks as though he's going to try to cling on.

It's how these boys work. Best get back onto Twitter to complain. Ha.

11 MARCH 2023

What? What? What?

Just a month after I got a warning shot across my bows from BBC management about tweeting politically, the BBC has suspended Gary Lineker because of a tweet the Tories don't like.

Let's be very clear. The BBC's social media guidelines are only meant to be applicable to staff and presenters who work on news and politics, not the rest of us working in other areas. Obviously, the Tories within the BBC want to close those voices down.

What's Gary done then?

Quoting the usual divisive nonsense from Suella Braverman, the current Home Secretary – in which she outlined her plans to ban people arriving illegally in the UK from ever claiming asylum – Gary Lineker said 'good heavens, this is awful'. Someone replied to him and then Gary tweeted:

Gary Lineker ✓ @GaryLineker   1hr ...

There is no huge influx [of immigrants]. We take far fewer refugees than other major European countries. This is just an immeasurably cruel policy directed at the most vulnerable people in language that is not dissimilar to that used by Germany in the 30s, and I'm out of order?

      ◯   ⟲   ♡   ⛶   ⬆

Braverman's supporters went over the top, the Tories piled in and yesterday the BBC suspended Lineker from hosting *Match of the Day* tonight.

But hang on . . . yesss! . . . other presenters including Alex Scott, Alan Shearer and Ian Wright have said they won't go on air either. Brilliant. And the commentators are walking out in support of Gary Lineker. This is a BBC meltdown. I don't think I've ever witnessed this before.

Earlier today, I hosted my little BBC Radio Wales show from Wogan House in London instead of from Cardiff. You do it from a tiny studio and the engineers patch it all together. Staff there are lovely. I spotted the statue of George Orwell outside BBC London

HQ and alongside it, inscribed onto the wall, the words: 'If liberty means anything at all, it means the right to tell people what they do not want to hear.'

As Gary Lineker had done about Braverman's statement.

I recorded a little video in front of it which seems to have gone viral.

I expect it'll be me next for the old heave ho.

13 MARCH 2023

Following a tense weekend for BBC management, with an independent review of social media guidelines, Gary Lineker tweeted:

Gary Lineker ✔ @GaryLineker   1hr ...

After a surreal few days, I'm delighted that we have navigated a way through this. I want to thank you all for the incredible support, particularly my colleagues at BBC Sport, for the remarkable show of solidarity. Football is a team game but their backing was overwhelming.

I have been presenting sport on the BBC for almost 3 decades and am immeasurably proud to work with the best and fairest broadcaster in the world. I cannot wait to get back in the MOTD chair on Saturday.

A final thought: however difficult the last few days have

> been, it simply doesn't compare to having to flee your home
>
> from persecution or war to seek refuge in a land far away.
>
> It's heartwarming to have seen the empathy towards their
>
> plight from so many of you.
>
> We remain a country of predominantly tolerant, welcoming
>
> and generous people. Thank you.

How right he is. We do remain a country of predominantly tolerant and generous people. And that's the very reason it's worth fighting for.

The one thing that keeps me going is that people who feel they have no voice, need to know that together we do have a voice.

I know hardship from my younger days, I know how bloody tough it is being poor and how you need help from family and good people and the 'state'. And I also know how cruel, thieving and manipulative this government is.

I'm just one voice, but if it helps anyone else at all, then I'll keep speaking up . . . let's go.

14 MARCH 2023

Well, life's never dull. I was tapped on the shoulder by Matt Hancock today and I lived to tell the tale!

My best friend Jules and I were at the Cheltenham Festival. I know Cheltenham well and have many mates who go every year. Richard Whiteley and I used to go 30 years ago and would be the last to leave, usually ending up singing badly in an Irish box somewhere. The Irish loved *Countdown* and we loved the Irish. One of my biggest sadnesses is that Whiters and I always said we'd go to Dublin once a year and we never did. He died too young.

For me, Cheltenham is a bit like catch up time at the youth club (except not so young any more). It's a brilliant atmosphere, half Irish, half whoever, with a lot of Welshies like me as we're only just over the border. Not posh like Royal Ascot and a great laugh.

Wandering through the crowds this year was different. Politics was writ large in our minds. Literally hundreds of people stopped me as I was wandering around and said, 'Can I shake your hand, Carol? Thanks for saying it all out loud.' Believe me, it makes a difference. But this passion isn't borne of anything to do with me; it's about all of us, and once you see the corruption, you can't unsee it.

So off we trotted (no horsey pun intended) to various bits of the festival to say hello. At one point, we were in the Royal Box, a huge box which has a large terrace outside. It had come to the most evocative part of the day when a famous Cheltenham racehorse, Honeysuckle, a beautiful Irish-trained mare who'd won three times before at Cheltenham, was running in the Mares' Hurdles. Her story is emotional on every level. Honeysuckle has always been ridden by the incredible female jockey Rachael Blackmore at Cheltenham and the two paired up once again. This time was super-charged. Honeysuckle's trainer was Henry de Bromhead, from Waterford.

He and his wife Heather were there, but everyone knew that their 13-year-old son, Jack, had died just six months before while riding in a pony race. The atmosphere was emotional to say the least.

The way Cheltenham is set up is different to most other courses. The horses ride out from the parade ring in front of and very close to the crowd. Once the race is over at the top of the steep finish, they come back down over 100 yards or more in front of the grandstands within touching distance of the crowd. It's spectacular and personal. So many of us wanted to see it all from beginning to end. My friend Jules and I went out onto the terrace of the Royal Box very early to see Honeysuckle trot out onto the course and to listen to the crowd and the singing.

While we were out there, more or less alone on the bottom step of the large terrace, looking out towards the course and soaking up the atmosphere, somebody tapped me on my shoulder, so obviously I turned round. Standing right behind us and one or two steps up from us were Matt Hancock and the lady he'd left his wife for (Hancock had resigned when he was caught very much not keeping a two-metre distance from this lady during Covid when he was health secretary).

She was standing behind me; he was behind my friend Jules. She had tapped me on the shoulder, I turned and she put out her hand and said, 'Hello, my name's Gina, and this is Matt.'

To be perfectly honest, I was so shocked by their ballsiness I just automatically shook hands with them.

'Matt's an amateur jockey,' she continued and, in fairness, tried to engage us in conversation. We exchanged a few sentences of small talk for around 30 seconds (no matter my feelings about Hancock's behaviour during the Covid years, I wasn't going to start a row in the Royal Box) and then I said, 'Please excuse us, we just want to watch Honeysuckle ride out,' and turned back around to face the racecourse.

Hancock then tapped me on the shoulder and said, 'I want to say thank you for all the work you do with your son about special educational needs. I'm dyslexic.' So I thanked him. I didn't know he was dyslexic, to be honest. After another 30 seconds talking about dyslexia, I said, 'Please excuse us, it's time to watch the race.' Jules and I turned round and that was it.

The crowd roared, we roared, Honeysuckle won, people cried and cheered, and the atmosphere was electric with 70,000 people realising the significance of what we'd just witnessed. It was a racing memory I'll never forget, a moment when time passes so quickly.

We stayed looking out and listening to the crowd until quiet descended, turned round to an empty terrace and went off to see some friends somewhere else in the festival. I thought nothing more about the Hancock thing until we got back home to Bristol and I looked at my notifications. Uh-oh.

The *Daily Mail* has done a classic and the right-wingers think they'd scored a point against me. It seems the paparazzi had positioned themselves to make a photo look like I was cheering and drinking with Hancock. Obviously I wasn't.

Unknown to me, Hancock must have sidled round behind me, further up the terrace steps. When the race was won and Jules and I were cheering and clapping as Honeysuckle was trotting down the hill in front of the massive crowd, looking in the direction of this amazing horse and being moved by the reaction and love of what seemed like the whole of Ireland, Hancock was lifting his glass entirely separately to me and two steps behind.

When you look at the picture, you can see Hancock wasn't in my eyeline at all. Why would he be when I didn't even know he was there? Ah well. Funny really.

It's a little nothing story in the great scheme of life, but the point is to show how desperate and manipulative the Tory-supporting right-wing press can be when they have you in their cross hairs. And I am most definitely in those cross hairs right now.

23 MARCH 2023

I'm proud to be a patron of the Menopause Mandate, chaired by the brilliant Mariella Frostrup.

We are a group of motivated women working to revolutionise the support and advice women receive during the perimenopause and the menopause itself. It's a strong list, including Davina McCall and Penny Lancaster, both incredible champions for other women. The group is supported by a number of members of Parliament, but particularly by Carolyn Harris, Labour MP for Swansea East since 2015, who is a Welsh powerhouse.

Most women are hit in some way or other when they go through the menopause. It absolutely knocked me out when it happened in my fifties. Back then, in the mid-2010s, women were meant to be quiet and not speak about their mental health at all. If you did, you would be labelled as 'odd'.

The truth is I suffered menopausal depression very badly. There was no explanation; my life was good in every other way imaginable and I tried to think of a reason why I felt as desperate as I did. Medical support was virtually non-existent and there was much less information readily available, but I eventually realised that the wave of utter blackness I'd feel was tied into my menstrual cycle. It was bad all the time and then for a week or so every month I felt desperate.

As a single parent with two children and my mother to look after, there was no respite. There were moments when I'd just think to myself, *I've tried so many ways to make this stop. The only way to make it stop is to make everything stop.* This darkness lasted for about a year and it got to the point I could take it no longer. I didn't want to go on anti-depressants as I felt that wouldn't fix the problem, just paper over the cracks, so I asked around and finally was recommended to go to a professor who specialised in hormonal depression. I couldn't find anything available on the NHS so I paid to see him privately. His name was Professor Studd and he probably saved my life.

Battling for many years against the opinions of many in the medical profession, Professor Studd was revolutionary in terms of the seriousness with which he dealt with women with hormonal depression. He took tests and gave me some manufactured and quality-tested bioidentical hormones. They came in gel form and I simply put them onto my skin daily.

Within just 48 hours of beginning this treatment, my hormones had begun to rebalance and my mood changed entirely. My depression had lifted and it felt like a miracle. I have never felt depressed in that way for a moment since then.

All of those desperate thoughts and tears had been linked to the menopause and a hormone imbalance which, in my case, could be easily fixed.

A few years later, I told my story on ITV's *Lorraine* show and it broke the taboo. The phone lines were inundated, many publishers wanted me to write a book about the menopause as there was little available back then, but I didn't want to do so.

The impact of telling my story and the response of so many women made me realise just how desperate most of us felt, with a lack of investment in this time in our lives from successive governments. The harsh reality was that you could be treated badly at work and in society and nobody cared. In fact, it was OK to call you 'a bit crazy' or for people to roll their eyes and say, 'Oh, she's having one of THOSE moments', to treat your physical and psychological symptoms as an issue which you'd somehow created because you're 'a weak woman'. In other words, to belittle the process. Well, it isn't all right. Millions of women are going through a bad menopause right now and with just a little of the right help, their experience could be much improved. Not only that, on a macro-economic scale, we need women to stay in the workplace. They may well need to stay in the workplace for financial and personal reasons, and they might want to stay in a career which they previously found enjoyable and fulfilling.

And yet 3.5 million women have considered leaving due to

menopause or menstrual issues, and nine out of ten want their employer to be more helpful around these issues. Around a quarter of menopausal women are thinking about leaving their jobs and one in six are actively planning to do so.[36] What an utter waste and an indictment of the lip service paid to a female workforce, many of whom will, for a number of years, go through a physical process and then come out the other end post-menopause feeling a whole lot better naturally.

I've lost count of the number of women I've spoken to about their issues regarding the menopause. The last time was to a lady in charge of the food trolley on a train. She's going through it right now and feels desperate but can't afford to give up work. What are her choices? They aren't good. We need a system which can flex with this to some degree. Only a quarter of employers have guidelines around this issue.

If you're a young woman, you will at some stage experience some form of menopausal symptoms. If you're a man reading this then it will likely happen to a woman you love, whether that's your partner, your daughter, your cousin or your mother.

As with all issues, to get change sometimes you have to beat the drum ever louder so that somebody in government will listen.

Carolyn Harris MP sits on the Women and Equalities Select Committee and she had organised for some of us from Menopause Mandate to give oral evidence to the committee yesterday.[37]

Whatever I do in the political arena, whether it's tweeting or being on the television or radio, it comes from a deep understanding that I'm grateful to be given a voice so that I can speak for people who feel that they don't have one right now. It's your voice that needs to be heard, not mine.

Earlier in the day, in preparation for the committee hearing, I went on ITV's *This Morning* to ask our viewers to tell me about their experiences, which I could then take with me. So many trusted us with their stories that day, and so many of those stories were awful.

Just weeks earlier, Kemi Badenoch, then the women and equalities minister, had been in front of the cross-party committee and, with her now familiar arrogance, had fierce words with the chair, the Conservative MP Caroline Nokes. When Caroline Nokes raised the issue of menopause being made a 'protected characteristic' under equalities law, Badenoch cast the notion aside dismissively, saying people asked for 'many things' to be protected in law such as 'carers, single people, having ginger hair or being short'.

This took my breath away. How insulting.

It riled me no end and if you watch her appearance in front of the committee it will probably anger you too.

Badenoch's junior women and health minister, the Tory MP Maria Caulfield, had been invited to give evidence to the Select Committee on the same day, 22 March. I was interested to see what she had to say.

However, Caulfield hadn't answered the letter of invitation dated 7 February from the chair of the committee and so on 10 March, Nokes had sent her a letter saying, 'I understand you are refusing our request [to give evidence at the committee meeting]. Attendance at a Committee is not an optional extra or a matter of convenience.'

She continued:

Your unwillingness to appear before us to discuss a high-profile part of your brief suggests that you are taking neither your role, nor the issue of the menopause seriously. It also demonstrates a severe lack of progress on the Government's commitments on women's health.

It's a discourtesy that you are abdicating your responsibility, to women and to this Committee, to answer questions about vital policy issues, such as current HRT supplies and pre-payment certificates, which the Government has only just now managed to implement.

The Government's, and your own, lack of serious engagement on this issue reflects a continued disregard for menopausal women everywhere.

Bear in mind that this letter was written by one Conservative MP to another Conservative, such was the strength of her feeling. Maria Caulfield didn't answer this severe letter until Carolyn Harris and I raised it on X on 21 March.

Put on the spot the day before the meeting, Maria Caulfield tweeted that she had written to the clerks the week before to offer new dates. Clerks are the people who run the admin of the committees.

Except, the clerks then checked all correspondence and Caulfield hadn't contacted them at all.

So in real time there followed a Twitter 'heated debate' (as Mrs Merton would say), in which Carolyn Harris showed evidence, including letters. I was amplifying it online. Caulfield was making excuses about what she had or hadn't said, and then deleting what she'd said in the first place. Eventually, she wrote to the committee at 4.38pm on 21 March.

Basically, Caulfield had either messed up or she had shunned the committee. But she wouldn't admit to either, which drives me nuts. Just own your nonsense and then we can all move on.

Before the Select Committee met, someone spotted Maria Caulfield sitting at a table in the atrium in Portcullis House chatting, which admittedly wound me up even more.

Four of us sat down in front of the committee to give our evidence. I read out a number of the stories sent from our viewers on *This Morning*, who were suffering badly with their menopause in their place of work.

I said: 'Jeremy Hunt in his budget last week was saying how we want more people to stay in the workplace. Really? Then why aren't your ministers here answering the Select Committee's questions? Why? Where are they? Maria Caulfield was having a cup of tea when we were having lunch over in Portcullis House. That's not much of an example, is it?'

I went on: 'The government has rejected in part or in full 11 of the 12 recommendations of the committee's report into the menopause. They've waved off problems in the workplace by saying sex discrimination laws will cover that; that'll do. But it won't do. It doesn't do.'

Caulfield has since blocked me on Twitter. And then today, after Thangam Debbonaire raised the issue of Caulfield's non-attendance, Penny Mordaunt did the usual Tory thing and defended Caulfield in the House of Commons and on X, saying that the story was 'confected and false'. Except we have the evidence, Penny – screenshots of Caulfield's tweets showing it wasn't false at all – something successive Conservative ministers seem to hate.

This is how it goes on. They come together to defend their party.

Just another example, yet again, of how we need a better and more honest political system.

3 APRIL 2023

The Tory party is the party of colour-changing chameleons.

Why?

They are now so unpopular, most of Tory MPs' online profiles don't say they are Conservative; no reference to their party is to be seen beyond the name of their constituency. Not only that, their literature is any colour but the colour of their party, blue.

Their heroine Margaret Thatcher would turn in her grave.

It's all kicking off online.

I really pay attention to what my 'followers' (followers sounds a bit pompous to be honest because we're all a team as far as I'm concerned) are saying. So many of the outrageous stories begin with some information from 'the team'. There are millions of good people out there who want to be able to give information or express their thoughts, it's just that so much of our mainstream media won't allow them to do it. So we go online.

We're coming up to the very important local elections in May shortly, so all political parties have been putting out their literature to try to persuade voters to tick their box. The Tories have now produced leaflets and all sorts of expensive campaign materials, a limited amount of which you'd ever know was from a Tory. Conservative Campaign Headquarters (CCHQ) knows that the word 'Conservative' is now so toxic that it turns off the vast majority of voters who can't wait for the first opportunity to get rid of them.

So I thought we could do a little exercise online. I've asked 'the team' to send me the bios of their Tory MPs, who aren't saying they're Conservative. Remember there are only about 360 of them. I'm laughing so much as it's gone viral and it looks like over 300 Tories don't say they're Tories. Hilarious.

This was my tweet today:

2.9 million views, 21,100 likes and over 6,000 replies later . . . and I am awaiting the Tory backlash. Counting down three . . . two . . . one . . .

Booommm.

Remember #30pLee, Lee Anderson, the former Labour party man who switched to Tory who said that there was no need for so many people to use food banks, as meals could be cooked from scratch 'for about 30 pence a day'? His Twitter bio says: 'Lee Anderson. Member of Parliament for Ashfield. All views are my own and the vast majority of the country. Location: The RealWorld.'

I kid you not. This is not the bio of a six-year-old. It's an actual Tory MP. And a deputy chairman of the Conservative party, the party leading the country down the Swannee right now.

Well, on cue, here he comes, with his chest all puffed out, replying to my tweet:

Lee Anderson MP ✓ @LeeAndersonMP   1hr ...
Replying to @carolvorders
Think you need to check my bio again and while your [sic] at it act your age.

He's so thin-skinned he's now bothered to change his bio to include: 'Proud member of the Conservative party.'

Bless his little cotton socks.

Anyway, this is a little lesson in how Tories are now trying literally any trick in the book to snake oil the electorate. Even by pretending they're not who they are by printing their literature in green. Give me strength.

28 APRIL 2023

Richard Sharp resigns. Sharpe attracted further scrutiny last month, this time for helping a close friend to get a paid job advising the BBC on editorial standards (the BBC said the relationship was disclosed to the corporation). The brief suspension of Gary Lineker didn't make him look great, either. And the fallout from the damning report[38] into his part in helping to facilitate a loan for Boris Johnson has rumbled on. Now his resignation day has finally arrived!

The sad part of this sorry tale is that the musical chairs and nods and winks in Conservative corridors have brought suspicion onto the BBC itself, one of the most trusted brands in the world. For the chairman to have to resign because of some alleged dinner party loan-facilitating role for the most dodgy prime minister in modern history is a disappointing chapter for the great organisation.

However, while Sharp is out, Robbie Gibb, Theresa May's former head of communications whom Sharp appointed to the BBC board, who I'm now calling the 'Tory plant', continues on and the BBC's political output is being endlessly criticised for its bias to the right-wing think tanks.

It isn't good enough. The BBC is owned by us, not them, and I worry for its future.

Meanwhile, various presenters on GB News, Tory MPs and other right-wingers keep calling for my sacking from my little BBC Radio Wales music and showbiz chat show. Hey ho.

I'm not stopping, of course.

28 APRIL 2023
(LATER THE SAME DAY)

The tension is building in the run-up to the local elections on 4 May. The polls are swinging further away from the Tories but we have such an archaic first past the post (FPTP) system of voting that we have to play the system in order to consign the grubby party to history for good. But how?

Excitingly, I might have found the answer. I've just tried out a new website called Stop The Tories. I've never seen this before – in fact, I think it's the first time it's been done. It's a tactical voting website for local elections. I've seen it done for a general election but never for locals before.

Jeez, it's good. It does what it says on the tin. Everywhere there is a Conservative councillor (in fairness, some of them will be good councillors but they represent a corrupt government so they'll suffer), it recommends who to vote for tactically to get them out.

So, here's a random, made-up example, just to show you. Let's say there's a Tory councillor and the votes last time were as follows:

CONSERVATIVE	1,060
LABOUR	850
LIB DEM	560
GREEN	340

You can see that the number of people who voted anything other than Conservative is 1,750 which is nearly 700 more than those who voted Tory.

So, if you encourage people to tactically vote, to lend their vote to a party they wouldn't naturally support, then you can change the result dramatically. That's what Stop The Tories does. So in this case, it would recommend those who'd normally vote Lib Dems or Greens to vote Labour. In other cases, where the numbers are different, Green, Liberal Democrat or Independent would be recommended as the tactical vote, or it says too close to call.

It's ridiculous, by the way, that we have to do this, but it's all we have right now before we push for proportional representation, where every vote would count.

Back to the plot. I love to be pragmatic. I think it's the engineering bit of my brain, to be honest.

Yes, write words.

Yes, show evidence.

Yes, poke a few thin-skinned political narcissists.

But let's be practical and achieve a goal.

And this website – StopTheTories.Vote – feels like it could work. I'm on X now – let's go and tweet the hell out of it.

30 APRIL 2023

It's working. Two days in and a quarter of a million people have already used the site.

Who's behind Stop the Tories? Well, I feel like I've joined a team of some damn clever political musketeers. All volunteers. Much younger than I am – I'm the 'pensioner'. Dozens of techies who've put the site together, programmers, marketing people, coders, all doing this because they believe in the cause. And so do I. Lots of famous people are now retweeting too.

This is going viral.

EXPLAINER: HOW THE TORIES CHANGED THE ELECTION RULES

Does every vote count equally in the UK? Absolutely not and I'll show you why.

In April 2022, the Tory government, under Boris Johnson (the man who illegally prorogued Parliament), passed the Elections Bill, which effectively took away the independence of the Electoral Commission. The commission had been introduced in 2000, recommended by the Committee on Standards in Public Life, in order to help set the electoral standards across the UK. In 2022, the Tories took it under their control instead, and with that, they changed a lot of the rules at their will.

Why does it matter? Read on.

Given the massive swing towards Labour we've just seen in the recent general election in 2024, you might ask why I'm even mentioning changes to the election rules which were brought in by the Tories before they lost power. But they're important and they will have repercussions for future elections when the results will undoubtedly be much tighter, so I want us to take a pause and look at them.

Boundary changes: baking in Tory bias

In 2023, the Boundary Commission brought in changes to constituency boundaries to even out populations in each constituency to within 5 per cent of the 'electoral quota' of 73,393, so around 70–75,000 people per constituency. Sounds fair enough on the face of it, but because of our ludicrous first past the post voting system, this has a disproportionate effect on the outcome.

Historically, boundary revisions tend to favour the Conservatives, as Britain's population shifts out of the cities and into the suburbs, and from the north towards the south. And this latest set of changes was due to favour them too. Professor Sir John Curtice, the pollster extraordinaire (I'm a bit of a statistical fangirl of his), explains: 'The new boundaries maintain and reinforce a substantial bias in the Conservatives' favour.'

This bias was baked in even before the 2024 changes. Analysis shows that in the last-but-one general election (2019), if both parties had tied in terms of their share of the vote uniformly across the country as a whole, then the Tories would have won 290 seats, 23 more than Labour's 267.[39]

Now, in 2024, if both parties had had the same share theoretically spread evenly across the country, then the Tories would have won 50 seats more than Labour. It's a bias system and a nonsense.

Ironically, the Labour party refuses to call out this unfairness because of its tacit support of our existing voting system which keeps our government either Tory blue or Labour red.

So what's the solution? There's only one way to make sure a party's share of seats reflects its share of the vote – and that's proportional representation (PR). I'm all for it.

It's time we joined the 100-plus countries in the world that use either proportional representation or a mixed system, rather than the archaic first past the post system we still use today. (See my Plan for Change, page 336.)

Now, boundary changes aren't the only electoral reform that's recently been brought in by the Tories. Voter ID is another.

Voter ID: a solution without a problem

Under the Elections Act (2022), the Tories introduced voter ID. Kemi Badenoch declared the change was necessary to 'eliminate election fraud and make elections more inclusive'.

Sounds bad, doesn't it? As if fraudulent bogeymen have been stalking the polling stations. Must be a big problem, surely, given that the previous Tory government agreed to spend around £180 million over a ten-year period to fix it?

So can you guess how many electoral fraud convictions there have been in the four years between 2019 and 2023 (including all the local elections)?

A few hundred?

A thousand, maybe?

I'll tell you.

Eleven.

Yes, you read that right. Eleven.

And even that number doesn't tell the whole story. In 2019, there were five convictions for electoral fraud, but only one was for 'personation' (i.e. the crime that voter ID has been brought in to prevent). The rest were candidates and others acting fraudulently, in matters including a forged signature on their nomination paper.

It's ridiculous.

In the 20 months of Rishi Sunak's premiership, 12 Conservative MPs were suspended from Parliament or resigned after facing criticism, accused of activities ranging from sexual assault to misuse of party funds. I repeat: there were more sleaze-ridden Tory MPs booted or pressured out of Parliament in under two years than there have been cases of voter fraud in four years.

So, if the UK has infinitesimally small levels of voter fraud, then perhaps the second part of Kemi Badenoch's claim is the reason for bringing this new rule in – to make elections more inclusive?

Er . . . not quite.

Polling company More In Common reported after the 2024 general election that more than 400,000 people might have not been able to vote because they lacked voter ID, with those from minority ethnic communities more than twice as likely to have experienced this. Absolutely extraordinary.

So what forms of photo ID were valid in the general election 2024? Let's take a look.

Permissible voter ID included:

- Older Person's Bus Pass
- Disabled Bus Pass
- Oyster 60+ Card
- Freedom Pass

Now let's look at what's NOT permissible:

- Student ID cards
- 18+ Student Oyster cards
- 16–25 National Railcards
- 26–30 National Railcards

Notice anything about these two lists? Lots of ID for younger people not being allowed.

In May 2024, a huge YouGov poll found that only people in the age bracket over 70 favour the Tories, with Tories at 37 per cent over Labour at 25 per cent. For the age group 18 to 39, just 9 per cent favoured Conservative to 59 per cent for Labour. It's safe to say the Tories knew this too when they brought in these voter ID rules.

Dr Jess Garland, director of policy and research at the Electoral Reform Society, said when the law was brought in in 2022: 'Allowing bus passes and Oyster cards for older voters but refusing to accept the same forms of ID for young people is the kind of democratic discrimination that makes this bill so dangerous . . . The Elections Bill is a full-fronted attack on our democracy.'

There was also a huge outcry when it was found that Veterans ID cards for ex-military could not be used in the local elections in 2024, after their use had been promised by the government.

Interestingly, Jacob Rees-Mogg let the cat out of the bag when he admitted in 2023 they had deliberately tried to gerrymander the result, though it perhaps didn't achieve the result they'd aimed for: 'Parties that try and gerrymander end up finding their clever scheme comes back to bite them, as dare I say we [the Conservative party] found by insisting on voter ID for elections. We found the people who didn't have ID were elderly and they by and large voted Conservative, so we made it hard for our own voters and we upset a system that worked perfectly well.'

For once, I agree with him. The blatant attempt to gerrymander was nothing short of outrageous. I hope Labour repeal these rules.

Mayoral election changes: making it harder to avoid splitting the vote

But there's more. The previous Tory government also changed the system for how mayors are elected, so if you live in London, Manchester, Liverpool or any of the other major cities, you are no longer able to write down a second choice on your ballot paper.

That second choice meant people could avoid splitting the

vote. So if you wanted to vote for the Greens or Lib Dems but your choice of candidate didn't have enough support, your second vote for, say, Labour, would be counted instead.

That option is now gone. Guess who that benefits the most?

Party donations

Finally, we come to another electoral change which has huge implications for how our country is run.

In November 2023, with the Electoral Commission now unable to present a case to stop it, the Conservative party quietly pushed through a massive and unprecedented hike in the amount parties could spend in elections, without even holding a vote in Parliament. The spending cap increased by a whopping 80 per cent, from £19.5 million to about £35 million.

They also changed the rules to increase the amount of money that an individual can give to a party without the party being required to declare who donated it.

As Jessica Garland from the Electoral Reform Society put it: 'Rather than fix the worrying loopholes that already exist in our system, such as the scandal of unincorporated associations which can donate under £25,000 a year without declaring the source, the government are just increasing the amount that can flood in. This decision to raise the cap shows we are moving in the wrong direction.'

She goes on: 'The concern here is that we end up with a politics for sale to the highest bidder, where the greatest influence is not wielded by ordinary voters but those with the deepest pockets.'

Britain for sale?

These rules matter because they rewire our system.

They make it easier for wealthy donors, including from outside of the UK, to influence politics and meddle in issues that affect us. From what I've seen, the gates have been both opened and widened in the last 14 years.

The system has to change. Will Labour bring in new laws to do so? I truly hope so but let's wait and see.

Meanwhile, we'll keep the pressure up from outside the Westminster Bubble. We can be strong together.

1 MAY 2023

Now then, it's been brought to my attention that the wife of Tory MP and veterans' minister Johnny Mercer, Felicity Cornelius Mercer – yes, that's a real name – has been trying to stir up trouble between me and the RAF. Yes, the wife of a minister working in the defence arena is using her position to stir up trouble for a volunteer (me), as she doesn't agree with what I'm saying. Hmmm. An abuse of position? Unquestionably. Let me explain.

I've been the ambassador for the RAF Air Cadets for almost

ten years. You might know that I love flying, I love engineering (my degree) and have spent most of my life encouraging young people to learn STEM subjects (science, technology, engineering and maths) through books, my online maths school, videos, TV shows and online programmes. You might have learned your times tables with your 'Aunty Carol' at some point yourself. Sorry! I've given bursaries to young people from a similar background to my own (free school meals kid at a comp) for years to help them to get through university. STEM and education are a critical part of who I am, and always will be.

My hard-working daughter, Dr Katie King PhD, is a research scientist now; she got her PhD from Cambridge in nano technology. Katie has a young space company, Bio Orbit, which is a positive disrupter in the chemotherapy and immunotherapy industry. Basically, taking new immunotherapy drugs to space means that the proteins can crystallise perfectly in micro gravity, something they can't do on earth. Why is that important? Well, it should mean that those drugs will be able to be injected under the skin at home (in a similar way to insulin for diabetes) rather than patients having to go into hospital to have them administered intravenously. This will be a game changer in medicine. The science is already proven and Katie's first prototype 'crystallisation factory' should be up in space within 12 months. The European Space Agency has also sponsored her. (She worked at NASA as an intern scientist in the Mars Rover lab years ago.) Typical proud mother getting in a mention of her kids!

Back to the RAF. After happily working for RAF charities for many years, in 2014, I was asked to become the RAF's first ever female honorary group captain, both as ambassador to Air Cadets and also as a representative for STEM subjects generally. What an honour. I felt so privileged as my ambition as a young woman had been to become a fighter pilot, but back when I was young, women weren't allowed to be pilots in the military. They are now, thankfully. All down to political decisions . . . again.

I accepted the offer with the biggest smile ever and until Covid struck, I spent about 20 days a year volunteering with the cadets, staying with them on camp, at airshows, celebrating our seventy-fifth anniversary, visiting squadrons, publicising their work and particularly that of the thousands of adult volunteers who fundamentally run the organisation through the goodness of their hearts and the triumph of their effort. I have been a volunteer, and it's been an utter joy to meet so many good people who are trying their best and achieving great things. The adult volunteers' love for the young cadets and their motivation is extraordinary, and they have made me feel universally welcome all over the UK for years. Also, it was lovely to be able to get our Pride of Britain Awards red carpet lined with Air Cadets many times; sometimes the young cadets even joined me on stage. I was asked by the RAF to renew my commission in 2019, which I did very happily.

Now, if you are a full-time member of the military you aren't allowed to comment about politics publicly. However, there is no such rule for anyone appointed as an honorary, as I am. In fact, the military is awash with Conservative politicians who hold similar roles to mine. For example, Shaun Bailey (who happily partied during Covid) is the equivalent honorary to me, but for an element of Army Cadets. Penny Mordaunt holds an honorary captaincy RNR in the Royal Navy and Scottish Conservative leader Ruth Davidson was made honorary colonel of her former Army regiment. The list goes on.

Quite obviously, none of these politicians are prevented by their honorary positions from expressing their thoughts about politics. They literally do it every single day.

But, of course, as ever, as far as Tories are concerned, it seems to be one rule for them and another for anyone who dares to challenge them. Me, in this case.

Now, the Mercer woman has form. One day last month, she sent me 60 tweets in a day moaning about how I shouldn't bring to the attention of the public the fact that the Tory MPs are not saying that they're Tory MPs in their online bios. I've just been ignoring her, to be honest.

She also swears a lot online – and I mean A LOT . . . using the C bomb, the F word, and pretty much everything else. All fine in private, but publicly?

Anyway, she's now attempting to cause trouble for me with the Chief of Air Staff by tagging him in, claiming I shouldn't be allowed to be political and remain as honorary group captain. Remember, she is the wife of the minister for veterans' affairs using that position. In my opinion, as I'm sure in yours, the military has better things to do than waste their time on the rantings of an entitled Tory with no substance to a claim. Jeez.

For now, I'm ignoring the little madam, and will wait and see what happens. The pattern of threats and abuse from Tories is growing. But first we've got the local elections to get through, which is far more important.

4 MAY 2023

It's today. The big test of our system and those who are going to come out and vote and do something to stop the tide of Conservative power.

With tactical voting we can make an enormous difference.

Around half a million people have now used the website and typed in their postcode. You can assume that most are tactically motivated and will vote, so let's see how it goes.

Right now, before voting, the numbers of council seats up for grabs in this election across the country are as follows.

CONSERVATIVE	3,365
LABOUR	2,131
LIB DEMS	1,221
INDEPENDENTS	954
GREEN	240
RESIDENTS ASSOCIATIONS	112

Come on, tactical voters. Let's get rid of as many as possible.

The political commentators are saying if the Tories lose as many as 1,000 seats (from their existing 3,000+) then it will be a disaster.

I'm hoping they'll lose more. I'm not politically affiliated. I just want to STOP THE TORIES.

Voting day is always strange on the news as they aren't really allowed to talk about politics as broadcasters are in political 'purdah'. Once the polls close at 10pm, that's when the juicy stuff begins. Best have a nana nap now as it's going to be a long night!

4/5 MAY 2023
(OVERNIGHT AND INTO THE NEXT DAY)

Star Wars Day. May the fourth be with you. Channelling Princess Leia.

Nana nap is done so I'm ready for it. Honestly, Geek Woman here genuinely gets more excited about an election night and the numbers than I do about a football match, that's how 'unusual' I am (unusual/weird/nerdy and other synonyms also allowed).

The thing is, you have to time it right.

5pm: Get a couple of hours' sleep in late afternoon/early evening.

10pm: Polls close so journalists can now comment. Watch the telly, switching channels between Sky, ITV and BBC most of the time to get updates.

11pm: Set the alarm for 1.30/2am and sleep.

1.30am: Get the teapot going, the laptop open for X, telly on for results/commentators and have a great time without leaving your bed! Some results will be in earlier as it's local elections so there are fewer votes to count in each ward compared to a full constituency in a general election, but the meat of the results will be after 1.30am.

This is going so badly for the Tories already.

3.30am: Plymouth council has turned red to Labour. A lot of cheering going on on the telly with a pompous Tory MP looking very cross.

4.48am: Boom. Tories have lost 100 seats. Just another 900 to go to target a meltdown! They've also lost Stoke council, which is an extremely bad sign for a general election as Stoke turned Brexit blue with three new Tory MPs in 2019. They can probably kiss their seats goodbye. Well done, Stoke.

5.10am: This is getting worse for the Tories. They've just lost Medway council which is a bellwether for indicating a trend for the general election results. Their total loss now stands at 134 seats.

5.30am: The Tories' recent policy of trying to hide the fact they're Tories on social media and campaigning leaflets didn't work well, did it? They've now lost 150 seats.

The Tories have lost about a third of their seats declared so far; a rough calculation means that they're on course for their worst results in decades. Make no mistake, this is all of us saying ENOUGH IS ENOUGH.

The results are coming in throughout the night. Professor John Curtice is as superb as ever in his analysis; I'm hooked.

6am: Time for some sleep, even though I'm now skipping around my bedroom. I've been having a right laugh with the 'team' online – it's been hilarious at times. It's like having a huge WhatsApp group. It's my nerdy numbers version of Glasto! Happy days.

After I woke up again, I switched the TV on. I've been watching on and off all day, waiting for the big moment . . . and here it comes . . .

8.30pm: EXPLOSION AND FIREWORKS in the studio please! The Tories have now lost 1,000 seats.

10.58pm: Looks like Jacob Rees-Mogg won't be around after the general election as the biggest council in his constituency has just turned from Tory majority to Liberal Democrat with a 45 per cent swing.

Final results (apart from one which is on a recount, weirdly) are:

LABOUR	2,675 (+537)
CONSERVATIVE	2,296 (−1,062)
LIB DEMS	1,628 (+407)
INDEPENDENT	865 (−89)
GREEN	481 (+241)
RESIDENTS ASSOCIATIONS	99 (−13)

So the voters have spoken and seemingly told the Tories that it's time for them to go.

Time for a general election NOW, don't you think?

7 MAY 2023

This is a strange one. A third recount has been demanded by Conservatives in the small Longbeck council ward in Redcar (part of the Redcar and Cleveland council, part of the Tees Valley combined authority).

A third recount is unheard of when someone can win a council seat with about 700 votes. My little detective nose is smelling a very big rat. Time to take to Twitter to ask the 'team'.

I swear you find out more through information on Twitter than through many standard channels – particularly the deep background behind, or leads to, stories. A lot of journalists believe this. Obviously you have to do your own research, as there is a plethora of misinformation online, but as long as you do that research, social media can be a great resource.

Redcar . . . hmmm. Sam Coates from Sky (excellent journalist) is questioning this too on X now.

Look for the pattern . . . always look for the pattern.

Steve Turner is the Tory who is trying to take the council seat and apparently demanding the recounts. Turner already earns £73,300 a year as the local police and crime commissioner (in an area with the worst crime rate in the country[40]). A former UKIP councillor, he's also on the board of the development corporation linked to the huge Teesworks site, part of Teesside Freeport.

A lot of information is coming through now about the Teesside Freeport and the local Teesside mayor, Ben Houchen, a Boris

Johnson favourite. Also a lot of news about the history of Steve Turner, including a caution for handling stolen goods when he was younger and an accusation and investigation into an alleged sexual assault – though last year the Independent Office for Police Conduct (IOPC) investigation was dropped. (The IOPC said they were 'satisfied all reasonable efforts to progress this investigation have been made and that no further lines of inquiry remain open at this time'.)

Wildly, in the run-up to the local elections, Turner made two official complaints about local Labour supporters, one of which was because a local Labour campaign leaflet was blue, which he said represented Conservative. Well, you could knock me down with a feather, given that most Conservatives have been campaigning using the colour green leading up to these elections!

Sam Coates reports: 'Sky News has been told by one of those interviewed that the plain clothes policeman said they were investigating because an election leaflet had "upset Steve". They added the police officers they were talking to "seemed a bit embarrassed to be dealing with it and said they're normally fraud officers but were working the election". At the end of both investigations, police concluded there was no offence committed.'

And all this while Turner is the police and crime commissioner. An abuse of his position? He says not. Of course.

All in all, you can see it's a highly toxic environment, whichever side of the political spectrum you're on.

9 MAY 2023

Well, the results are in. Both Steve and his wife Andrea Turner have lost their bid to be councillors on the Redcar council.

The elected councillors are Luke Myer, Labour, and Vera Rider, Independent.

But the investigative information from *Private Eye*, *Yorkshire Post* and others about Teesworks and Teesside Freeport – well, that's an entirely other matter . . . off to find out more.

EXPLAINER: WHAT ARE FREEPORTS AND SPECIAL ECONOMIC ZONES?

Some of you might not have heard of freeports. Or if you have, you might think they sound quite dull. But read on because the Tories have been quietly introducing them around the country, and it's high time we shone more of a light on them. As with many things Tory, they were sold to us in one way, then smoke and mirrors were applied, and now it seems they are something else . . . And I am deeply suspicious and concerned about them. I may, of course, be wrong but it's worth taking a deeper look.

Essentially, freeports are designated areas where normal UK tax and custom rules don't apply. So goods can come into the country with simplified custom procedures and without anyone paying tariffs. Businesses operating inside the designated freeports can manufacture goods there using imported parts, then export them again without ever paying the full tariff on the original imports.

Special economic zones (SEZs) act in a similar way, though they are even broader in scope. As well as tax incentives, businesses located in SEZs enjoy looser regulations around labour law and foreign investment, even planning laws and compulsory purchasing of land and buildings. The zones amount to enormous swathes of the country.

Rishi Sunak has long been a fan of them. When he was a backbench MP in 2016, he wrote a report for the right-wing think tank Centre for Policy Studies in which he claimed that freeports could create a whopping 86,000 jobs.

Later studies, however, suggested this dazzling figure was highly questionable. In fact, it's more likely that business would simply be diverted from other parts of the country, leading to what former SNP leader Nicola Sturgeon called 'low-cost, low-wage, low-value opportunities' (though that didn't stop the SNP later waving through their own versions in Scotland).

Despite these concerns, in 2021, the government announced eight new English freeports, in East Midlands airport, Felixstowe and Harwich, the Humber region, Liverpool City region, Plymouth, the Solent, the Thames and Teesside. All but one are now operational in some form.

Why are they controversial?

You don't have to be a genius to realise that criminals and others who possibly have some matters to hide are going to be attracted to this kind of zone, given the fact that the freeports actively advertise that you can do business there with less scrutiny and a lower-level paper trail. Wherever freeports have been introduced around the world, they have provided ripe opportunities for tax evasion, not to mention money laundering, smuggling and trading in counterfeit goods.

Then there's the issue of the lack of regulation. This means businesses in these zones can, in theory, ride roughshod over workers' rights and bypass environmental laws that apply elsewhere in the country.

The Teesworks redevelopment project in Teesside has been dogged with controversy from the start, with many allegations of wrongdoing and cronyism. Ninety per cent of the shares in Teesworks ended up in the hands of private companies, while hundreds of millions of pounds of taxpayers' money was pumped into the scheme. A review published in January 2024 found 'no evidence' of corruption, but nonetheless stated that the project was excessively secret and lacked oversight as to how public money was spent: 'There are issues of governance and transparency that need to be addressed and a number of decisions taken by the bodies involved do not meet the standards expected when managing public funds.' In total, the panel made 28 recommendations to improve transparency and decision-making.

It will come as no surprise that freeports and SEZs have not brought the post-Brexit sunlit uplands that we were promised. The laxer regulations and tax benefits only serve to line the pockets of shareholders and owners, not the workers who may well be on zero-hours contracts. These shadowy economic zones are, in my opinion, home-grown tax havens; they don't foster genuine growth but divert business from elsewhere and they do nothing to help local businesses which fall outside of their boundaries.

So perhaps it's time to ask ourselves a few questions.

How do we feel about the UK becoming more of a centre for money laundering?

Are we happy about the UK's laws and regulations being undermined within our own country?

Do we care about the erosion of workers' rights for greater profits, which benefits those at the top?

And ultimately, who benefits? Not the taxpayer, it seems.

As ever: look for the pattern and follow the money.

8 JUNE 2023

This was a lovely day. I've been into Global Radio many times before to promote books or TV shows or whatever is on the PR round. It's a huge commercial base for a number of stations, including Capital, Heart, Smooth, Classic FM, Radio X, Gold and LBC. A very buzzy building, like the old BBC TV Centre and LWT tower used to be many years ago, full of young people, all of whom seem to love what they do. Happy days.

Today, I was in to see James O'Brien, the hugely popular LBC broadcaster, who has a podcast called *The Full Disclosure*. Though, I wasn't sure what I was going to be disclosing! Ha.

I really enjoyed it. It was good to be able to chat about what motivates me politically. I guess it all comes back to what you've experienced through your life. It's funny, as I've got older, I know exactly who I am and what I'm prepared (or not) to put up with. Decisions become much simpler than ever before. And it's increasingly important for people who feel they have no voice to speak up and be heard. And if I can help people to do that in even the smallest way, then that is more than enough for me. I like James O'Brien. Brilliant broadcaster.

9 JUNE 2023

Boris Johnson's Resignation Honours list was published today. It's a disgrace, shows his utter contempt for us and democracy and, in my opinion, reads like a who's who of people who shouldn't be near government, let alone be rewarded for their behaviour.

Let's remind ourselves: Johnson was only prime minister for three years before he was forced out of the job by a mass revolt of ministers after a series of scandals. Then he resigned as an MP following a Privileges Committee investigation into Partygate, to avoid the humiliation of being suspended from Parliament and the possible by-election that might have ensued.[41] And yet the system is so crooked, he's still allowed to have a Resignation Honours list!

The word 'honour' is meant to mean 'respect, integrity, prestige, morality, kudos, distinction'. It's a sorry day for etymology.

The rundown

Johnson wanted to put 15 people into the Lords. The House of Lords Appointments Committee has rejected eight of them, so Johnson's list is down to seven new peers.

This brings the total number of new peers he alone has created since 2019 to 93, including his brother Jo Johnson, now Lord Johnson, naturally. Jeez.

There are many on the list but some of the new honours have gone to:

- Ben Houchen, the Teesside mayor, goes into the House of Lords.
- Jacob Rees-Mogg – now a sir.
- Andrea Jenkyns, MP for Morley and Outwood, and the one in the yellow dress who stuck her middle finger up outside Downing Street – now a dame.
- Priti Patel – now a dame.

- Charlotte Owen becomes a baroness. Who? I hear you cry. Well, she is a 30-year-old who worked briefly for Johnson in his office. There is literally no reason for her to be near the House of Lords. There is nothing much to say about her other than she played the flute at school and is a Conservative.
- Evgeny Lebedev, the Russian-born son of a KGB agent.

Nowhere else on earth can randoms be elevated to be legislators for life. Nowhere. Welcome to Britain.

Let's all celebrate Partygate

Johnson also gave a number of honours for those involved in the Partygate scandal. Remember that Number 10 became the address with the most Covid fines in Britain: 126 fines were issued to 83 people, including Boris Johnson, his current wife Carrie and Rishi Sunak. Twenty-eight people received between two and five fines. Let's see who's been rewarded:

- Martin Reynolds – the man who became known as 'Party Marty' after inviting over 100 people to a party at Number 10 and telling them to 'bring your own booze'. He receives a CB.
- Shaun Bailey – the disgraced London mayoral candidate

who was partying at Conservative campaign HQ on 14 December 2020. It took years for the evidence to come out. He becomes a lord.

- Ben Mallett – also at Bailey's party. The man in the red braces. He now has an OBE. And is a friend of Zac Goldsmith.
- Shelley Williams-Walker – the 'DJ' at the party held the night before Prince Philip's funeral. She becomes a dame.
- Jack Doyle – who, when *Daily Mirror* journalists began to investigate Partygate, advised his colleagues to 'just be robust and they'll get bored'. He gets a CBE.
- Rosie Bate-Williams – a press officer who continually issued denials about Partygate. A CBE for her, naturally.

It's a long list and this is just the tip of the iceberg but it makes me feel queasy so I'll stop here.

Angela Rayner, deputy Labour leader, has said, 'It's a sickening insult that those who planned Covid parties and held boozy lockdown bashes while families were unable to mourn loved ones are now set to be handed gongs.'

And she's right.

Absolutely sickening.

I hope if Labour gets in, they do something to change this ridiculous system of political so-called honours. It debases the awards given to those who truly deserve them.

EXPLAINER: THE HOUSE OF LORDS

The House of Lords acts independently of the House of Commons. None of the peers (the people who sit in the House of Lords) have been elected by us; they have largely been nominated and placed there by other politicians. It's known as the 'second chamber' or the 'revising chamber', and the purpose of it is to check and to challenge the work of the government, predominantly through Select Committees (see page 96 for more on this). It attempts to hold government to account with varying degrees of success – for example, the Lords voted for many amendments to the Rwanda Deportation Bill, which delayed its passing into law. The Lords cannot block a bill altogether, but can hold it up and attempt to amend a piece of legislation for up to a year.

Currently made up of nearly 800 members, the House of Lords is the only 'second chamber' of any parliament that is bigger than the elected chamber (i.e. the House of Commons). In fact, it's the largest parliamentary chamber in the world other than the Chinese National People's Congress. This is clearly a ridiculous and expensive situation and, as with everything, it's wise to know how we have arrived at the position we're in today – so time now for an extremely potted history.

The House of Lords first developed in medieval times from the King's 'Great Council', where noblemen would advise the

King and recommend which taxes to inflict on the population. It held its exceptional power until relatively recently, apart from a short period in the seventeenth century after the English Civil War, when Oliver Cromwell dissolved it entirely. (Incidentally, I studied at the same college as Oliver Cromwell, Sidney Sussex College in Cambridge; in 1960, his severed head was buried in a secret location in the college grounds. I never found it!) Once the monarchy was restored in 1660, the Lords reverted to their previous position.

Before the First World War, fundamental changes were put forward by the Liberal government but the heavily Conservative House of Lords kept rejecting them (the rich were clinging on to power – sound familiar?). Eventually, some of those reforms were passed, but it wasn't until 1958 that the biggest revolution of the Lords happened.

Up until this point, the House of Lords was largely made up of hereditary peers, all of whom were male – their privilege of birth and penis giving them rights above and beyond the rest of the monarch's 'subjects', no matter what they did or said. When the daddy peer died, his title and seat in the Lords would pass automatically to his eldest son.

In 1958, the Conservative prime minister Harold Macmillan put through an Act to make life peerages possible for the first time, meaning most newly created lords would have a position in the House of Lords for life, but this privilege couldn't be handed down from father to son. Women were also allowed to become peers at this point too. The Labour Leader of the Opposition at the time was Hugh Gaitskell, who argued that the whole of the House of Lords should be disbanded and all peers should be elected. He may have been right. You will still hear this argument today and I for one feel that it's time for enormous reform to happen (see my Plan for Change on page 340 for more on this).

Incidentally, there are still hundreds of hereditary peers, but 'only' 92 are now allowed to sit in the House of Lords (there shouldn't be any in my opinion, and Keir Starmer has pledged to remove them all). When one of these men dies, an election is then held to see who will replace him in the Lords – but to be a candidate, you have to be a hereditary peer, which in this century is a pile of utter privileged nonsense.

Some facts at the time of writing in July 2024:

- The average age of those in the House of Lords is 71.
- 71 per cent of peers are male; 29 per cent are female.
- Most peers don't receive a salary; they get an allowance of £342 per day for attendance plus travel.
- The total cost of the life peers' allowance and expenses was around £21 million for 2022/23.
- Many hardly vote at all.

In 2024, the 790 members of the House of Lords who are eligible to attend are made up of the following:

- 674 life peers
- 91 hereditary peers (maximum 92)
- 25 bishops (maximum 26)

Before the July election, the largest blocks of life peers by political party were:

- 278 Conservatives
- 173 Labour
- 80 Lib Dems
- Plus 182 crossbench (non-party political) peers

It's claimed that the House of Lords is less partisan than the Commons, but in practice the difference is marginal. In 2016/17, 78 per cent of Tory peers failed to vote against their own government while Labour peers voted against the Tory government in 90 per cent of votes. So however you look at it, that's pretty much Tories voting for Tories and Labour voting against them, which brings into question the point of the House of Lords.

There are many fine people with good hearts and determination in the House of Lords, of that there is no doubt, but drastic reform is still required.

Two years after Labour won the 1997 general election with a landslide, it introduced the House of Lords Reform Act. It was sorely needed: by October that year, the House of Lords had reached a record size of 1,330 peers. After Tony Blair's reform, the number was reduced to 669, with a maximum of 92 hereditary peers and 26 bishops, the rest mainly life peers.

However, when Tory David Cameron became prime minister in 2010, things changed again. Between 2010 and 2016, an additional 214 new life peers were created, a faster rate than under any other British prime minister in history. Tories, eh?

In 2014, the wonderful Betty Boothroyd said of this ennobling frenzy: 'All prime ministers, including this prime minister, are very keen to put a lot of new members in here so they can get their legislation through . . . it's what I call lobby fodder. They go through the lobbies and they vote for the prime minister who put them there.' It seems she was right.

The number of new peers reached a high of 826 in 2015. During these years, when trust in politicians has slumped to a new low, many of those appointments were hugely controversial. Those two facts are linked.

David Cameron of course put the proven liar Michelle Mone into the House of Lords. She's currently taken a leave of absence but could walk back into the Lords any time she likes, such is the nonsense of it all.

What's even more absurd is that after just 49 days as an unelected prime minister (voted for by Conservative party members and not the electorate), Liz Truss was allowed a Resignation Honours list. Despite her dismal track record in her short time in office, she still managed to put two highly controversial men into the House of Lords: Matthew Elliott (former Vote Leave chief executive and leading figure in the group Conservative Friends of Russia) and Jon Moynihan (chair of Vote Leave and a Tory donor who helped to devise the catastrophic mini-budget). Note that the Electoral Commission found that Vote Leave's campaign 'broke the law on electoral rules . . . Serious offences such as these undermine public confidence in our system.' And now both of these men are in the House of Lords deciding on laws which we must obey.

There are many questions about the legality of obtaining a peerage. The Honours Act 1925 made it illegal for somebody to be put into the House of Lords based on an exchange of money. But over the years, many allegations have been made that major political donors receive their peerages thanks to their hefty contributions.

Since 2010, ten Conservative party treasurers have been elevated to the Lords, many of whom have donated more than £3 million to the party. It's been said that the chance of that happening randomly is like winning the National Lottery 12 times over.

Between 2013 and 2023, 68 out of a total 284 new peerage nominations from political parties had donated a total of £58 million, with £53.4 million going to the Conservative party. Money seems to talk.

In 2006, Tony Blair nominated several people for life peerages, but they were rejected by the House of Lords Appointments Commission (HoLAC), an independent body which advises the PM about specific appointees, as they had apparently given large financial loans to the Labour party. You may remember the media was full of stories about this for about a year – it was known as the 'cash for honours scandal'. The Labour party's Lord Levy, who was in charge of party fundraising, had somehow managed the loans from wealthy businessmen to the party's coffers, meaning they weren't technically donations. Lord Levy was arrested; Tony Blair was interviewed by the police; but in the end, nobody was prosecuted and the Labour party paid back the loans. At the time, it damaged the reputation of the Labour party hugely; it would barely register these days, so debased has the appointments system become.

In 2022, the former Labour prime minister Gordon Brown published a report, commissioned by the Labour party, about future reform for the House of Lords. In short, he proposes that:

The House of Lords is abolished and replaced by an elected assembly of around 200 people.

Members are elected so that the regions are better represented than currently, with London and the south east overrepresented.

We wait to see if Keir Starmer will bring in all of these changes. I hope that he does, and fast. It's important for us all to feel that Westminster is being held to account before trust in government will grow.

3 JULY 2023

Johnny Mercer's wife has been having a rant into the void again about yours truly. This time on Rachel Johnson's (sister of Boris Johnson) podcast. 'She's a celebrity attack dog who knows nothing about politics,' she said. 'She drives me up the f**kin' wall.'

Sweary woman, isn't she? I'll let it go. It's nice to get under the skin of the wrong 'uns. I still haven't responded or acknowledged the Mercers in any way, such is the unburnished shine on my halo of patience . . . ha.

7 JULY 2023

Well, what do you know? Johnny Mercer creating bad headlines all by himself with a car-crash interview on Sky News earlier this week. I think my halo of patience may need removing shortly!

The channel had recently run a piece by their Defence Correspondent Deborah Haynes, in which she'd been talking to military personnel who were using food banks. Last month, it was reported that military morale had hit a five-year low over poor pay and housing, after a pay freeze for many years followed by a below-inflation pay offer. The military are not allowed to strike. Housing standards are dropping, with Royal Navy base HMS Collingwood being forced to shut down an accommodation block after maggots and silverfish were found in the fridge freezers.[42] There are very many similar stories.

On Tuesday, Kay Burley was interviewing Johnny Mercer on her breakfast show and she asked him about the food banks story.

He put on his 'look here, I'm very important and I'm speaking' face and said, 'These are personal decisions around how people are budgeting every month.'

Kay Burley pressed him, saying, 'But they don't have any alternatives.'

To which Mercer replied, 'Well, in my experience, that is not correct . . . I don't think food bank use is an accurate portrayal of where levels of poverty – relative or absolute poverty – are in this country.'[43]

Try telling that to the Trussell Trust, who estimated a record 3 million food parcels were distributed in 2022.

Mercer gave short shrift to the outcry that followed, claiming that anyone who disagreed with him is a 'bedwetter'. As he put it on X: 'Enjoying the collective bed-wetting on this. Military personnel should not be using food banks – period. Disagree if you like, but that is true.'

You know when you get a feeling that there's a little Tory Story hidden in the background? (Let's be fair, there usually is.) Well, I had that feeling. So I went on the Independent Parliamentary Standard Authority's website. IPSA was set up after the MPs expenses scandal in 2009 with responsibilities including the regulation of MPs' business and staffing costs. It contains a wealth of information if you ever want to look. I found out that Mercer has been paid in one year

£86,564 for his MP's salary and £31,680 for his ministerial salary. In 2019, he was also on a contract worth £85,000 a year for 20 hours' work a month in a second job with a company which eventually went bust. He left the company in 2019, when he had to resign in order to become a minister in order to comply with the ministerial code.[44]

No food bank necessary for Mercer, obviously, nor should there be.

But hidden within his 'business costs' on the IPSA website was a little gem. Ooh, I do love detail, it's where the devil lies.

While he was telling people that food bank use doesn't indicate poverty, the biggest hypocrisy of all is that the taxpayer is paying MPs' staffing costs circa £45,000 a year in order for him to employ his wife in his office. Not something which is widely known.

Not only that, while the military has suffered a real-term pay cut since 2010, her full-time salary received, as stated by IPSA, went up from circa £15,000 in 2015 (when Mercer became an MP) to circa £45,000 just six years later. An extraordinary set of promotions which means her income went up by circa £30,000 of taxpayers' money (in response, he denied the figures in the public domain were correct, said that the rise was due to her moving 'between full and part time' and claimed that 'she is worth every penny'[45]). I wonder if there were other people invited to apply for this remarkably well-paid position in Plymouth, where the average salary is around £29,000?

So their basic joint income from taxpayers seems to be £163,000-plus before expenses.

In 2017, this cosy system of an MP employing his/her partner or offspring, or 'connected party' as it's known, was banned – EXCEPT for those MPs who were already doing it. Ridiculously, no time limit was put on this arrangement either. Around 70 MPs (mainly Tory) are still using this system in 2023. Nadine Dorries employed two of her daughters in her office under this arrangement.

In 2016, before the rules changed, the total expenses bill for 'connected parties' across all MPs was £3,693,250 – not far off £4 million of OUR money.

Anyway, I thought I'd draw attention to this information about the Mercers on X. Boy, has it got a bit wild.

Over the course of a few days, Johnny and Felicity Cornelius have called me many names, from 'grim' with lots of puking-up emojis – yes, this was from a minister – to quoting 'plastic surgery' and 'inciting hatred' (a common refrain from the Conservative party aimed at anyone who dares to call them out) and much more.

To people who dare to criticise either of them, Mercer's wife has been giving a volley of abuse: '@CarolVorders isn't going to shag you', 'thunderf*ck', 'prick'. And so on it goes, from a taxpayer-funded member of staff for a minister.

Apparently, I'm the one with the issue. Hmmm.

Last night, Mercer appeared on *Question Time* and had a total meltdown, shouting over other panel members so much that somebody in the audience told him off for it. It is trending on social media as the worst performance on the panel for years. According to the *Daily Express*, he also had a very long rant about me in the show's green room.

Now, this genuinely isn't about yours truly, even though it's been a week of sticking my head above the parapet; it's about the bullying methods of the Conservative party, which I've tried to bring to everyone's attention, while getting trolled every day. You take them on and they use all their friendly press to attack you. I'm way past the point of caring nowadays. Speaking truth to power and showing people evidence – that's where I'm at.

Anyway, it's been a bit of a week all in all, with a very sweary pair of Plymouth Tories not happy with me for pointing out the truth, and the newspapers following it all with daily headlines. Ah well.

13 JULY 2023

Headline on the front page of this morning's *The Times*: 'I WANT A CAROL VORDERMAN DAY RIGHT NOW' by Deborah Ross. She suggested there should be a national holiday 'to applaud the one person who has relentlessly spoken truth to power'.

Awww . . . thank you! You've no idea just how much this lifted me after the onslaught I've received from right-wing media and Tory MPs this week. It's a very funny piece and I love it. You're brilliant, Deborah. I'll take the 'win' because I just know a storm is brewing! Ha.

31 JULY 2023

Whoa, the onslaught of abuse and bullying from Tories has been turned up a notch or seven over the last few days. Now the combined forces of the *Daily Telegraph*, *Mail*, *Express* and Tory MPs are saying I should be sacked by the BBC. Hey ho. I have a feeling the writing is on the wall.

13 SEPTEMBER 2023

It's been brewing for a while but it's now been announced that the new BBC social media guidelines are due to be published at the end of the month.

I've been working at the BBC for decades, on and off. I think the first show I ever made with the BBC was in 1987. It was called *Take Nobody's Word for It*, a science programme for BBC2 with Professor Ian Fells and I hosting. It was a big success, won awards, and featured guest appearances by Margaret Thatcher (who had been a scientist) and a young Myleene Klass (aged about eight) when she won our children's competition for an engineering design using paper. I think she built a Ferris wheel, if I remember rightly. Years later as grown-ups we became friends and even spent some time sharing a camp in *I'm a Celebrity*. Funny how life turns out!

Anyway, back to the BBC. In the nineties I hosted *Tomorrow's*

World for the BBC, was on *The MidWeek Lottery* every week with Carol Smillie, presented *Mysteries with Carol Vorderman*, a big ratings winner, and hosted *Points of View* and numerous science-based shows among others. The BBC and I go back a very long way.

In 2018, I started hosting a Saturday lunchtime show on BBC Radio Wales, my first little radio show since the early 1980s, as TV had become my mainstay since then. I said yes to BBC Wales as I'm Welsh, grew up in Wales and there's a thing we call 'hiraeth', pronounced 'he-rye-th'. It's a longing for your homeland – and I'd been feeling it pretty deeply since Mum had died the year before. It's a deep and heartfelt feeling of belonging to your country, to the land.

Where I grew up in Prestatyn, we were on the coast so you could smell the salt of the sea air and the wind blowing in from the Irish Sea, but at the same time you could see the mountains of the Vale of Clwyd and Snowdonia (Eryri) beyond. It really was beautiful.

Once we'd moved some miles inland to Denbigh, every journey in my teens to school in Rhyl was past miles of fields and hills and castles. There was a sense of permanency, of solidity, a sense you belonged.

There are over 600 castles in Wales, about one for every 5,000 people nowadays, many of which were built by the English kings who were trying to control a feisty bunch of Celts. We've always been 'troublesome', now I think about it! We had a beautiful castle in Denbigh at the top of the town . . . stunning . . . with a view of the whole of the Vale of Clwyd. If I could live my life again, I'd make more time to stop here and there and take in the view.

So working on BBC Radio Wales over the last five years has been lovely. I've made some wonderful new friends and re-engaged with the country. Our little show on a Saturday lunchtime has always been a laugh; we end up dancing most of the time, joking and chatting to showbiz people who might be on tour in Wales. We have lots of lovely listeners so we all feel like a family.

BBC Wales, in fairness, has been thorough with their advice about social media and the new guidelines that are about to be introduced. I'm pretty sure I'm seen by some at the top in London as a troublemaker they'd rather see quieted (my words, not theirs). I've been given a list of content which would probably break the new social media guidelines – fundamentally it covers most of what I say online!

I still find it ridiculous that I am not allowed to have a political view at a time when it's more important than ever for people to speak out. Of course, I totally understand that Ofcom regulation and broadcasting guidelines determine what a broadcaster is able to say or do on air, and I have adhered to this code during 42 years on TV and radio. Furthermore, if you are a newscaster (which I am not), there are extra rules about impartiality, all of which I understand. BUT my BBC Radio Wales show is a showbiz chat and music show, and never once have we mentioned politics in the five years I've been hosting it.

So now the BBC wants to govern the opinions a part-time presenter (it's a once-a-week show) may or may not express outside of work. To me, that feels ludicrous.

As you might imagine, I'm resigned to the changes about to be imposed, but not happy.

We are now living at a time when the reach of social media prevails in many age groups over and above that of broadcast stations. Social media is now a key part of any broadcaster's portfolio. Within that online presence, opinions are actively encouraged.

If we're not careful, female BBC presenters could easily now be reduced to just smiling and wearing dresses, which is fine for those who want that, but not for the rest of us who don't!

I see this change as an unwarranted curb on the activities of those who contribute to BBC programmes. I can't see how this is going to work out well, but here we are.

23 SEPTEMBER 2023

Daisy Cooper (deputy leader of the Liberal Democrats) has become an ally. I like her.

I've been asked to make a video to be shown at the Lib Dems' conference this year. This is about my belief that our first past the post system of voting maintains a system of 'democracy' which is wholly unsuitable for today's world. I want proportional representation, but with the system we have now, tactical voting is our best hope.

Steve Coogan has also made a video in which he says how the current system means 'millions of people's voices go unheard'. He said, 'I'm not a member of the Lib Dems; despite the beard and the fleece, I generally vote Labour. But where I live in Lewes, the candidate best placed to kick the Tories out is the Lib Dem candidate, so I vote for them.'

I've never belonged to any political party, and I doubt I ever will, but happy to help the Lib Dems with this one.

29 SEPTEMBER 2023

With the BBC social media guidelines about to be announced, which I know will lead me to a decision to leave my Radio Wales show, and yet another row, it's lovely to get a lift every now and again.

This month, I've been named as one of the 'British *Vogue* 25 women defining and redefining Britain', which for a near-pensioner at the age of 62 is a lovely accolade. But really, it's for all of us – all of us who felt we had no voice and now we're finding that we do.

The list includes some incredible women: Jodie Comer, whose one-woman play *Prima Facie* drew attention to the legal problems of securing convictions for sexual assault; Raye, whose brave decision to part ways with her label and record independently has catapulted her to new heights; Baroness Louise Casey, who chaired the damning inquiry into the Met Police following the murder of Sarah Everard and so many others.

Vanessa Kingori, Condé Nast's chief business officer, hosted a beautiful dinner and a lot of the *Vogue* 25 were there. Vanessa herself is a powerhouse who is regularly named on lists of the UK's most influential Black Britons.

Raye sang barefoot and powerful, an utter joy. There is a sense of women feeling a shift in power today, which we haven't felt before. It's really our time, girls, to speak out and not accept bullying any more, not from politicians or any institution.

We can change it for our daughters and nieces and the babies of today.

Time to not be 'shamed' for being independent, or not stick thin, or choosing to not conform. We have nothing to apologise for and now it's time to step up and speak out.

One of the things I love about the world today is that the younger generation do exactly that, including many young men who are so supportive of women. Times they are a-changing.

Together we're heading for a better world. Although there are a few potholes in the road to negotiate first and we have to do it together. We really do. Please don't be silent.

8 OCTOBER 2023

Over the last year, I've met and been in touch with Rachel Reeves: she really is an impressive and kind woman. No ego. Enormous sense of justice. Huge brain and she listens. I've always passed on YOUR views and emotions about particular matters to her, such as the VIP PPE lane.

We're in the middle of rehearsals today for our twenty-fourth *Daily Mirror* Pride of Britain Awards at the Grosvenor House Hotel, with my co-host Ashley Banjo and ITV. There's bad phone signal in the Great Room where we hold the event as it's underground, so it wasn't until I got back to the dressing room when I let out a special yelp of joy. Why?

I've just received a message to say that I'll be very pleased with an announcement Rachel is going to make at the Labour party conference tomorrow. Keeping my fingers crossed that it's about the VIP PPE lane!

9 OCTOBER 2023

Pride of Britain went so beautifully last night. The winners and their bravery and their stories made me cry; they always do. They really make you feel that there is something in the human spirit, in good people, that makes us better and makes our world better for having them in it. Every year, our award winners surprise us and even knowing that they are there makes you feel that there is always hope.

Next year, we will celebrate 25 years of the Pride of Britain; I'm the only one left in the team who has been there from the very beginning. Peter Willis, an editor with the *Daily Mirror*, established the idea in 1999 and we worked together to take it to ITV. A much younger me was hosting quite a lot of primetime shows on ITV back in those days so I worked with ITV bosses pretty closely. We lost Peter recently and I miss him very badly, as all of us who worked with him do. I loved him as my friend; I still can't believe he isn't here laughing out loud and causing mischief. He gave his all to make sure the Pride of Britain was everything our winners could want it to be. That's our mantra, to give our winners their best time, and I'm pleased to say the team delivers that year after year.

Feeling very emotional about last night, so to hear Rachel Reeves announce today that should Labour win the next election, she will immediately appoint a Covid corruption commissioner made me burst into tears.

She said, 'Today, the cost to the taxpayer of Covid fraud is estimated at £7.2 billion. With every single one of those cheques signed by Rishi Sunak as Chancellor. And yet, just 2 per cent of all fraudulent Covid grants have been recovered.' She continued, vowing to 'chase down those who have ripped off the taxpayer, take them to court and claw back every penny of taxpayers' money that they can. That money belongs in our NHS. It belongs in our schools. It belongs in our police . . . we want our money back.'

Bravo, bravo, bravo.

I fully expect that her Covid corruption commission will also go after the associates of the Conservative party who profiteered during the pandemic while frontline NHS staff put themselves into danger because this government had failed to protect them. It is, in my view, the worst example of corrupted politics in my lifetime.

I've become heavily involved in showing the evidence of the VIP PPE lane and taken a lot of abuse by doing so, but I know it's the right thing to do. They'll come after me again I know for sure, but let's take the wins when they happen.

So thank you, Rachel Reeves. You're a good woman.

4 NOVEMBER 2023

I've been trying hard – well, hardish – for about a month to abide by the new BBC social media guidelines. Hmmmmm.

But now I'm on my holiday with my best mate and there have been a few political stories which are truly worrying me.

One of my grave concerns is the use of ever more right-wing rhetoric by some government ministers.

The Israel–Hamas situation has intensified after the horrific Hamas attacks on 7 October, with the taking of hostages and the bombing of many civilians, including children, in Gaza by Israel. Consequently, many want to protest and voice their opinions.

Suella Braverman, the Home Secretary, has described those wishing to march in London next Saturday asking for a ceasefire in Gaza as 'hate marchers'. She tweeted: 'It is entirely unacceptable to desecrate Armistice Day [11 November] with a hate march through London.'

She has also attacked the Met Police, who refuse to stop the planned march, for choosing 'favourites'.

Mark Rowley, the Met Police Commissioner, has been criticised in heavy terms by both Rishi Sunak and Braverman, who both insist that the pro-Palestine march must be banned. But Rowley is standing for the principle of operational independence from politicians. Asked on the *News Agents* podcast about Braverman's term 'hate march', Rowley said, 'She's picked two words out the English language and strung them together.'

Little by little, we've witnessed an erosion of our freedoms in this country. Perhaps it is a hangover of the government's sense of how they should govern after using emergency powers during Covid, but there are many precedents including the proroguing (suspension) of Parliament by Boris Johnson in August 2019. This was later deemed unlawful. There's a pattern.

Braverman and her words – it needs a tweet. So today I wrote:

> **Carol Vorderman** ✔ @carolvorders   1hr ...
>
> Mark Rowley (Met Commissioner) saying he has no idea what Suella Braverman is talking about. We've come to this . . . This iteration of the Tory party needs to be utterly dismantled at the next election.
>
> ○   ♻   ♡   🔖   ⬆

Today, Braverman has a new target and is attacking the street homeless. She's pushing for a new offence which would fine charities if they provided tents to rough sleepers. In a cost of living crisis of the Tories' creation, with a proliferation of food banks, the crashing of the economy and the numbers of rough sleepers more than doubling since the Tories took over, they want to yet again pick on the most vulnerable.

I'm afraid I can't hold back any longer. Quote-tweeting Braverman, I'll keep it civil but mimic her words, 'What I want to stop, and what the law-abiding majority wants to stop . . . ' So here goes another tweet:

> **Carol Vorderman** ✔ @carolvorders   1hr ...
>
> @SuellaBraverman What I want to stop, and what the
> law-abiding majority wants to stop, is your vile government
> clinging onto power for a day longer.
> You don't speak for us.
> Every week you debase democracy further.
> We're ashamed of you.
> Go now.
>
> 　　　　○　　　⟲　　　♡　　　◻　　　⬆

I feel better for that. But it's a matter of time before the BBC bosses come knocking, I know that full well. The countdown to leaving the BBC starts now!

5 NOVEMBER 2023

The abuse of women is growing. Rape convictions only stand at around 2 per cent of those reported. The message seems to be that you can do as you like and you probably won't be caught.

I've always believed that the singular thing any government should represent is a sense of protection and security for a population. Now, there is a revelation at the very top of the Tory party itself, which beggars belief.

A Tory MP has apparently been under investigation on numerous counts of sexual offences, including rape. The former Tory chairman

NOW WHAT?

Jake Berry has alleged in the *Mail on Sunday* that the party attempted a cover-up, with only limited action taken, which has allowed the MP to continue offending after the alarm was raised.

Berry is quoted as saying that he wrote to the police after he discovered that, shockingly, the Tory party had paid for one of the alleged victims to receive treatment at a private hospital.

Oliver Dowden, the Tory deputy prime minister, has been interviewed on the media rounds this morning and when asked about the hospital payment he said that he 'can't say for certain' that the party did not pay the alleged victim's hospital bills.

'I'm not denying that it could be the case that those payments were made, but it's not something that I authorised or was part of as chairman of the Conservative party.'

My tweet says it all:

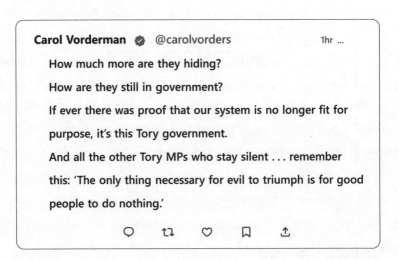

Carol Vorderman ● @carolvorders   1hr ...

How much more are they hiding?

How are they still in government?

If ever there was proof that our system is no longer fit for purpose, it's this Tory government.

And all the other Tory MPs who stay silent . . . remember this: 'The only thing necessary for evil to triumph is for good people to do nothing.'

It's a subject so serious that I think damn the consequences with the BBC. It's my decision and I'm happy with it.

(NOTE: The MP at the centre of the allegations has always denied the charges. The police investigated but he was never charged.)

6 NOVEMBER 2023

This morning, there's been a bombshell exclusive from journalist David Conn who has been brilliantly covering the VIP PPE lane and the Michelle Mone story in the *Guardian*.

Finally, for the first time, Mone and her husband have admitted that they had both been involved with PPE Medpro deals. Mone's lawyers have consistently told the newspaper previously: 'She [Mone] has no involvement in the business . . . She has never had any role or function in PPE Medpro, nor in the process by which contracts were awarded to PPE Medpro.'

Now it seems that isn't the case.

Time for a tweet or two:

Carol Vorderman ✅ @carolvorders   1hr ...

Michelle Mone story courtesy of Led@ByDonkeys ... up until today's revelations.

£65 million transferred to a trust – beneficiary Barrowman ...

from there £29 million to a trust – beneficiaries Mone and her 3 grown-up children.

I hope criminal proceedings come soon.

   ○   ↻   ♡   ◻   ↥

> **Carol Vorderman** ✓ @carolvorders   1hr …
>
> Finally, the lies unravel . . .
>
> Let me be very clear. What she and her husband Doug
> Barrowman have done disgusts me. The money MUST be
> retrieved and I hope criminal proceedings follow.
>
> To profiteer in the pandemic and lie and spend and mock
> the good people in this country, while our NHS frontline
> workers risked their lives for no reward whatsoever, is
> beneath contempt.
>
> ○   ⇄   ♡   ☐   ⬆

I could have been more expressive, given that they are both guilty of pandemic profiteering while so many suffered. But I'll leave it at that.

7 NOVEMBER 2023

Today my contract with the BBC has been terminated. Just like that. No surprise there. Five tweets from the last few days are deemed to have broken their brand new social media guidelines. There is absolutely no doubt in my mind that the social media guidelines have been put in place to close down political debate, particularly from those who criticise the Tory party. I have not broken broadcasting rules. I have not mentioned politics on my radio show. The people moaning, and MPs making complaints to the press about my online political views, are all Tories.

According to the BBC I have breached three principles in their nonsensical social media guidelines:

Principle 1: Do treat others with respect, even in the face of abuse.

Principle 2: Don't use offensive or aggressive language and DO conduct yourself with courtesy.

Principle 4: Don't attack individuals, even when you disagree with their views.

What do you think? Should a person be sacked for calling out the rhetoric of a Tory Home Secretary inciting discord; the horrors of a ruling political party alleged by its own former chairman to have attempted to cover up allegations of multiple sexual offences and rape by one of its own MPs; and a Tory baroness who has lied consistently about her involvement in one of the biggest scandals of modern times?

I have no regrets about a single word of those tweets.

My fury remains targeted at how low this Tory government has brought the country.

Right. Let's crack on with the announcement. As my best friend says, 'OWN YOUR SH*T.'

Quick story.

I remember the last time I was 'let go' by the BBC. (I think I must now be the only presenter to have been effectively sacked twice; I really must get a badge made.)

The first time was back in the mid-1990s when I was the main anchor for *Tomorrow's World*, the BBC's flagship science and technology show. I'd been on *Countdown* for many years by then and the BBC courted me after a poll apparently indicated that I was the easy favourite to take the role. I wasn't sure if I wanted to do it but after a while I said yes.

The issue began over this – I had by then already signed a contract to present commercials for Ariel washing powder. Contractual negotiations with the BBC were continuing after I started hosting the show.

Months later, and *Tomorrow's World* was going really well; meanwhile, we made a new commercial for Ariel and it was broadcast.

My agent got a phone call from the BBC to say that I had to return from filming in Australia immediately as someone senior at the BBC had complained that I shouldn't be appearing on the adverts. (Note that we were told complaints had not come from viewers.)

So I came home from Australia early, some heavy conversations took place and eventually the BBC allowed me to carry on.

We signed a contract which said that the Ariel advert could continue but if another one was made, the BBC would have the right to not renew my contract.

Sure enough, Ariel and Saatchi & Saatchi (the advertising agency) were thrilled with the response to the advert and they wanted to make another. So the BBC terminated my contract immediately.

Not only that, they stopped my column in the *Radio Times* and they stopped me hosting a new education series I was contracted to make. It was an axe falling at a time when I was making my way as a presenter onto primetime TV.

Well, I'm not one to take an injustice without speaking my mind.

Other (male) presenters had appeared in commercials over the years, including Noel Edmonds on the 'Noel's Maxwell House Party' coffee ads and Gary Rhodes the famous chef advertising Tate & Lyle sugar. I had no issue with that, and strangely neither did the BBC. Apparently, I was the problem, and the other BBC presenters weren't.

One rule for them (and I had no issue with them advertising products) and another me. Sexism was rife.

I pointed this out in newspapers and it seems the public agreed with me. Ratings for *Tomorrow's World* fell.

A few months later, the BBC offered my job back to me but I felt so let down by them at that point, I considered it for a while and then finally said no just before the show was meant to come back on air. I was happy with that decision. They weren't. But years later I was given many more shows to host by the bosses and times were good once more.

That was about 30 years ago. Swings and roundabouts.

Now, here we go for another ride on the roundabout, except this one is far less serious than the big one back then. This is just a tiny little bumpette in the path of life.

I want to stress here that I do love the BBC, that the people we have been dealing with at BBC Radio Wales in recent months have been very lovely and I only have fond memories of all my times there over the years.

The issue for me is that, in my opinion, this comes from a government pressure. I doubt that many others will receive similar treatment.

In fact, I received some kind words from BBC Radio Wales: 'I wish to put on record my heartfelt thanks to Carol for everything she has done for BBC Radio Wales over a number of years.'

I know that those words are meant. So thank you, lovely people. I'll see you sometime soon.

Time now to put together my own statement and issue it tomorrow. Some words have been suggested, but I prefer to do my own. I'm feeling very calm, and pretty relieved about it all, if I'm honest. I'm free to do what I like now. I'll think about my statement overnight.

8 NOVEMBER 2023

Here's my statement:

The BBC recently introduced new social media guidelines which I respect.

However, despite my show being light-hearted with no political content, it was explained to me that as it is a weekly show in my name, the new guidelines would apply to all and any content that I post all year round.

Since those non-negotiable changes to my radio contract were made, I've ultimately found that I'm not prepared to lose my voice on social media, change who I am, or lose the ability to express the strong beliefs I hold about the political turmoil this country finds itself in.

My decision has been to continue to criticise the current UK government for what it has done to the country which I love – and I'm not prepared to stop. I was brought up to fight for what I believe in, and I will carry on.

Consequently, I have now breached the new guidelines and BBC Wales management have decided I must leave. We each must make our decisions.

I'm sad to have to leave the wonderful friends I've made at Radio Wales. I wish them, and all of our listeners, all the love in the world. We laughed a lot, and we will miss each other dearly.

But for now, another interesting chapter begins.

Diolch yn fawr iawn i chi i gyd [thank you all very much]

Heck. The response online has been off the scale. Quite extraordinary, so thank you if you're reading this and you replied. Some of my 'celeb' mates including Alan Carr, Sally Lindsay, Joe Lycett and others have been lovely online too. It's an odd industry; many hide away in times of trouble but others don't, but there we are. It's just life and I am a very lucky woman.

I feel 100 per cent better than I did a few weeks ago, I felt tied down back then but now I'm full of fight to get rid of these Tories within the next year when we come up to the time of the general election.

Here's to life.

An interesting new chapter begins.

13 NOVEMBER 2023

Today the Tories are having ANOTHER Cabinet reshuffle.

It's like musical chairs. No ideas left.

Sunak has sacked Suella Braverman after her disgraceful she-nanigans around Remembrance Day, in which she revved up the far-right yobs by calling the pro-Palestinian protests 'hate marches'.

James Cleverly – the man who in the House of Commons called the town of Stockton-on-Tees 'a sh*thole' (he later claimed he said the MP was a 'sh*t MP' – too many syllables, James, to match what we heard!) – is shifted sideways from Foreign Secretary to Home Secretary. He won't like that.

Others are shuffled around.

And now the press is expressing a little bit too much awe for my liking as David Cameron comes striding along Downing Street as the new Foreign Secretary. It seems the Tories have run out of both ideas and people.

If you need a reminder, Cameron is an old Etonian who took us to a Brexit referendum, then lost and resigned, and after 'leaving' politics became involved in the biggest lobbying scandal in modern history. It's called the Greensill scandal, it involved over £400 million of our money and David Cameron was at the heart of it.

In Tory world, his reward is to become Foreign Secretary.

2 DECEMBER 2023

The fallout from the BBC continues. It was always going to be that way, I guess.

Now that I've made the decision, I'm all in and devoting all my time to calling out the Tories. Next year is going to be critically important, even though we don't know when the general election will be.

A lovely part of the year that's just passed is that I've come across wonderful people and organisations who dig deep into one issue or more. They won't accept the status quo and, as such, provide a full-throttled voice against the cruelties and lies of the last 14 years.

One of those is the Good Law Project, a crowdfunded organisation run by lawyer Jolyon Maugham, which works to investigate particular issues and bring legal cases where it can to hold the government and others to account. I really like the work they do.

I've been a bit daft not making many political videos, despite the fact that, as a TV presenter, talking into a camera is what I do! Idiot! So the Good Law Project and I have decided to start a series of videos specifically about the VIP PPE lane and I can't wait.

5 DECEMBER 2023

Nadine Dorries resigned as an MP last August, after months of anger from her constituents for a host of reasons. So today I had to laugh out loud. My agent, Josh, sent through an email this morning. It was from Nadine Dorries' agent suggesting that she and I might do a podcast or show together. Whaaat?!

Well, I'm sure that her agent is a very nice man and is thinking, as he should, about his client, but I think we can all agree that's a polite NO. Life's never dull, eh?

6 DECEMBER 2023

I went off to the gym this morning to squat, scream, jump, collapse . . . and just when I was finishing up, Neil Reading (my press agent for when I'm promoting things) rang me and said that he'd received a funny story from the *Daily Mirror* and that he needed to check with me if it was true.

The *Mirror* had been told by someone at GB News that the boss of GB News had made me a job offer and I'd said no.

It's one of those unimportant but bizarre stories.

It's bizarre partly because GB News slates me on air most weeks, often devoting chunks of a show to right-wingers saying pretty disgusting, rabid stuff about me to persuade their viewers that I'm some kind of anti-British activist with devil's horns.

I'd met the boss years before through my old TV friend Eamonn Holmes, before it became the right-wing station it now is. So he had my number and the day after I left the BBC back in November, he sent me a text, offering to show me around the station. Sometimes I think it best not to say anything, so I didn't answer and forgot about it.

So now the *Daily Mirror* has told my press agent that they have a quote from someone at GB News saying, 'Carol wouldn't touch GB News because she thinks it's full of right-wing nut jobs.' Which is pretty accurate, to be fair.

But what was really weird to me is that it was leaked by GB News, like a classic own goal. The newspaper headlines duly screamed: 'Carol Vorderman snubs GB News offer'.[46]

Some days you just have to laugh!

Anyway, now seems a good moment to explain how press works for 'celebs'.

I didn't have a press manager for the first 40 years of my career (yes, I'm an old bird). Odd really, I suppose, but when you are hosting various shows, the channel you are working for will have a press person for that show, who deals with the enquiries. So, for instance, *Loose Women* has a press officer who'll also look after other shows. The BBC Science department will have a press officer, BBC Wales has a press officer – you get the idea.

Although *Countdown* used to go through Channel 4 press office, the show was made by Yorkshire TV, now part of ITV plc. As we were based up in Leeds, filming at the YTV Studios, we were largely forgotten about by the bosses in London, which suited Richard Whiteley and me, to be honest. Untrendy, innocent, happy to just do our little thing, we would often get random press stories about us, which were daft and nice and not earth-shattering.

I know I'm switching off politics for a bit here, but it's nearly Christmas and this has to be my favourite *Countdown* press story of all time . . .

Countdown used to be a huge show, pulling in about 4 to 5 million viewers every day; it was the biggest show on Channel 4 for about 15 years. We would pre-record our Christmas Day show months beforehand and one year, Richard pulled me into his dressing room to help choose the best tie for him to wear. One had been beautifully hand-painted by a Countdowner (our name for *Countdown* viewers). It was silk and the wonderful Countdowner lady had painted the word COUNTDOWN, starting at the top of the tie and running down it, and then painted some Christmas decorations around the word. It was lovely, so he wore it. We recorded the show, all of us went to the bar for a drink after, the show was edited and weeks later, on Christmas Day, it went out on air. How nice! Or not . . .

Boxing Day: we wake up to the whole front page of one of the tabloids showing a photo of Richard in his *Countdown* chair from the Christmas Day programme, with the headline RICHARD IS A SILLY . . . with four arrows pointing to his tie.

NOOO!

The tie had the word 'COUNTDOWN' painted vertically downwards. Fine. But when Richard sat in his chair, the letters DOWN disappeared from view, leaving the word COUNT visible on the tie. Then, unnoticed by the rest of us, he'd clipped his little microphone on his tie covering the letter O . . . so only C–UNT was left in view. And there he sat, smiling away through the whole show, and we were completely oblivious to it. OMG . . . we laughed for years about that. Total innocence.

By hell, I loved my days with him. I've been a lucky woman. Twenty-three years together laughing and loving each other as friends until he died very suddenly in 2005. I have never been so struck with grief as I was by his death. For many weeks after, I would still sit bolt upright in bed in a cold sweat in the middle of the night, unable to think, and all I could feel was an overwhelming blackness.

I still cry happy tears if someone reminds me about him. I loved our time so much.

When I eventually was forced off *Countdown* three years later, I mourned Richard all over again.

It was only a TV show, I know that, but it was loved and we loved it and everyone who watched or appeared on it was part of our *Countdown* family.

To mourn so deeply means that the love was real. I don't regret a single day of our 23 years, or any of them since. Old *Countdown* was a part of us, and we were a part of it, and I'm very proud of that. And I wish 'New *Countdown*' all the luck in the world. It's always been a special show.

7 DECEMBER 2023

Today was Boris Johnson's second day in front of the Covid inquiry. The crowd included people from the Covid-19 Bereaved Families for Justice group, who stood outside holding placards saying, 'The dead can't hear your apologies' and jeered while he entered and exited the building. What an absolute lowlife Johnson has proven to be. It seems about 5,000 WhatsApp messages on his mobile from 30 January to June 2020 were 'unavailable'. Why? Johnson told the inquiry: 'I don't know the exact reason, but it looks as though it's something to do with the app going down and then coming up again, but somehow automatically erasing all the things between that date when it went down and the moment when it was last backed up.'

Sunak has lost his WhatsApps too.

And they expect us to believe any of it? Really?

It piles insult on top of insult, yet the system allows it all to happen without recourse. One rule for them and another rule for us, yet again. It must be extraordinarily difficult for those who lived through the worst of it to have to sit through his testimony. Unbearable.

Johnson has run up a big bill for his lawyers for this Covid inquiry, all paid for by the taxpayer. We don't know how much that bill will be yet, but the lawyers paid to advise him in his evidence to the Privileges Committee in relation to his Partygate antics cost us £265,000. Johnson was found to have committed five 'contempts' of Parliament in that inquiry and the National Audit Office judged that the Cabinet Office effectively failed to follow proper processes by expecting us to pay his bills.[47] We also know that the Tory government has set aside £55 million for legal bills for the defence of the government at the Covid inquiry.[48]

I hope Rachel Reeves' Covid corruption commissioner looks into all of this and demands some of it back.

10 DECEMBER 2023

Here we go. This morning, the woman who can't lie straight in bed, otherwise known as Michelle Mone (yes, her again), has put out a marketing video – or, as she describes it, a 'World Exclusive Investigative Documentary' to 'give my side of the story' – in which she finally admits she's been lying like hell for three years about her and her husband grabbing £65 million of OUR money in exchange for some very dodgy PPE.

This piece of marketing puff is an abortive attempt to try to play the world's smallest violin, begging us to feel sorry for them and explaining how the nasty Tory party are picking on them.

'I'm not an angry woman,' Mone whines in her disastrous piece of aggrandisement and self-pity.

'We've done nothing wrong,' she and her husband bawl.

Jeez. So you set up a company to profiteer from the pandemic, you recommended it to the government days before it was even registered, you lied about it and threatened people, you whipped out £60 million-plus, you're being sued for £122 million of it not being useable by the DHSC and you've been raided by the National Crime Agency – and then you bleat? Really?

For three years, let's remember, since the discovery of her involvement with PPE Medpro, Mone and her husband have threatened newspapers and issued lawyers' letters to anyone who implied that she and he had anything to do with the company.

Now, in this video, Mone admits she 'made an error' and says 'I regret not telling the press of my involvement' with the company. More importantly, she says she lied to the press on 'legal advice'. Wow. This means Mone has now made an extremely serious allegation that her own lawyers told her to lie to the press. If true, that would be enough to have a lawyer struck off.

You didn't make an error, girl; you lied time and time again.

Without a shred of self-awareness, Mone then continues about how what with all of these (true) accusations from the wicked journalists, she can't sleep and suffers panic attacks.

I tell you who's suffered, Michelle. The people on the frontline of the NHS who had crap PPE during Covid, the hundreds of frontline workers who died, their families who lost them, the one in seven health workers who thought about self-harming such was their trauma, and the NHS staff who contracted Covid, who weren't protected, and who are still suffering today. I'll save my tears and sympathy for them. Not for a lying profiteer like you.

I get so angry about the Covid contracts, and not just this one. I need to let off steam.

Anyway, back to the 'Mone Marketing Enterprises one-hour-long commercial'. Since its release, Mone, her husband Doug Barrowman, and the so-called 'reporter' who was paid to appear in the video have been destroyed on social media. She has been, as it's called online, 'ratioed', which means that the number of negative comments far exceeds the number of likes and retweets a post may have gathered.

So why have Mone and Barrowman admitted to their involvement with PPE Medpro now, after years of saying they had nothing to do with it?

The reason (which hasn't been highlighted that much) is fairly simple. They had to or it would have come out anyway.

Three days ago, on 7 December, lawyers representing the Department of Health and Social Security, which had issued the two contracts to PPE Medpro, went to court for a pre-trial hearing. The government lawyers are claiming more than £130 million in damages. The trial will be based upon the £122 million second contract, which PPE Medpro received through the VIP lane. Government lawyers said that the '25 million sterile gowns' were 'not sterile when delivered'. PPE Medpro contends this, insisting that its gowns 'passed quality inspection in China' and were manufactured to the 'correct quality standards and specification'.

In the meantime, it continues to cost us millions of pounds to store all these unusable gowns until the court matter is concluded. The total storage bill is already more than £10 million. A reported estimate for the total claim by DHSC, including storage and disposal, is nearly £133 million, not including interest.

By the way, it's unlikely that the trial will take place before the next general election. Well, there's a thing.

DARVO and narcissism yet again

Just to note, this is a classic case of narcissism and the DARVO technique, so much so it should be included in school textbooks going forward.

D for Denial. Mone LIED for three years, vehemently, through her lawyers.

A for Attack. Threatening legal letters were issued at the drop of a hat.

R for Reverse the roles of . . .

V for Victim.

O for Offender. They quite laughably spouted how they were being victimised by being taken to court.

Nah, not a lot of sympathy coming from me.

11 DECEMBER 2023

The Good Law Project and I have been working to make our new VIP PPE lane videos short but full of the key information, so here we go with the first of our episodes in #TheVIPFiles. Posted.

What a great reaction. To hundreds of thousands of Insta and

TikTok followers, this is new news, something which hasn't necessarily been presented to them before. Quite rightly, they are as shocked as I was when I first learned about the profiteering deals made through the VIP lane, all linked or referred through the Tories.

13 DECEMBER 2023

On the days where the BS and staggering levels of ineptitude/ corruption become apparent, I do a little list to get my thoughts in order. I have to make a tweet list and get back to it at the end of the day once I've finished at work.

Normally it's just a note on my iPhone, but some days it can get a bit too complicated for that. You know that feeling when you have three shopping lists (one for food, one for Boots the chemist and one for B&Q) and a to-do list (worky things, house chores and bills), and that's before you've even got the kids off to school . . . Well, the Tories supply such levels of nonsense most days that I sometimes end up with my own 'political shopping list' of whose activities to, er . . . enhance that day!

Tweet list for the day to show you how sometimes it's difficult to keep up with the Tory fountain of nonsense

ONE: RISHI SUNAK AT PMQs

Wednesday is always Prime Minister's Questions (PMQs), beginning at noon. Today, Sunak was brought down by Chris Bryant. Bryant is a long-term Labour MP from the Rhondda in South Wales. At PMQs, he asked Sunak: 'What's worse? Losing your WhatsApp messages as a "tech bro"; losing £11 billion to fraud as Chancellor; presiding over the biggest ever fall in living standards; or desperately clinging to power when you're even less popular than Boris Johnson?'

Superb parliamentarian. I hope he becomes a powerful minister after the election.

I try to stay out of the Westminster Bubble as it's just not me at all – I don't like the playground nature of it. But the braying and pointless nature of PMQs where nobody answers a bloody question drives me particularly nuts.

TWO: THE ECONOMY HAS NOW FLATLINED

A recession is defined as two consecutive quarters of a year where the growth in GDP is less than zero. In one quarter of the last two, GDP fell by 0.3 per cent, and now the results for the next quarter say it's flatlined. So we are not technically in a recession . . . yet. The Tory spin is it's all fine and 'we're sticking to the plan'.

Actually, please don't.

THREE: TORY LEGAL COSTS FOR
THE COVID INQUIRY

The Tory legal costs alone are £55 million, payable by the taxpayer, for lawyers to go through documents before they're handed to the Covid inquiry, including trying to stop messages between ministers being handed in. Why not just hand them in? It's as though they may have something to hide . . . Sunak losing his WhatsApps. Johnson also losing his WhatsApps. It's one insult after the next. Some days you want to round them up and march them out of Westminster, the whole lot of them.

FOUR: DAVID CAMERON

As mentioned earlier, we have a new Foreign Secretary, David Cameron. This is the man who, when he was prime minister, brought in austerity for the masses and oversaw wealth creation for the already super-rich. The one who closed youth clubs while cracking on with privatising the NHS by stealth so that money was steered into the profits of private companies, many of whom then gave donations and/or jobs to the Tories. The one who cut the core funding to councils so they're now going bust, encouraged water companies to invest less in the infrastructure and, above all else, the one who kept the super-rich paying less tax through offshore funds, while the rest of us pay more tax than ever before. Yes, we now have the highest tax burden for 70 YEARS.

David Cameron and his dad were caught out in the release of the Panama Papers, a leak of 11.5 million records relating to secretive offshore tax funds, when it was found that Cameron Senior had squirrelled away money which was then passed on to his son. In 2016, after four days of stalling and partial statements, David Cameron finally admitted he benefited from offshore trusts in Jersey and Panama. Great for a prime minister in charge of our tax system, don't you think?

So last month, Cameron came ambling down Downing Street as the new Foreign Secretary – an extraordinary position, one of the great four seats of state (the others are prime minister, Chancellor of the Exchequer and Home Secretary).

But to be in the Cabinet of any government, you either have to be an MP or a member of the House of Lords. So Rishi Sunak put his friend into the House of Lords to make him Lord Cameron of Chipping Norton. However, as a lord, Cameron can't go into the House of Commons, so he has a different person to answer his questions in the lower house. You really couldn't make this up.

Andrew Mitchell MP (of 'Plebgate' fame) now speaks on behalf of Lord Cameron. Cameron can now effectively go about his 'work' without hindrance. Exactly what you don't want one of these Tories to be able to do. They should be constantly hindered.

Here is the biggest issue of all. Mr Eton Mess resigned as prime minister when he lost the Brexit referendum. But don't worry, he's fine (of course). In fact, he started lobbying for a firm called Greensill Capital, where he earned an estimated £10 million-plus to push the company in front of Sunak and Johnson and others in power around the time of Covid.

He sent them dozens of messages, spoke to Richard Sharp (the now disgraced former BBC chairman) and persuaded the British

Business Bank (owned by the taxpayer apparently – I know, I hadn't ever heard of it either) to guarantee loans of over £400 million for Greensill . . . then Greensill went bust.

Well, guess what? We, the taxpayers, are left high and dry with the fallout from the Greensill fiasco. It became the biggest lobbying scandal for many years.

Now he's back in government, David Cameron has quickly moved all his assets behind what they call a 'blind trust', just like Rishi Sunak has. This is a handy little system where they effectively say, 'I don't know what is happening with those shares and money so I can't have a conflict of interest.' It's all bullsh*t, in my humble opinion.

14 DECEMBER 2023

More tweet planning.

FIVE: ANOTHER TORY MP SUSPENDED

I forget sometimes how many have been suspended during this Parliament now. This one today was for many counts of bullying and one count of sexual misconduct to a member of staff. Oh, hang on, that was the last one. Today's reason for suspension is lobbying. His name is Scott Benton, MP for Blackpool South. He was caught in a lobbying sting back in April and the Commons standards watchdog has now recommended that he should be suspended for

35 days. Scott Benton was caught by *The Times* offering to lobby ministers and table parliamentary questions on behalf of gambling investors. Right.

Now more Tory MPs have been suspended since 2019 than there are Lib Dem MPs in the House of Commons. It beggars belief.

SIX: ROBBIE GIBB

I've mentioned Robbie Gibb before. He is a former head of comms at Number 10; his brother is Tory minister Nick Gibb. Robbie Gibb was a founding director of GB News. You'll remember that Richard Sharp – appointed BBC chairman by Boris Johnson – had to resign. But this was not before he'd overseen the appointment of Robbie Gibb onto the board of BBC directors.

Gibb has enormous influence. Alan Rusbridger, former editor of the *Guardian* newspaper, has spotted that in Nadine Dorries' recently published book, *The Plot*, she has claimed that Gibb tried to influence her, when she was the Secretary of State for Culture, Media and Sport (I know, it's an absurd situation) as to who to appoint as the new chair of Ofcom, the media regulator. Later, Dorries denied this was correct, saying, 'Alan Rusbridger completely got hold of the wrong end of the stick.' Hmmm.

Whatever happened between Gibb and Dorries we should be concerned, and someone should be looking into it now the question has been asked. Any hint of that sort of influence would be a VERY serious matter,

17 DECEMBER 2023

Michelle Mone and her husband have been interviewed by Laura Kuenssberg for the BBC in Spain. It was broadcast this morning and resulted in a Prince Andrew-level car-crash interview. Yes, it was THAT bad.

'Saying to the press that I was not involved to protect my family is not a crime. I was protecting my family. I think people will realise that.' Cue the tumbleweed. Absolute textbook gaslighting.

After it was confirmed that £29 million of their £65 million profit had been transferred to a trust in Mone and their children's name, Kuenssberg asked, 'Do you admit . . . that one day you and your children will benefit from that money, because you right now are listed as the beneficiaries of the trust?'

Mone replied, 'If one day, if God forbid, my husband passes away before me, then I'm a beneficiary as well as his children and my children, so yes, of course.'

So that's a yes then.

Then, quite extraordinarily: 'I can't see what we've done wrong.'

And there we have it.

That, my friends, is how corruption and cronyism works, with a healthy splash of 'nothing to see here'.

'The Narcissist's Prayer'

I'm keen that we all become aware of how a system can become as corrupted as ours seems to be right now, so let's look again at narcissism. What we've been seeing with Mone and others is a pattern of action which compulsive liars follow. They start by stretching what you and I would consider as the truth, then they just stretch it a little bit more until it morphs into an outright lie. This continues until they find they can get away with it, often for years, so the lies become bigger. At some point, they've lied so much, they then believe what they have said. It's a key psychological aspect of narcissism.

I bet you've witnessed it with someone at some point yourself. This is how the appalling 'Circle of Acceptable Behaviour' (see page 48) grows.

My son Cameron showed me a wonderful poem by Dayna Craig called 'The Narcissist's Prayer' and it very simply shows the techniques of a narcissist. This is what they will say when something bad happens:

That didn't happen.
And if it did, it wasn't that bad.
And if it was, that's not a big deal.
And if it is, that's not my fault.
And if it was, I didn't mean it.
And if I did, you deserved it.

Every line tells its story.

Firstly the narcissist denies, with an attempt to rewrite history.

Then they minimise what has happened, saying to the real victim that what the narcissist thinks is important is the only thing which matters.

The narcissist minimises a second time and adds in gaslighting, so that the victim starts to doubt their own reality.

A narcissist cannot ever feel shame, as a normal person would. They can never apologise and truly mean it. The apology, such as it is, must be to their benefit.

Finally, the narcissist will never accept blame, always pushing it onto the victim, as the narcissist must keep up their outward image of superiority at all costs. Any politicians you can think of?

Classic.

By the way, and I know I shouldn't mention it, but . . . the world couldn't help noticing that in the interview, Douglas Barrowman's shirt didn't fit over his belly particularly well. Thousands commented online that it was, er, distracting. That bit isn't political but that's what happens when you appear on telly – I should know, I've worn many outfit shockers over the years!

19 DECEMBER 2023

Alastair Campbell (Labour) and Rory Stewart (Conservative) have the biggest political podcast in the UK. It's called 'The Rest Is Politics' and is made by Gary Lineker's company, Goalhanger Productions. The podcast is so big that this year they sold out at the Royal Albert Hall. Political rockstars.

Someone has just sent me a message to say that Alastair C has put me down as one of his political heroes of the year in an article in the *New European*! Heck.

I'm delighted to be named alongside Feargal Sharkey, formerly of The Undertones, and who had the ever-popular solo hit 'A Good Heart'. He's pretty amazing and is encyclopaedic in his knowledge about the privatised water industry. Unafraid to call out the environmental organisations, regulators, successive Tory ministers and, of course, the water companies themselves, Feargal is incredible.

So the two of us are on the list. Plus also someone I have loved for decades: Sue Campbell. My mum worked for her in the 1980s, at the National Coaching Foundation in Leeds. Mum and Sue adored each other. Sue has always been a grafter, and was rapidly promoted through the ranks of sport, and Mum was always very proud of her from a distance. Sue became a baroness, was one of the key figures along with Seb Coe to organise the London Olympics and, as Alastair Campbell (no relation) puts it, 'Her leadership role in women's football is one of the reasons why England women beat the men in the national sport of trying to make 1966 a thing of the past.'

Incidentally, Mum lived with me and my children until she died in 2017. We came as a team, and she would have been beaming away and so proud that Sue and I were linked in this way. Today's news has really made me think of Mum and our lives in poverty in those early years. It made me think of Richard Whiteley too, and the years spent in Lucky Leeds and how happy and welcomed we were there in the 1980s. Counting my blessings tonight.

22 DECEMBER 2023

I needed to get some last-minute bits from the shops before Christmas but I found myself freezing cold, standing in a shop doorway as stormy weather is raging. Sadly, I was not chatting to a friend or badly singing a carol to anyone down the phone, but – on three days before Christmas – I was having to talk to a defamation lawyer as Michelle Mone has been slinging out made-up stories about me to the *Daily Mail* . . . again.

While I'm doing this, despite my numb hands, I burst out laughing at the thought of how ridiculous it is. Here I am in my scruffs in the howling wind, having to talk to a lawyer to get my message across to a newspaper, the *Daily Mail*, that even Wikipedia won't take seriously (Wikipedia won't accept a *Daily Mail* reference as a reliable enough source), against a woman who is a proven liar, Michelle Mone.

So what's happened this time?

Earlier in the day, Neil Reading, who looks after the press side of business, was contacted by the *Daily Mail* as a certain 'friend' of a certain baroness has told the *Daily Mail* a new pack of lies about me and they wanted my comment.

Let's be honest, the *Daily Mail* just wanted clickbait over Christmas; it's how their business model runs. I'm not sure if you're aware but the more time you spend on their website, whether you like the story they've published or not, the more money the *Daily Mail* earns, so if you keep looking at their pages because you're so angry you might want to write a comment, it's even more money for them. In that way, certain 'celebs' make them more money than others, as they are just clickbait to feed their readers' emotions one way or another. Bear that in mind in future. Also, if you don't like any publication, don't put a link to an article on your feed, just a screenshot of their title, they earn nothing that way.

Back to Mone, Neil told the *Daily Mail* that the story that had been concocted was all a pack of lies, but the paper then refused to confirm that they would not print the lies in an article over the Christmas period. Well, I was in no mood to be waking up every day over Christmas waiting to see what the bloody *Daily Mail* printed and then, when it was too late, be forced to go to a lawyer (if I could find one over the holidays). So I took the bull by the horns. I spoke to one of the bosses at the paper and told her, 'You have had stories about me told to you via a proven liar, a woman who has admitted that she lied. She's lied to press, she's lied to the public, she's lied to her lawyers and she's even lied *about* her lawyers. I'm telling you she's lying about me again. You won't confirm that you will not print the story so I'm afraid that three days before Christmas, I have no option but to send you a lawyers' letter for the first time in these circumstances.'

So that's how I found myself in a shop doorway today, hiding from the wind and talking to lawyers. We sent the lawyers' letter late this evening, and at least I know I will sleep better over Christmas but that shouldn't have to happen. I have the money to do it but if you don't, you're subject to bullying of all kinds. I know many 'celebs' who've suffered in this way, or they're frightened of the unwritten rules, and that is the way the world goes round. So when you read something about a 'celeb', whoever that may be, read behind the headlines and think, 'Why is this paper telling me this story about them? Why are they saying terrible things about someone I thought was quite nice?' It's usually (not always) just clickbait and you viewing the adverts on their pages adds to the papers' profits. I've lost count of the number of articles where papers will go to someone's Insta page, look for a few bad comments from trolls and use that to generate a story with the word 'outrage' in the headline about the 'celeb'. It's an old trick. There is no 'outrage', just a troll or two, but a reader will go to that headline, and hey presto, ker-ching, more money in the bank for the publication.

A year ago now, I started to fight the fight about corruption and political lies. The essence of this diary, perhaps, is that in order to speak truth to power, the amount of abuse, harassment and bullying that you have to go through from the right-wing establishment would test the patience of a saint. It's why so few 'famous' people take it on. But I wouldn't have swapped it and we will win. Good will win in the end. I believe that. But by hell it can be tiring.

On a specific political note, the regulation really does need to be looked at. It's what Hacked Off Hugh (Hugh Grant's organisation) has been fighting for on behalf of those who have no voice, when they find themselves in the glare of the press without regulation. Remember Hillsborough, the Leveson inquiry, the phone hacking scandal, Millie Dowler and countless more issues. There are some excellent journalists and publications, but please be aware of the differences and check out a few sources of a story before you believe and quote what you read. Together we're stronger.

24 DECEMBER 2023

The *Daily Mail* continue to be quiet. It's my birthday, I'm 63. Hell, where did those years go? I've had thousands of lovely 'Happy Birthday Carol' messages. Thank you everyone. The difference between a year ago and now is that me and 'the team', we've kind of found each other; we've found evidence and seen data showing how cronyism and lack of accountability works in this appalling government, and we have a way of dealing with it come the general election.

The Mone saga continues. In a Liz Truss scale of delusion, Mone has claimed this morning, 'I've been treated like Pablo Escobar', after her bank accounts were frozen by the National Crime Agency

(NCA) a year ago. The NCA is investigating both Mone and Doug Barrowman amid allegations of conspiracy to defraud, fraud by false representation and bribery. The bribery one is interesting. I've no idea who they might have been bribing, by the way, or even if it relates to them.

What we do know is that Mone is still whining, via a 'friend', this time to the *Sunday Times*. 'It's been an extremely tough year of pain,' she said.

Considering that around 24 hours ago, she was issuing a whole pile of lies about me to the *Daily Mail*, all's well that ends well.

Just off North now for Christmas with another branch of our family, with lots of children and youngsters and laughing and love. It's going to be a lovely, lovely, lovely Christmas, and here's the bonus for an endlessly travelling 63-year-old – my son Cam's driving. Result.

27 DECEMBER 2023

Today it was revealed in a new report that homelessness for veterans has risen by 14 per cent this year, awful.[49]

This fact was pointed out by Fred Thomas, a former officer in the Royal Marines,[50] who will be standing as the Labour candidate against Tory Johnny Mercer, the pompous veterans minister in Plymouth.

I found a link to an interview in which Mercer had vowed to

end homelessness for veterans this year and he said we could hold him to it.[51]

So I did.

Obviously, Mercer took it badly, as ever. He's becoming extremely predictable.

Back in October, he was found not to have told the entire truth when he answered a question from his local paper asking if he'd received £17,000 severance pay when he was previously sacked as a minister. Mercer said at the time, 'No, I did not get a £17,000 severance payment and I just don't talk about that stuff' – the inference being he hadn't received taxpayers' cash as a result of being sacked (twice, by both Boris Johnson and Liz Truss). It turned out he did receive a total of £13,513.[52] I posted this observation and of course he insulted me with his usual array of throwing-up emojis.

Never an apology from the minister, just attacks.

Then in November, he was told to stop spending taxpayers' money on 'vanity snaps', as he'd claimed hundreds of pounds in expenses for a photographer who had taken photos of him walking out of Downing Street.[53] He has form for a previous wrongful claim, incidentally – in 2019, he was ordered to pay back £930 after an investigation into his expenses.[54]

But back to the far more important issue of veterans' homelessness increasing. Remember, Mercer had promised to end the problem and said, 'Hold me to that.'

I pointed out he hadn't achieved what he'd set out to do, as the numbers are still rising. He blew a gasket.

Mercer replied to me on X, claiming I was deliberately misleading people – his argument being he was only talking about *street* home-lessness – 'because that makes your sh*t lonely life feel better. No one normal really cares about your view. They think you're mad.' With yet another handful of puking-up emojis.

He then attacked Fred Thomas as 'only being in uniform for five minutes', thereby mocking a man who'd been in the Royal Marines for seven years and is now a 'veteran', one of the people for whom Mercer, as Minister for Veterans' Affairs, is supposed to protect.

Why can't these Tories just behave?

28 DECEMBER 2023

The morning began with Mercer trending online quite vigorously – 99 per cent of replies were against him. I think we've all had enough of the narcissism and gaslighting.

He's also been shown up in the newspapers – yes, even in the *Daily Mail* – for saying that I have a 'sh*t lonely life' and for the other abusive messages he sent to both me and Fred Thomas. I was told that his wife has closed her account on X – good job I screenshotted her obsessive tweets before she did so (including the time she charmingly declared she was going to take 'a massive sh*t on your front lawn' to someone on X). I've learned to always keep the receipts!

1 JANUARY 2024

Happy New Year! Regardless of how you feel about resolutions, I always think this is a good time to count your blessings and look back at how far we've come.

So, one of the greatest blessings: a thought about how wonderful the younger generation is. How much more equal and less judgemental they are than mine. Not perfect, but so much better than the deference, accepted misogyny and snobbery instilled into my generation. I think we've generally done a good job of bringing up a fairer society; I hope we have.

How far have we come?

A very long way since I was born in 1960. Politics and new laws have changed so much for the better.

When I was growing up, homosexuality (between men) was illegal; if you were a child born out of wedlock you were called a 'bastard'; poor people were meant to stay poor and 'know their place' and it wasn't until 1975 that women were allowed to open their own bank accounts. Finally, in 1975, the Sex Discrimination Act made it illegal to discriminate against women in work, education and training.

I wasn't allowed to join the RAF as a trainee pilot because I didn't have a willy. Who knew that you needed one to fly a plane! In 1980, I was the only woman working underground on Europe's largest construction site – so that's me (a very junior civil engineer) and 2,000 men. Being 'good at maths' was not a thing for women to be. And on and on it goes.

Thank goodness things have changed. Though there's still a long way to go.

When things look bad, I ask my female buddies this: 'If you could choose any year to be born in, as a woman living an average life (you can't choose to be a princess or a particular film star, ha!), in which country and when would you choose to be born?'

What's your answer?

Mine would be around the 1980s in the UK or the Netherlands I think, although I change my mind occasionally.

5 JANUARY 2024

Something on GB News was brought to my attention last week and I haven't had time to address it properly, because I was having some time off. So time now to come back to it. Apparently, Shaun Bailey (put into the House of Lords by Boris Johnson) was spouting off on GB News (where else!) about me.

I wouldn't normally comment as I never watch the channel, but I'd received a number of unpleasant online threats after they said they'd be featuring me on the show. It's become relatively common for the channel to do a specific feature about yours truly and it usually ends up with someone saying something abusive. It's the same reason why some newspapers feature certain 'celebs': more readers or viewers leads to more money for them.

So what about Shaun Bailey?

This Partygate 'Jingle and Mingle' failed London mayoral candidate had to resign from two London Assembly Committees after his Covid partying became public. He was made a member of the House of Lords in Boris Johnson's Resignation Honours list and regularly appears on GB News.

I could give you a list of other Shaun Bailey delights but I don't want to waste your time. You get the picture.

On 28 December, on GB News, Bailey was having a very shouty rant about me: 'Look, on the one hand, she's got all that stuff, you know. She's a serious political commentator [he rolls his eyes] and then if you look at her Instagram, it's all pictures of her bums and boobs. So what is it here? She can't be both.'

How strange – I didn't know I had more than one bottom! Or that wearing a bikini means you aren't allowed an opinion. It doesn't say that on the label! We all know what Bailey was doing; it's that classic narcissist manoeuvre, huffing and puffing and attempting to pigeonhole women in order to keep us down. You know, I've lived a life where others have tried to do this so often it's become dull. Once when I was 39 and wore a short dress to the Baftas, the media went berserk for weeks. The BBC even featured it on a programme; the question on the show was: 'Should a woman aged 39 wear a dress above the knee?' I kid you not. This was in the year 2000. Outrage over a dress. Baffling. It seems that 24 years later, some of the predictable places are effectively still broadcasting/publishing the same pile of petty nonsense.

Anyway, today I put Shaun Bailey's video clip online under the hashtag #SexistShaun and it went viral. It clearly struck a chord.

What is sensational is the many thousands of comments which women have left: 'Come on, Vorders', 'You know we're right behind you' – that kind of thing. It was overwhelming.

To be clear, this isn't anti men at all; the majority of men are good guys and support and love women – they love their partners, wives, mums, sisters and aunties. This is not men versus women.

This is a win against the trolls and the abusers, both in and outside of government (Bailey is a part of the Tory government now he's in the Lords). Attitudes in society generally – other than in certain predictable quarters – have changed largely for the better, and amen to that.

7 JANUARY 2024

Bailey has laughably accused me of bullying him. He doesn't seem to like people remembering that he partied during Covid, funny that. I've said he's ridiculous (which he is). We go back to the narcissist's technique of DARVO again, where the narcissist attempts to reverse the role of victim and offender. Watch out for that if you come across a narcissist in your private life; it's their classic twist. For instance, if a narcissist has been discovered sending messages to someone they shouldn't, they would accuse their partner of 'always looking at their phone', 'you're always so suspicious', 'it's your fault I do this', 'I have to be secretive because you spy on me' . . . all the usual DARVO lines. They're turning themselves into the victim.

My tip: get out fast if you're going through this in your private life right now. Fast as you can and don't look back.

Back to Bailey and the issue of misogyny has really struck a chord.

I have been asked to write a piece for the *Evening Standard*. In it, I laid out the events of the last few days and how within 20 minutes of my tweet going out, #SexistShaun was trending at number one on X.

I ended the piece:

What Shaun Bailey and the rest of his ilk don't like is that those of us without a voice have found a voice.

All of those who felt that they didn't have any way to express what they suspected about this government, or didn't have the evidence, or thought that the government would always get away with it, now we speak as one.

It's laughable that Shaun Bailey and all the right-wingers like him are so thin-skinned because, quite simply, they can't argue with a woman about the subject matter.

To quote their heroine Margaret Thatcher, 'If they attack one personally, it means they have not a single political argument left.'

I never thought I'd be quoting Thatcher in my defence, but such is the nature of my life now being lived without apology.

9 JANUARY 2024

When *Mr Bates vs the Post Office* hit our screens last week, I don't think any politician had a clue what the reaction of the British public would be. We were rightfully angry and disgusted with the system of political unaccountability, and furious that so many innocents, so many families, so many good people had been destroyed by lies and cover-ups on every level.

The series is the dramatised story of the greatest miscarriage of justice in modern British history, where more than 900 subpostmasters were falsely accused of theft from the Post Office.[55] There have been a number of suicides, thousands of lives ruined, and all because of a fault in the Fujitsu Horizon system of accounting which the Post Office had introduced and subsequently lied about.

The drama centres on the true stories of a number of subpostmasters, including Jo Hamilton, who suffered a 'horrendous ordeal' after being wrongly accused of stealing £36,000 by the Post Office. She hadn't stolen a penny. She had to find the money from friends and family and, after she was told – along with all the others – that she was the only one complaining about the system (another lie), she pleaded guilty in 2008 to false accounting to avoid going to prison.

In 2021 – 13 years later – her conviction was overturned.

Hundreds more have been sent to prison and their convictions currently remain.

It's been shocking how this week, many new cases have been

coming to light, via social media. This Post Office scandal has continued for decades and is still going on. Without the ITV drama it would no doubt have continued for many more years.

I've been contacting a number of subpostmasters online to give them the chance to speak on LBC and to offer them support. I know that every tweet and message they get gives them confidence to shake off the completely unwarranted shame they have felt for years.

This week, politicians of all stripes (it's gone on for years) are pointing fingers at each other. Nothing to see here. It's a disgrace and does nothing for our belief in our democratic system.

To be fair, a few have done their level best to help for years, most notably Lord Arbuthnot – a former Conservative MP who had previously been mired in the MP expenses scandal, particularly for claiming for having his swimming pool cleaned. But the postmasters' supporters have been few and far between.

Honourable exceptions are investigative journalist Nick Wallis, who has been covering this story for a long time and was a consultant on the ITV series, and *Private Eye* magazine, particularly their journalist Richard Brooks (who covers some tough subjects in forensic detail). They have been dogged and superb for many years.

Today, Paula Vennells, the former CEO of the Post Office, has announced she will give back her CBE. There are calls for those involved to be prosecuted at some stage.

Dan Neidle (one of our favourite tax lawyers) has said this week: 'The executive team at the Post Office boasted about it becoming profitable . . . one third of their bonus package is linked to that profitability . . . but the Post Office was never profitable at all . . . so they should be thinking about clawing back those bonuses.'

It's often reported that there are hundreds of victims.

There aren't.

There are thousands.

More than 4,000 victims in total.

And all the while they were being told, 'You're the only one with this problem.'

Fujitsu was in charge of the Horizon computer system, at the heart of the whole case. It seems some Fujitsu staff were able to access and change individual accounts within a sub post office and/or Crown Office branches. This was denied endlessly but it turned out to be true.

In 2019, in a court ruling about the Post Office, the judge said he would refer two former Fujitsu engineers to the director of public prosecutions for possible further action. Since the judge said that, what's happened? Has the government held them to account?

No. The opposite is true. The Tory government has given Fujitsu £3.4 BILLION of solo and joint public-sector contracts, including £3.6 billion AFTER SUNAK BECAME CHANCELLOR. It is also noted that the IT firm Infosys, founded by Sunak's wife's family, also has a long-standing partnership with Fujitsu. Just saying.

I want my politicians of the future to have absolutely NO CONFLICTS OF INTEREST (see the Plan for Change on page 309).

Do you?

11 JANUARY 2024

In December, I signed a new contract with the commercial political radio station LBC, for a Sunday afternoon show every week, but I couldn't tell anyone.

Today we announced it and 'Congratulations Carol' was trending on Twitter all day. God, it started me off crying happy tears again. After all the issues with the BBC, and the fights on and offline for so long, it all came pouring out. Guess I'm a softie after all.

After the whole BBC nonsense, it's been wonderful to have garnered so much support from inside and outside of my industry. From producers, bosses of other stations, many celebs, commentators and, most of all, from 'regular' people. It's overwhelmingly lovely. Thank you, if you're in that number. Thank you from the bottom of my heart.

14 JANUARY 2024

Today is my first official show on LBC. I'm on every Sunday from now on and I'm so looking forward to it.

I love live broadcasting, I love the immediacy, talking to real people, asking questions, and I particularly love radio – slippers on and wearing scruffs . . . well, beneath the desk anyway! Bliss.

Connor and Ellie are my producers today, an absolute joy and super bright.

A new chapter has begun. Thank you, LBC.

25 JANUARY 2024

Led By Donkeys make incredible political short films and have a huge following online. Journalist Gavin Esler often voices their films but they've asked me to voice one about the rotten system in the House of Lords. I said yes and it's a privilege to be able to help.

They projected the film onto the House of Lords from the other side of the Thames. It's stunning and shows the questionable nature of how some Lords are selected. It highlights a number of recent shocking appointments, including some of the peerages that Liz Truss gave out after her disastrous 49 days in Downing Street (one honour for every four days she spent there), as well as some of the baffling peerages given in Boris Johnson's Resignation Honours list, such as to the former political journalist Ross Kempsell. Since being inaugurated, Baron Kempsell of Letchworth has spoken in the Lords chamber a grand total of zero times yet has still found time to set up or relaunch three companies, one of his first clients being none other than . . . the office of Boris Johnson.[56]

The film concludes: 'It's time to reform the House of Lords.' I couldn't agree more.

14 FEBRUARY 2024

This is a funny little story. Someone sent me a letter at LBC in an official House of Commons envelope. When I got into the office, I was messing around with the young producers, saying, 'Have a guess, is this a threatening legal letter or an invitation to something?' It wasn't bendy so we concluded it must be an invitation. We opened it together to have a laugh. Heck. It was a Valentine's card.

On the cover it says: 'You Make My Heart Sing'. Inside, hand-written:

Oh my goodness. Lady, you are complete sauce!!
Happy Valentine's Day
?
Xxx

Your guess is as good as mine! I'm assuming it wasn't from a Tory, but it made us all laugh and it was taken in good humour.

20–24 FEBRUARY 2024

Please just make it stop. It's exhausting, but maybe that's their intention.

As Boris Johnson once admitted, 'I've got a brilliant new strategy

which is to make so many gaffes that no one knows what to concentrate on. You pepper the media with so many gaffes that they
are confused.'

I think it's part of the Tory training manual now.

This week, I've been wondering if I've woken up in a parallel universe, where the Conservative party has turned into something akin
to the Mad Hatter's tea party, full of anger, arguments and riddles.

In Lewis Carroll's *Alice's Adventures in Wonderland*, the strange
characters at the tea party are lost in a place where the world isn't
turning and hands aren't moving around the clock face, and the
characters shuffle endlessly around the tea party table. Very much
like the Conservative party, who rotate prime ministers and ministers in a never-ending sequence while achieving nothing but more
chaos.

In the Mad Hatter's world, dirty dishes accumulate, the guests
talk in riddles and there doesn't seem to be any food. No one even
seems to be taking tea.

'We're all mad here,' said the Mad Hatter.

Welcome to this week in Tory Story world.

Here's a summary:

20 February: Michael Gove

On Tuesday, Michael Gove was being asked to address why he didn't
register two hospitality football tickets which he'd received from his
political ally and donor David Meller.

Meller's family firm, Meller Designs, received £164 million of PPE contracts through the VIP lane in 2020. Michael Gove was involved in PPE procurement. Meller Designs boosted their profits from less than £200,000 in 2019/20 to £16 million in 2020/21 after receiving the government contracts.

Meller also donated towards Gove's bid to become Tory party leader in 2016. Hmmm.[57]

21 February: Ceasefire chaos in the Commons

Wednesday saw utter chaos in the House of Commons with three political parties putting forward separate amendments for various forms of ceasefire in the Israel–Hamas situation.

The Speaker chose the Labour motion above the others, which then prompted a walkout by SNP members of Parliament. Then the Tories started shouting and kicking off.

Sir Lindsay Hoyle, the Speaker of the House of Commons, then apologised for the chaos, by which time most of us had lost track of points of 'order' or 'principle', and who had said what to who, and why anyone was being called Right Honourable at all.

A total shambles.

If ever it was clear that our ancient democracy needs a complete overhaul it was today.

22 February: Suella Braverman

Spurred on by the events in the Commons, Suella Braverman wrote some insane claptrap in the ever more right-wing-lurching *Daily Telegraph* (unrecognisable from its days as a serious newspaper).

She said: 'We need to wake up to what we are sleepwalking into: a ghettoised society where free expression and British values are diluted. Where Sharia law, the Islamist mob and anti-Semites take over communities. This is a crisis.'

Really? I think not, Suella.

I think we're all waking up to what you and your angry followers are trying to turn this country into, but you won't win. There is unquestionably a need to look at the levels of migration, both legal (study, work, people from Ukraine and Hong Kong and so on) and 'illegal' (around just 5 per cent of the legal number). Post Brexit and under the Tory government it is the highest net figure for 200 years. But this rabble-rousing rhetoric is still truly shocking.

23 February: Lee Anderson,
MP for Ashfield and GB News host

Also known as 30p Lee (31.17p Lee with the current rate of inflation), after claiming that people didn't need to go to food banks as you can cook a meal for four for 30p, Anderson has taken his trusty political dog whistle and blown as hard as he's able.

This time, Sadiq Khan was his target. 'I do believe that Islamists have got control of Khan, and they've got control of London, and they've got control of Starmer as well,' he said on GB News today.

What an eye-rolling . . . [complete this sentence as you see fit].

Fresh from his romantic moment spoonfeeding cold baked beans to Tory MP Brendan Clarke-Smith on (where else?) GB News,[58] 30p Lee is now spouting nonsense with the full intention of causing division.

Anderson refused to apologise so, under pressure, Sunak has suspended him from the Tory party.

All the Tory MPs are currently doing the media rounds saying 'Lee was wrong', but when asked if what he said was Islamophobic (which it was), they refuse to answer the question and just repeat, 'What Lee said was wrong.' They all became so robotic it was meme-worthy. 'Lee was wrong.' 'What Lee said was wrong . . .' dozens of times a day, but they didn't say why it was wrong.

The question now is at what point will Anderson switch to Reform? Probably within days, knowing how he's flip-flopped from Labour to Conservative in the past!

24 February: Liz Truss

Liz Truss (still paid as an MP by the way and with a lifelong Public Duty Costs Allowance of up to £115,000 a year as a former PM, despite crashing the economy) has just been over to America.

'Why, sometimes I've believed as many as six impossible things before breakfast,' said the White Queen in *Through the Looking Glass* at the Mad Hatter's tea party. How true.

Liz Truss packed up her right-wing conspiracy theories in what must be a very tiny executive briefcase and went to a conference where she spoke alongside Trump's inner circle, including the former Cambridge Analytica director Steve Bannon.

Truss is famously known as the prime minister of the shortest tenure in history, just 49 days, and within that time, she managed to crash the economy so badly that millions are still recovering from the fallout. She doesn't care. Recently, she's even claimed that her mini-budget was right, it was the response to it which was wrong!

Truss claimed in her speech that Conservatives are 'now operating in what is a hostile environment and we essentially need a bigger bazooka in order to be able to deliver' and that 'left-wing elites' will be 'aided and abetted by our enemies overseas' in China, Iran and Russia.

I think what we need is a bigger bazooka to drown out the Mad Tory Hatter's noise. I look forward to a general election and the future possibility of some sanity around Westminster.

25 FEBRUARY 2024

The misery of Covid and the scandals which have emerged have taken a long and devastating toll on the NHS. A lot of misinformation prevails and those who call it out online are often pilloried by the trolls, so it takes a brave woman to say 'enough'.

In the wake of the impact of *Mr Bates vs the Post Office*, ITV is broadcasting a series called *Breathtaking*, starring Joanne Froggatt. It's the story of the frontline staff, their lack of PPE and the way they were treated, as well as the lies of our government during the early days of the pandemic. It's based on someone I've been following on Twitter for some time, Dr Rachel Clarke.

I went to see the first screening of it in London the other week and it was great to meet some people I know well online, like Rachel and also Peter Stefanovic (very good to follow him). It's now available to view online.

It's shocking and accurate and I think it will be a hard watch for many people.

Thanks, Rachel, for telling the truth when so much was hidden from us.

1 MARCH 2024

This has been a significant week for talk about protests. While the Israel–Hamas conflict has shown us more and more horrendous examples of the suffering of humanity as the weeks go by and protests for a ceasefire in Gaza intensify, hundreds of thousands of people are peacefully protesting every week and those numbers seem to be growing.

However, there have also been disturbing incidents followed by arrests, including the projection onto the Houses of Parliament of the phrase 'From the river to the sea', which many say is anti-Semitic. Many Israeli hostages are still being held by Hamas after the horrific attacks of 7 October 2023.

There was also a protest outside the MP Tobias Ellwood's family home, which some claim was not intimidating, but I'd strongly disagree. I would have felt intimidated by it for sure. I've been stalked and harassed close to my home at a much lower level and it was frightening.

We've also had the fallout of the Lee Anderson Islamophobic statements about Sadiq Khan; the non-fallout of Liz Truss happily sharing a far-right platform in America and the inaction over Suella Braverman's words that 'Islamists are in charge of Britain now'.

Amid all this heightened tension, the Rochdale by-election took place on 29 February. Just weeks before the by-election, the Labour candidate Azhar Ali was withdrawn by the party after making controversial statements about Israel and the Hamas attacks on 7 October. Rochdale was a Labour seat. George Galloway won with a landslide victory saying, 'This is for Gaza.'

Clearly, feelings are running high. But ministers don't seem to think people's views about the now reported 30,000 deaths in Gaza are important.

With regard to the protests, Home Secretary James 'Stockton is a sh*thole' Cleverly has told us, 'You've made your point', and that protestors should now stop.

James, this was still some form of democracy the last time I looked, so as long as people aren't breaking any laws, it's up to them when they stop.

Let's face it, the Conservative party has been stoking up the rhetoric for a very long time.

So, in the typical style of this government, Sunak has come out with some highly emotive language about 'mob rule'.

In a meeting with regional police chiefs on Wednesday evening, Sunak – who is under pressure from his party to take a tougher line with protestors – said, 'There is a growing consensus that mob rule is replacing democratic rule.'

I don't believe that there is a growing consensus about mob rule at all.

Inevitably, #MobWatch is now trending on X where people are absolutely taking the mick out of Sunak. I love it when X/Twitter does this.

With a picture of an empty street in Inverkeithing, Scotland, @SCM_BD reports:

With a photo of traffic lights, @Richard57318238 says:

> **Richard Brown** ✅ @Richard57318238   1hr ...
>
> #Mobwatch dastardly stuff in Godmanchester. They are now signalling to each other! They've just flashed red, now orange, hang on, green, no orange, back to red! If only I could crack their code.
>
> 　🗨　　⇄　　♡　　🔖　　⬆

A picture of a cat watching the garden through a window has been captioned #Mobwatch.

> **Carol Hedges** ✅ @riotgrandma72   1hr ...
>
> #Mobwatch reasonably quiet in Beckenham so far today. Thought I saw a couple of right-wing extremists planning something with an Islamist, but it turned out to be my neighbour and his wife showing off his new tattoo to the postie. (@LoxyFlo)
>
> 　🗨　　⇄　　♡　　🔖　　⬆

Thank you, Twitter, I mean X.

We have to remember that here is a prime minister on the lowest ratings since 2019. He's months away from a general election in which the Tory party will hopefully be wiped out for a generation. Many of his MPs have gone rogue. He's losing by-elections with historic swings to Labour.

So this evening, seemingly to make himself appear to be more in charge than he is, he stepped outside Number 10 and talked the big talk, which took me aback. He was describing a Britain I simply don't recognise.

I'd hoped he was calling the general election. Sadly, he wasn't. But his speech seemed sinister in its promise to take away part of our police independence.

And it made me think about our freedoms. Afterwards, I chatted to my son Cameron about his freedoms and how I was seriously concerned that this government, if it ever got back in, would reduce them dramatically.

Sunak's words were divisive to my ears. Here are just some of this government's restrictions on our freedoms. I'm sure you can think of many more:

- A new police law that restricts protesting and increases penalties for protesters
- An election law requiring voter identification for the first time in history
- A reduction of the independence of electoral oversight
- A law limiting a person's right to judicially review social security and immigration tribunal decisions

In my opinion, our democracy *is* under threat – from this government. They inflame all debate, then attempt to crush others who wish to speak out. We have the lowest grade of parliamentarians in my lifetime.

Sunak also spoke, without flinching, of how the system isn't rigged against poor children. And yet social mobility in this country is now at its worst in over 50 years. Never in living memory have families become so much poorer over a single Parliament. In fact, the UK has just been ranked by Unicef – the United Nations Children's Fund – as the worst among the world's richest countries in child poverty levels.[59]

Utterly ignoring the facts and any truth, Sunak was there to blow his dog whistle and sure enough, his media kennelmates came running.

2 MARCH 2024

This week, I studied an amazing piece of research showing in graph form how the Conservatives have wrecked the economy over years.[60]

- We now have the highest level of debt as a percentage of GDP since the 1960s, standing at well over £2.3 TRILLION.
- NHS waiting lists are more than three times higher than 14 years ago.
- Our economy has shrunk. The National Institute of Economic and Social Research estimates that the UK's annual growth rate has fallen from 3.4 per cent a year

postwar until 1973, to 2.3 per cent until the 2008 global financial crisis, to just 1.2 per cent since then.

- The UK goods trade has fallen 15 per cent below the G7 since Brexit.
- Great Britain average weekly earnings in real terms in 2023 are below their 2008 peak.

6 MARCH 2024

Today is budget day.

This budget, so we're led to believe, is the Conservative party's last chance in the last chance saloon.

We're in recession; our public services are in a desperate state.

Time for feet up on the couch, a pot of tea and the remote control to hand so I can press pause while I intermittently yell at the telly.

With the House of Commons full of jeering, ra-ra-ing and hear-hearing, Jeremy Hunt, the latest in a long line of Tory Chancellors, will get to his feet and deliver the last budget of this appalling government, and hopefully the last budget of a Tory for many years to come.

Jeremy Hunt has been doing the rounds in recent days with a lot of word salad.

'The Tories are the party of cutting taxes.'

Oh really . . . ? We have the highest tax burden since the Second World War.[61]

'We want net zero.'

So we've granted new North Sea oil and gas licences which won't alter the price we pay for both energy sources at all, as it's all sold on the international market anyway.[62]

'We have cut HS2 to improve transport links to the north.'

And then we use the money to fill in potholes in London and call it Network North.[63]

'We have to learn to run public services more efficiently.'

A bit rich from the Tories, who spent £8,000 on alcohol alone at a party at Number 10 in January 2020 to celebrate Brexit.[64] Just in case you were wondering why your child's school can't afford books!

Jeremy Hunt tries desperately to sound responsible. But is he?

The Office of Budget Responsibility (OBR) is the independent body that gives the Treasury various reports upon which it makes its decisions – a check and balance on the bank account of the government, if you like.

A few weeks ago, the head of the OBR, Richard Hughes, was in front of the Lords' Economic Affairs Committee where he made a scathing criticism of the government's financial predictions:

'Some people call [the projections] a work of fiction, but that is probably being generous when someone has bothered to write a work of fiction and the government hasn't even bothered to write down what its departmental spending plans are, underpinning the plans for public services.'[65]

That is not how you run a country. Not in any way, shape or form.

The OBR doesn't trust them.

I certainly don't trust them.

Do you?

The budget itself held few surprises and passed off without much fanfare. A slight drop in National Insurance, some promises about looking at things, an attempt to laughably blame Labour and the Lib Dems for the mess we're in and a lot of Hooray Henrys behaving like they're from a public-school debating society. Most importantly, very little change to help most people in this country who are struggling to get by.

7 MARCH 2024

Feeling grateful this morning to be on the *Independent* List of 50 Influential Women 2024.

Apparently, they're including women who their readers may disagree with or disapprove of. Uh oh. 'Influence does not mean adulation and some of the most influential figures of history are difficult and controversial, to say the least.'

I think I might fit into that difficult category nowadays!

Number one on the list is the incredible Esther Ghey, who refuses to be broken by the murder of her daughter, Brianna. How she has managed to listen to the heart-wrenching evidence in court and still survive is extraordinary in itself, but Esther Ghey has used it to campaign for change. She's a hero.

Also on the list (too long to include all names here) are:

- Mary Earps, who with her Lionesses has influenced not only a younger generation but my generation too.
- Hugely bright, comprehensive school-educated Rachel Reeves, who will become the first woman Chancellor in history.
- Most women's girl crush, actress Hannah Waddingham.
- Labour's Bridget Phillipson, who will hopefully become the new Secretary of State for Education, booting out the unpleasant Gillian Keegan.
- The presenter Kate Garraway, who has shown remarkable fortitude looking after her husband, Derek Draper, during his battle with Covid.
- Sue Gray, writer of the damning report into those lockdown-busting parties at Number 10.
- Rosie Jones, the comedian who has been subjected to reams of ableist abuse online (she has cerebral palsy). I love her.
- Baroness Hallett, the first female Lord Chief Justice, who is doing such sterling work holding the government to account in the Covid inquiry.
- Merope Mills, who lost her daughter Martha when NHS staff failed to listen to her concerns, and has fought for Martha's Law, which gives families a right to a second doctor's opinion.

I feel really humbled to be in the company of these inspirational women.

8 MARCH 2024

Michelle Donelan is the science minister. This week, she has been forced to apologise and reportedly pay £15,000 to an academic after wrongly accusing her of 'sharing extremist views' and supporting Hamas.

Donelan deleted a tweet and accepted what she termed a 'clarification' from Professor Kate Sang at Heriot-Watt University after Sang launched a libel action.

Last year, Michelle Donelan published a letter encouraging the UKRI (UK Research Institute) to cut links with Sang and another academic, describing her 'disgust and outrage'. She doesn't mince her words, does she? The UKRI did as Donelan suggested but the academics fought back.

I've come to know that there is always at least one more layer lying beneath any Tory Story. The excellent journalist Poppy Wood from the *i* newspaper then found that it was the taxpayer who has had to settle this libel bill; yes, we have had to pay the £15,000.[66]

Defending the taxpayers having to pay Donelan's libel bill, Penny Mordaunt – she of the weighty sword-bearing prowess – ludicrously claimed that Donelan didn't take her redundancy payment as education secretary, 'which speaks volumes about [Donelan's] character'.

Michelle Donelan was the Secretary of State for Education from 5–7 July 2022. That was 36 hours in total. For that, she was due a 'redundancy' of £16,000-plus but she didn't take it.

'Stand up and fight' Sunak fangirl Penny Mordaunt (if you haven't seen her 'stand up and fight' speech given at last year's Conservative party conference, then I strongly recommend it for a laugh) says we should be grateful to her for not taking that sum of money! Well, I'm not.

A little extra information: Michelle Donelan's now husband heads up the commercial unit at a family-held company which was awarded numerous PPE contracts. Stronghold Global landed deals to supply NHS hospitals, government Covid testing sites and universities. Just saying.[67]

(NOTE: Figures released a few days later put the figure taxpayers spent on Michelle Donelan's libel bill at £34,000.)

11 MARCH 2024

One of my pet subjects has become political donations and their possible influence on governmental policies and/or contracts.

Today's headlines are full of Frank Hester, the owner of a tech company called Phoenix Partnership. The firm has received over

£400 million in government contracts since 2015, mainly through the NHS.[68]

On income of £80 million last year, the firm made £40 million profit . . . quite a profit.

At the same time, Frank Hester and his firm donated £10 million to the Conservative party. It's rumoured he's also donated another £5 million but that has yet to be confirmed.

Today, it was reported that Frank Hester said truly the worst things about Labour MP Diane Abbott. I hate to repeat them, to be honest, but here they are: 'She makes you want to hate all black women' and '[She] should be shot'.[69]

The Tories disgust me more by the day.

Last year, Sunak accepted a £16,000 paid-for helicopter flight from Frank Hester. And so the tie-ups continue.[70]

Conflict of interest? Call it what you will.

12 MARCH 2024

The Tories are now on their countdown to the local elections on 4 May – 'Star Wars Day', May the Fourth Be with You. Somehow I don't think it will be with them.

In this week of absolute chaos – in which the Tories plotted to put in their FOURTH PRIME MINISTER in as many years, their biggest donor Frank Hester has been shown to have made racist comments about Diane Abbott and hospitals continued to crumble – I think of this wonderful place where I grew up and all the opportunities I was given.

When I think of it, I cry at the loss of so many of those incredible opportunities which have been taken away from those who need them.

Then I remember a few of the amazing people who have won Pride of Britain Awards over the years and what they could have done with just a whiff of the money handed to the super-rich by this lot of Tories . . . those people are amazing, and with the right support they would and could do even more good in the world. And my heart fills up with hope again, just knowing that they, and so many like them, are all around us.

31 MARCH 2024

With just weeks to go before the local elections, and with our tactical voting website StopTheTories.Vote getting primed to give advice depending on your postcode, today's front page splash in the *Sunday Times* brought a huge smile to my face: 'TORIES WILL WIN 98 SEATS TO LABOUR'S 468, SAYS NEW POLL'.

A wipeout. The story of what would be the most devastating result in Conservative party history was running as the lead item on every news outlet this morning.

How could I possibly ignore it for my LBC show later on in the day! Oh, OK, I was laughing all day and couldn't wait to read out the names of those predicted to lose their seats (not counting the 65 who've already stated they are going to stand down).

About a year ago, I said to a few friends that I felt we could get the Tories down to 70 seats or fewer at the next general election. They said it was a nice thought but scoffed at the idea. Now it seems I might have been somewhere near the right lines. Here's hoping. I like numbers, they're my friends too, and forgive me if it sounds a little odd, but just like musical notes speak to musicians, numbers (and lots of them) have always spoken to me. They tell me a story.

I started to realise that the power of social media (which costs you nothing but your time) and its ability to give people evidence they haven't been getting from a lot of the mainstream media, together can influence an election. After all, that's what newspapers endlessly try to do, isn't it? Added to that, there is the practical measure of tactical voting, as 38 per cent of voters are saying that they will tactically vote to rid themselves of a Tory MP in their constituency.

Today, thanks to the pro-democracy group Best for Britain and Survation (the polling company), the prediction of Tory MPs numbering fewer than 100 following the next election was leading the news.

Right now, according to the pollsters, Rishi Sunak and Jeremy Hunt would cling on by a whisper . . . and a very quiet whisper at that.

Those who the poll thought might lose their seat include:

Jonathan Gullis	Mel Stride
Penny Mordaunt	Jacob Rees-Mogg
Robert Jenrick	David Davies
James Cleverly	Gavin Williamson
Alex Chalk	Liam Fox
Grant Shapps	Thérèse Coffey

Those left in their very safe seats might include:

Suella Braverman

Kemi Badenoch

Liz Truss

Looks like Badenoch might be the next leader of the Conservative party after all. I don't mind that, as she'll rate worse than Truss, lead them into another electoral chasm in five years' time, and then it's 'bye bye, Conservatives'.

From here on in, I'll be concentrating on getting information out there about voter ID and encouraging as many people as possible to get out and vote tactically at the forthcoming local elections. Wish us all luck.

1 APRIL 2024

Last Saturday, 30 March, was perhaps a line in the sand, or a paddle in the water, for the privatised Thames Water, and the billions of litres worth of sewage they have pumped into our waterways.

As the Oxford–Cambridge annual boat race took place and the eyes of millions around the world were on the River Thames, many of the rowers declared they'd been ill leading up to the race, with vomiting, high temperatures and diarrhoea. They have also been warned not to enter the water in the Thames due to E. coli levels being around ten times higher than our environmental agencies consider the maximum for public bathing. When the race ended, the winning cox stayed on dry land rather than be thrown overboard as is the tradition. Who can blame them!

Afterwards, one of the Oxford rowers said his team 'had a few guys go down pretty badly with E. coli this morning. I was throwing up. It would be a lot nicer if there wasn't as much poo in the water.'

Today, the Lib Dems released some new analysis of the official data.[71]

In 2023, there was an 80 per cent increase from 2022 in the amount of sewage deliberately put into rivers and seas.

In 2022, sewage spills lasted for 125,808 hours.

In 2023, that went up to 228,098 hours. And that just includes data from the places which have monitors and where those monitors are working. Many don't.

On average, 86 sewage spills took place, every day, for the whole year.

In January 2023, 292 Tories voted to allow sewage spills to continue and grow for another 15 years, only recommending weak targets to be met by 2038. Water company top executives had by that point paid themselves £51 million in 2021/22, including £30.6 million in bonuses. Bonuses for what exactly? Putting up bills and killing rivers?

This week, Thames Water said that they would have to put up consumers' bills by 40 per cent to pay for infrastructure. Yes, you read that right. Consumers will pay AGAIN for what the water companies should have been doing themselves with their monopolies over years.

Thames Water was privatised in 1989 and all the debts were written off. Thatcher told us at the time it would be marvellous for consumers.

She was utterly wrong.

All the privatised water companies (bar Welsh Water) are now fundamentally owned by foreign companies. Thames Water's owners include the China Investment Corporation, for instance.

Since privatisation, when they had no debt, the companies have paid out around £85 billion in dividends.

In the same amount of time, they've also borrowed a similar amount, according to Ofwat.

During that time, spending by the ten largest water companies on waste infrastructure (excluding Thames Tideway, which is a separate project) has been less than £300 million in each year. Hmmm. You do the maths. Follow the Water Guru, Feargal Sharkey, to keep up to date on water matters and how you can help to protest.

18 APRIL 2024

This is the story of the witch hunt of a working-class woman who frightens the pants off the Tories and their allies. Angela Rayner is the deputy leader of the Labour party who could become the deputy prime minister, and I, together with a lot of people, think that would be bloody marvellous.

Angela Rayner is a VERY funny, strong and caring woman. We've spoken a few times and she's the kind of woman you really would want to go out and have a laugh with.

Who is she? Angela Rayner was born in 1980 in Stockport in Greater Manchester, growing up in a council house where her mum suffered from severe depression. As a child, Angela would bath her mum, feed her and care for her. Her mum couldn't read or write and Angela remembers they had shaving cream once instead of cream with their jelly because her mum couldn't read the label.

Angela left school when she was 16 when she became pregnant. She went to college after having her baby son, Ryan, and became a care worker working for Stockport council. After becoming a trade unionist, she later achieved something extraordinary. At the age of just 35, she became the MP for Ashton-under-Lyne in 2015, and later she powered her way through to become the deputy Labour leader. A grandmother by the time she was 37, she's a fighter.

This particular Tory witch hunt (there are many) began in February 2024.

The Tories' client media – there have been dozens of *Daily Mail* front pages about this – have been publishing tales about whether or not Angela Rayner might (and that's a big might) owe around £1,500 of capital gains tax on the sale of the council house she bought 17 years ago.

It's a gossip-level story of ifs and buts and Tory media desperation. So come with me on a rollercoaster ride of utter Conservative hypocrisy.

Before the witch hunt began, the Conservative party was already 20 points behind in the polls with no hope of winning the next election and every chance of a total Tory wipeout. And every week seems blessed with yet another Tory misdemeanour, scandal, disgrace. Trust in politics is at an all-time low, our infrastructure is at breaking point, the cost of living crisis has hit millions and people have generally had enough.

A co-ordinated attack on Rayner seems to be the best, but most pathetic, counter-narrative Tories have in their bag. It's small beer compared to their scandals, but their friendly media has been helping them through. Which is where the rest of us come in nowadays, trying to bring some perspective on social media and other platforms.

At the heart of the 'story' is the complicated issue of how the tax system treats two unmarried people who own properties very differently to two married people in the same situation. Angela and her husband Mark Rayner owned two separate properties before they were married. In 2007, when she was 27 years old and bringing up her son as a single parent, she bought her council house in Vicarage Road, Stockport, on the 'Right to Buy' scheme. Now, when you do that, you get a 25 per cent discount on the current market value, so she paid £79,000. She sold her house in 2015 for £127,500, making a profit of £48,500. If she had continued to live in the house in Vicarage Road until that time, then it would be her home and no capital gains tax would be due (I'm not going to give you the ins and outs of allowances, including investment in renovations in a property and the rules of principal private residences, as they're pretty complex.) The *Daily Mail* has been trying to show that Rayner moved in with her husband before she sold her house in 2015. Note that even if she did move in beforehand, then it could still be the case that no capital gains tax is due to be paid (like I said – complex). Angela Rayner says that her legal and tax advice has been that she does not owe any tax and has not broken any laws.

These odd tax claims come from a book by 'Lord' Michael Ashcroft. Ashcroft is reported to have allegedly avoided over £100 million in UK tax by being registered offshore in Belize for many years. He is a billionaire. He was a deputy chairman of the Conservative party and one of the Tory party's biggest donors. For a number of years, Ashcroft lived in the UK enjoying non-dom tax status. The Conservative party elevated him to the House of Lords in 2000, when it was widely stated that he would voluntarily change his status and become liable for full UK tax. This did not happen. He resigned from the House of Lords in 2015. Then, in 2017, when the leak of the Paradise Papers exposed a large number of offshore investments, it was revealed that Lord Ashcroft had remained a domicile of Belize. The BBC *Panorama* programme pursued the story.

So Ashcroft and the *Daily Mail* have been using their joint power to attempt to pillory a woman who grew up in a council house and has strived all of her life because they want the public to believe that she might (and almost definitely doesn't) owe £1,500. Why? Because the system is made so that those with power can do more or less what they want.

However, the levels of hypocrisy are wild. While the right-wing media attempts to derail Rayner, they say nothing of the tax affairs of Ashcroft, the man who made the accusations, or the complex structure of ownership of the newspaper, the *Daily Mail*, that is amplifying them.

It's how the system will continue to work while the super-rich hold the strings of power.

Has the pursuit of Angela Rayner over more than three weeks achieved what they want? To some degree, they've achieved a 'no smoke without fire' thought in some minds, but overall it seems to have backfired, as all the polls are showing that generally people understand what this is and see through it. By attacking her, the Conservatives and their right-wing media allies are seen to be attacking all of us too.

So many Tory scandals have come to light over this same month.

For example, a week or so ago there was the story of Conservative MP William Wragg and the catfishing fake account on Grindr to which he sent compromising images. Wragg then gave the contact details of a number of members of Parliament to the catfisher. This happened over a period of time with at least two other Conservative ministers and MPs sending compromising images to the catfisher(s) as well. Those names have not been revealed.

Today, the headlines have been dominated by Mark Menzies MP, who was found to have rung a 78-year-old Conservative volunteer in his constituency in December at 3.15am begging her for £5,000 cash as he was being held in a flat by 'bad people'.

A long, unbelievable (but true) story continued with claims of him meeting a man online, going back to a flat with the stranger, then on to another flat with another man, which is the point at which it seems Menzies believed he had been 'kidnapped' and wasn't being allowed out of the flat.

The elderly woman he'd asked to help him rang another woman who worked in the local Conservative party office. First thing the following morning, she cashed in her ISA to send £6,500 to the MP. She was then recompensed through local party funds, or so the story goes. The entire course of events was reported to Conservative party HQ in December but little was done until *The Times* got the story.

Now, these are just two scandals that have taken place in the short time the Tories have been attacking Rayner. Obviously, to distract from this mayhem, they needed to have one more go at cornering the deputy Labour leader.

James Daly, the Tory MP for Bury North, has reported Rayner to Greater Manchester police, who are now having to 'investigate'. Daly is part of the 2019 Conservative intake and has a tiny majority of 105 votes and is hugely likely to lose his seat in the coming election. He's the MP who said that most children who struggle in his town are the 'products of crap parents'. This bastion of righteousness has pushed the Greater Manchester police to open an investigation into whether or not Angela Rayner, by spending time in two houses, has broken electoral law. I doubt very much that she has.

Rayner herself has said that if she is found to have broken the law – and she's pretty insistent that she hasn't – she will resign.

A point to ponder: if Angela Rayner is cleared, now that it's reported that more than 12 police officers are on this investigation, will Tory MP James Daly be charged with wasting police time? I had a spat this week online with the chairman of the Tory party, Richard Holden, about this very issue.

I wanted to show the relative size of the £1,500 that Angela Rayner may or may not owe to HMRC in relation to huge and questionable Conservative party sums of money, often taken from the taxpayers' purse. So I came up with the concept of an 'Angela Rayner Unit' equal to £1,500, compared sums and put them out on social media in graph form. They went viral. Here's what I posted:

With Tory hypocrisy reaching explosive levels, I thought it would be a good exercise to see how this claim of theirs relates to just some of their waste, fines and dodgy dealings (all numbers rounded).

£7,897 Boris Johnson booze bill for his Brexit party, 31 Jan 2020.

5 #AngelaRayners

£15,000 Liz Truss in-flight catering on one private jet single trip to Australia.

10 #AngelaRayners

£34,000 libel bill that Michelle Donelan got us to pay after she libelled an academic.

23 #AngelaRayners

£61,000 fine for Vote Leave breaking electoral law. MD Matthew Elliott given a peerage.

41 #AngelaRayners

£67,801 illegal donation (broke electoral law) for Boris Johnson's flat refurbishment.

45 #AngelaRayners

£334,803 spent by Foreign Office in 2021 on alcohol alone.

223 #AngelaRayners

£370,000 paid out after Philip Rutnam claimed Priti Patel bullied him.

247 #AngelaRayners

£993,086 severance payouts to Tory ministers during Johnson/ Truss debacle. Some had only been in office a matter of days or weeks but were due taxpayer-funded payouts anyway.

662 #AngelaRayners

£2 million for eight by-elections caused by Tories' bad behaviour/ quit under Rishi Sunak.

1,333 #AngelaRayners

£40 million VIP helicopter contract which Ben Wallace was cancelling. Sunak intervened and kept it.

26,667 #AngelaRayners

£65 million PPE estimated profit for Michelle Mone and husband
    who are under investigation by the National Crime Agency.

43,333 #AngelaRayners

£4 BILLION wasted on unusable PPE.

2,666,667 #AngelaRayners

I love working with brilliant journalists and some were on form with this story. Yesterday, Russell Scott, an excellent investigative journalist who often works with the Good Law Project, took a stroll through PPE Avenue – the houses bought with Covid profits.[72] Here's a tiny list of some of those properties bought by executives and others who benefited from enormous PPE deals during the pandemic:

- £1.5 million pad bought by Tory donor and former Tory councillor Steve Dechan after he secured a £200+ million contract for PPE.
- $9.5 million Australian pile bought by Gareth Hales, the founder of Unispace, which secured £679 million in PPE deals via the VIP lane after contacting Michael Gove.
- £30 million Caribbean villa bought by owners of the PPE suppliers Full Support Healthcare after receiving over £1 billion of PPE contracts.
- Two new Gulfstream jets and two multimillion-dollar homes bought by executives in an American firm, Innova Medical Group, who benefited from UK

government Covid deals. Innova was eventually awarded
£4.3 BILLION of contracts for Lateral Flow Tests.[73]
By June 2021, the National Audit Office reported that
Innova was still 'the only supplier of LFDs [lateral flow
devices] for self-test approved by the MHRA'. The NAO
warned that there were 'risks to value for money due to
a lack of competition and normal regulatory processes.'

So are you angry about Angela Rayner and whether or not she
possibly owes £1,500 of capital gains tax or are you angry about the
Conservative party saying 'nothing to see here' about PPE contracts
and hundreds of millions of pounds in contracts going to companies
who then donate massively to the Conservative party?

I know which one bothers me the most.

27 APRIL 2024

This week we've all had to endure the pointless Rwanda debates.

My summary is this: the Tories haven't got a clue, the courts
keep booting out their policies, the cost is now around £2 million
per refugee even if they get the flights off the ground, it's cost
£500 million already (don't ask who gets the contracts with our
money!) and I predict it'll all come to nothing.

In the meantime, the Tories haven't concentrated on the asylum
processing system, so many refugees have been 'lost', children have

disappeared, Robert Jenrick ordered a Disney cartoon mural on an immigration centre wall to be painted over (kind man!) and on *Question Time*, the policing minister Chris Philp had to ask if the Democratic Republic of Congo and Rwanda are two different countries. I give up.

But they blindly continue on.

This was meant to be Sunak's BIG WEEK. Yes, another one.

We saw him putting on his best bib and tucker for various trips abroad, standing next to various leaders in Germany and Poland, talking defence, Ukraine and Russia.

With headline after headline predicting a catastrophe for the Conservative party in the lead-up to next Thursday's critical local elections, last week was labelled as 'Shore up Sunak' week and Rishi's 'Reset week'. Things aren't looking good. But Sunak looked pretty pleased with himself and his supporters have been saying it's been his best week in the job. Which leads me to ask: are they living in some parallel universe?

Meanwhile, we have been testing out our tactical voting website StopTheTories.Vote on the local elections. Voters have been typing in their postcodes to receive their instant advice. It's a shame as some of the Tory councillors are undoubtedly good, but they will suffer as the party is rotten to the core and those at the top don't seem to care about the country, or seemingly their grass roots either. Hundreds of thousands of views so far. It's going well. I should point out that all of this is run on tiny amounts of money and everyone involved is a volunteer. I'm glad to be a part of it.

4 MAY 2024

It's local election time with about a third of councils being voted on today (the local elections operate in a rota as they can't all be held at the same time), along with one Westminster by-election and the big metro mayoral elections too across the country. I always use a postal vote; it's just easier and I've been doing it for decades. So let's see how today goes, shall we? Hoping for the Tories to lose another 500 seats here in the lead-up to this year's general election, whenever that might be. As ever, the polls open at 7am and close at 10pm. Exciting.

5 MAY 2024

As usual, I got out my thermal teapot (very handy when you're watching telly in bed) and sat up most of the night to see the results . . . Heck.

By any measure, what the Tories have just gone through is a catastrophe. They have lost almost half of their council seats overnight.

The Westminster by-election in Blackpool South saw a 26 per cent swing from the Conservatives to Labour, the third biggest swing since the Second World War.

They lost every single mayoral election except one. A lot of media attention has been on the mayoral election in London, where Sadiq Khan, up against Susan Hall, increased his majority by over 4 per cent, and also in the West Midlands, which went to the wire last night. Andy Street had been the Tory West Midlands mayor for the last seven years; he was defeated tonight by Labour's Richard Parker, in a shock to the Conservatives. Andy Street had been very popular and not seen as a part of the Tory crowd but even he was diminished by the unpopularity of this Tory government down in London.

The Conservatives came THIRD in these local elections in terms of the number of councillors elected, losing to both Labour and the Liberal Democrats. That's the first time it's ever happened.

So by any measure this was an utter disaster for them.

Sir Keir Starmer said in the *Observer* newspaper today that it's time for a general election. I think it is too, but then maybe I'm a teeny weeny, tiny winy bit biased?

What do the Tories think? They're all saying this morning 'we just need to stick to the plan'. They don't even know what their plan is, for goodness' sake! The longer they leave the election, the more of them will lose their seats. Their plan isn't working at all.

It's now looking likely that any Tory MP with a majority of below 15,000 is going to be out of their cushy job nodding from the back benches at the latest drivelling/divisive/destructive/money-draining policy their government comes up with next. A lot of them will be waving goodbye soon to their very nice life at the taxpayers' expense.

So who will be gone at the general election, whenever it comes? You can give yourself sweet dreams thinking about them.

We've had more government losses in this parliament through by-elections than ever before. So ignore the whole current Tory spin about their poor results being due to people not getting off their sofas to vote. Let them believe that is the only issue if they want, but they're only going down, down, down.

17 MAY 2024

The politics we have right now is full of people with obvious conflicts of interest; it's endless and it's in plain sight. Here's just one example.

Rishi Sunak is married to Akshata Murthy, whose family founded the Indian firm Infosys. She owns around £590 million of shares in the company. Her family, including her brother and her parents, cumulatively own around £4 billion of Infosys shares.

Every year, as with all companies, a firm pays dividends to shareholders at a certain price per share. It varies according to what the board of directors chooses to do and depends on the profit for the year. The higher the dividend, the more attractive it is to many investors, as they get a greater return on their share purchase.

Sunak's wife has been paid many millions of pounds in dividends while living in the UK. She actively chose to claim non-dom tax status on dividends earned in India on her Infosys shares. Non-domicile status is a legal tax avoidance scheme where on dividends from companies based abroad, you opt to pay a flat fee of £30,000 a year dividend to HMRC instead of the 45 per cent income tax you would normally pay at that level of dividend income.

In the time from when Sunak became an MP, it is estimated that she saved around £20 million of tax payments in this way. In 2022, this legal tax avoidance by the then-Chancellor's wife was discovered by the press. Sunak was angry; he defended his wife, saying the reports were 'unpleasant smears'. But the couple eventually backed down and from that time, she has stated that she is no longer claiming non-dom tax status and is now paying full tax. Hmmm.

The recently published *Sunday Times* Rich List estimated that the wealth of the Sunaks rose by £122 million to £651 million last year, based on the rising value of her Infosys shares.[74] In other words, they had gained a third of a million pounds of wealth *a day* for every single day of the year.

Now, Infosys is a global company but it has been given over £100 million of UK government contracts in recent years, including a £44-million contract in 2022, and it has just been put on a government contract framework for £750 million with a number of other tech companies.

The government says that ministers (even the prime minister) have nothing to do with the contracting process.

From the time Sunak became Chancellor in February 2020 to early 2022, the value of Infosys shares more than tripled from around 500p when Covid struck to a high of almost 2,000p two years later, the first year the Sunaks entered the *Sunday Times* Rich List. Obviously, the use of tech also increased in that time with many working from home so a high-tech company like Infosys would benefit from that naturally. But the problem is a potential conflict of interest between someone who signs the cheques as Chancellor and contracts given to a company that increase the wealth of him and his family.

The number of scandals surrounding the Conservative party and its leading players – such as the VIP PPE lane and others – brings everything they do into question. In Sunak's case, he received a police fine for his involvement in Partygate at Number 10. He couldn't present his WhatsApps to the Covid inquiry. When asked by Hugo Keith KC, the main Covid inquiry legal counsel, about the missing messages, Sunak said: 'I've changed my phone multiple times over the past few years, and as that has happened the messages have not come across.'

Neither he nor Boris Johnson, the two most powerful men in the country during Covid, could produce their WhatsApps at the inquiry. At the same time, both receive police fines for partying at Number 10 when the rest of the country was operating under strict lockdowns. What are the chances of all of those things happening?

Naturally, therefore, the granting of multimillion-pound government contracts to a firm in which Sunak's wife's family has billions of pounds invested, will raise questions.

Surely as a country our system of protection from political gain must become far better than this? (See my Plan for Change, page 309.)

22 MAY 2024

Great excitement. Everyone has been called to Downing Street for an announcement at 5pm by Sunak. It can only mean one thing. It's either a declaration of war on a galaxy far, far away (you never know with the Tories) or we're going to have an election sooner than we thought.

Oh no (hehe!). The rain has started . . .

The Number 10 lectern is out in front of the famous black door in Downing Street. It's gone 5 o'clock but no one has come out. Has Sunak changed his mind?

Some amplified music has started up from somewhere out of view of the cameras. It's the 'Imperial March', the Darth Vader *Stars Wars* theme . . . That has to be from Steve Bray, the Welshman with the EU hat famed for 'interviewing' politicians on the streets around Westminster.

This scene isn't going to go well. You just know it. We're still waiting. It's now gone ten past five.

Here comes Rishi Sunak, wearing a strangely fake grin. The rain is beginning to fall fast.

OMG . . . Steve Bray (it's got to be!) has started playing the Labour theme tune from 1997 'Things Can Only Get Better' VERY loudly. I can't stop laughing. Sunak needs subtitles. What's he saying? I can't hear him.

Rishi's getting soaked. Someone get him an umbrella or his pants will shrink even further up his legs. This is a shambles. Funny, though.

'Now is the moment for Britain to choose its future.'

Too right, Rishi. Let's crack on with doing just that.

'We will have a general election on 4 July.'

Booommm.

Our general election will be on 4 July ... AMERICAN INDEPENDENCE DAY.

And now it will be ours too – independence from this pile of incompetent charlatans. Bring. It. On.

24 MAY 2024

I think about the future, what comes next in a time after I've long since gone, and how good and innocent people must be protected.

Two of the biggest government and public scandals in modern British history have been in the headlines within a week, showing how when people aren't protected many thousands have suffered.

Last week, we heard the results and the report from Sir Brian Langstaff about the infected blood scandal, in which infected blood and plasma was knowingly given to thousands of patients in the UK. Many contracted hepatitis C, HIV, AIDS, and more than 3,000 people died.

In other countries which also received the infected blood products from America – Canada, Ireland and France – the scandal was dealt with very quickly, in the 1990s.

In the UK, by contrast, it has taken decades for an inquiry to be held. The compensation scheme for those involved will amount to some £10 billion.

As far as I'm aware at this time, no company will be giving money towards that and no one will be held up for any criminal prosecution.

Also this week, the biggest miscarriage of justice in British history, the Post Office scandal, has been in the news again, taking us further into the detail of the cover-ups and misery caused by executives at Fujitsu and the Post Office.

We've just had three days of evidence at the Post Office Horizon IT inquiry from the PO's former chief executive officer Paula Vennells and we witnessed her cry many times.

All the subpostmasters' convictions were overturned this week. But this is decades after the events took place. It began in the 1990s and many of those affected have since died. Some took their own lives. And all the time, there were people who knew what was going on with the Horizon IT accounting system, run by Fujitsu.

As I mentioned earlier, since the huge Post Office scandal report was published in 2019, Fujitsu, far from being seen as questionable, have been given upwards of £4 billion pounds' worth of new government contracts.

It seems to me that nobody is ever held to account.

Is it good enough? No.

Is it time for us to hold both politicians and also executives to criminal account? Absolutely.

(For more on this, see my Plan for Change on page 320.)

25 MAY 2024

We're six weeks away from the general election and now is the time to explain to people that this is a once-in-a-lifetime opportunity to eviscerate the Conservative party for what they've done to the country. The number of Tories who've said that they're going to leave or stand down at the election has surpassed any previously. I think it's 78 now, including Michael Gove and Andrea Leadsom. They've probably got very nice opportunities lined up for themselves somewhere else. Who knows.

Rishi Sunak has had a disastrous few days. He went to a biscuit distribution centre in Derbyshire. Adam Bienkov at the *Byline Times* newspaper identified two of the men in high-vis jackets asking Sunak questions – who were meant to be locals – were actually Conservative party councillors.[75] A Tory spokesman said, 'We do not control who asks questions – anyone can try and ask one.' What a load of snake oil.

Then, on the same day, Sunak went to Wales and said, 'It's all about the football', in relation to the Euros, which will be starting soon. Well, the Welsh football team didn't qualify for the Euros this year, so it was a bit of a faux pas to make in Wales.

I wish he'd stop trying to pretend to be a man of the people when he clearly isn't.

As if things couldn't get worse, some idiot decided to take Sunak to Northern Ireland to go to the *Titanic* exhibition. I mean . . . the metaphors with the sinking ship, the Conservatives about to hit an iceberg, the now infamous photo of Sunak in the rain outside Number 10 – they make the memes too easy.

The enormous backlash is building and it's building fast.

Our StopTheTories.Vote website is up and running with some of our recommendations for tactical voting to oust the Tories depending on your postcode. We're monitoring every poll and adding recommendations when the options become clear. We've also had a few Twitter Spaces broadcasts. I haven't done one before and they're great fun. Steve Bray (he of the 'Things Can Only Get Better' song during the general election announcement) has just told us what happened on that rainy afternoon last week.

He said his first big amplifier had got wet in the rain so he sent his friend Gareth to their car at nearly five o'clock to get their second amp. By the time he got back, Sunak was ten minutes late, the first amp had sprung back into life, he pressed play on 'Things Can Only Get Better' and boom, both amps worked perfectly, which is why, in that iconic moment seen the world over, the music was so incredibly loud! More by error and rainfall than by judgement, but oh, it was glorious, Steve. Absolutely glorious.

29 MAY 2024

Lo and behold, the police have said they have nothing more to do with the investigation into Angela Rayner and her council house sale. The *Daily Mail*, having done about 1,322 front pages (!) about

. this non-story in an attempt to smear her, says nothing about her being cleared. If ever you need to know how certain elements of our national media work, that says it all. Cowards.

Meanwhile, the *Mirror* has a story about four Tory MPs over the years who collectively made a profit of £5.4 million when they sold their expenses-funded second homes in London, all of whom have repeatedly declined to reveal if they paid any capital gains tax on their profits. No questions asked by the *Mail* on that![76]

3 JUNE 2024

Nigel Farage has just announced he's standing as a candidate for Reform in Clacton. Of course he is. The interesting thing is that he will kill the Tory vote there. Farage has enormous support from a section of the population who feel that Westminster is out of touch with their lives, and that politicians don't care about them. They're absolutely right to think so, which is why the system MUST change. Having lived nearly all of my life outside of London and the Westminster Bubble I feel the same. Why? Because it's true. I have hugely different motivations and politics to Farage and Reform, obviously, but I do understand the sense of hopelessness the Westminster 'elite' has created, and I know it will be the motivation behind many votes which will be cast for them. One thing is for certain, the Tories are now having to defend on all fronts, not just against Labour.

5 JUNE 2024

Last night, ITV hosted the Starmer versus Sunak television debate. The first one in this run-up to the election.

Sunak was very tetchy and basically just kept shouting. He claimed that NHS waiting lists have gone down, which was later shown to be a lie. They are up. Peculiarly, he also claimed that boat crossings had gone down, which they haven't. They need an on-air fact checker nowadays, working in real time to give viewers any hope of finding the truth.

Sunak then said, 'Labour will cost you £2,000 in tax.' Now, politicians do that all the time – they claim this, they claim that – but Sunak went one step further and said very stridently that this figure had been 'independently verified' by the Treasury.

Except of course it hadn't – and this morning, Starmer has accused Sunak of 'deliberately' lying about it.[77]

Labour have now put out a letter they received two days ago from the Permanent Secretary to the Treasury – the most senior Treasury official – in which he basically says that this £2,000 figure wasn't independently verified because the numbers were given to them by the Tories.[78]

So what has happened? Well, let's say I'm the Treasury and a sneaky person (the Tory SPADs) gives me a pile of numbers and says that they are prices in a shop – but I don't know if they are the real prices in the shop, they're just telling me that they are. They then ask me to add those numbers up and give them the total. They then tell everyone that I have 'independently verified the prices in the shop'. But I haven't done that at all, have I? All I have done is add up the numbers they have given me. My addition is correct but I don't know where those prices came from or even if they have been made up or not.

In the same way, the Treasury was given numbers by the Conservatives and did some calculations on those numbers. But as the source of the data was the Conservatives themselves, the final total is invalid. It's nonsense.

By saying this £2,000 number was 'independently verified by Treasury officials', Sunak and all the Tories now repeating it are lying, in my opinion. Lying in politics, particularly in the run-up to an election, must be dealt with firmly in future. This is appalling.

7 JUNE 2024
(MORNING)

Yesterday, millions of us watched the incredible eightieth anniversary commemoration of the D-Day landings on the Normandy beaches on the BBC.

The D-Day assault involved Allied forces from Canada, America, Poland, British Commonwealth countries, the Netherlands, France and so many more. The number of personnel who took part is staggering: 18,000 paratroopers, 14,000 air sorties, up to 7,000 ships and landing craft delivering 132,000 men. Some 4,400 Allied troops died that day, and 9,000 were wounded or missing. They fought and died for us, for our future.

The commemoration was spectacular, with many veterans present. Those who are left are now in their late nineties, some fine men over 100 years old. They are amazing.

President Macron was at the commemoration representing France. Rishi Sunak was there. King Charles, who has prostate cancer, had apparently brought forward his treatment so that he could be there. He and Queen Camilla were visibly moved.

It meant something to them. And it means something to all of us, particularly those of us over the age of 60. Most of our parents were involved in the Second World War, even if not on D-Day. Our parents would often speak about the war, and the struggles and the sacrifices of the time. Even those left at home would talk of 'the war effort', of food rationing and how millions were displaced from their homes. TV shows would reference it all the time in soap operas and comedies (think *Dad's Army*); in that way it became a part of our collective childhood memories, even though we hadn't even been born when those brave men and women were fighting. But we were always conscious of the ultimate sacrifices they made for our freedoms and we forget that at our peril.

Celebrations like this bring so many tears; every family has a story of loss, bravery and pride in members of their own family during the war, and so they should.

The BBC covered the commemoration of the British involvement magnificently in the morning. There was palpable gratitude for those who gave their lives for our freedoms. It was stunning. Then the international commemoration, recognising the contributions and sacrifice of all of the Allies, took place in the afternoon. President Biden was there. President Zelensky was there. Chancellor Schultz was there. President Macron was there . . . and Rishi Sunak wasn't. He was missing.

He'd flown back to do a television interview with Paul Brand on ITV. It was extraordinary. An insult not only to the British veterans, but the international veterans too. It was an insult in a way to all those who lost their lives and who fought throughout the war, not just the brave men on D-Day, and for all of those reasons it's why what he did was significant.

For a prime minister to do this was a grave insult.

7 JUNE 2024
(AFTERNOON)

It's seven years today since Mum died, in 2017. She died at home with all of us around her. I often think how terrified she would have been had she been on her own during lockdown, as so many elderly people were.

I can't and won't get past how the Tories partied to the point of puking down the walls of Number 10 while people died alone in torment. While they sent the elderly back to care homes knowing that they carried the deadly disease. Johnson has been accused of saying, 'Let the bodies pile high.' Then there are the 'lost' WhatsApp messages from two prime ministers. What did they say and how have they 'disappeared'? And the billions siphoned off to their cronies for often useless PPE. I will never forget that. I don't think most of the public will ever forgive them for it, either.

With just four weeks to go until the general election, Sunak has now apologised in an almost robotic manner for skipping the D-Day ceremony.

Sky News's Sam Coates interviewed Sunak and asked him about why he had left the D-Day celebrations and Sunak just repeated his apology almost verbatim. Then Sam said that he had spoken to Ken Hay, one of the veterans at the commemoration, who said Sunak's actions had 'let the country down'. Sunak just repeated his lacklustre apology.

So that has been leading the news and all over social media.

This evening, there was another TV debate. I think we're going to tire of these pretty quickly. I know my hair looks crap most of the time, but Penny Mordaunt – whose hairdo was like a Lego-doll version of cosplay Thatcher – was just shouting, which was quite odd to witness.

She kept pointing at Angela Rayner and shouting about the £2,000 in tax, which everyone watching now knows has not been independently verified.

It's absolutely baffling how quickly they are imploding.

This evening, the Tory MP for Stoke Central, Jo Gideon, has given her reasons why she is standing down at the election, and her reasons make the Tory party sound like some sort of political mafia. She used phrases like 'unethical', 'persistent bullying', 'intimidation', 'toxic culture'.[79] Just quite extraordinary.

Four more weeks of this to go and I'm not sure that I can take it!

Every day, the polls show the gap narrowing between the Conservative party and Reform, which means that the Tory vote is going down into the dungeons of political hell.

I predicted a year ago that the Lib Dems could become the opposition. Now the media is beginning to talk about it. I realise it would be a stretch, but a girl has to have a dream!

12 JUNE 2024

Beth Rigby hosted the Sky News leaders' debate between Starmer and Sunak. She's very good. In fact, Sky News has some truly great journos.

In a snap poll afterwards, two-thirds of people watching said that they thought Keir Starmer 'won' the debate. And Beth Rigby didn't give him an easy time at all. But people are just openly laughing at Rishi Sunak now. I almost feel sorry for him. Almost, but not quite.

As well as the leaders' debate, the already infamous 'D-Day interview' with Sunak conducted by the excellent ITV journalist Paul Brand was broadcast tonight. Oh God.

Paul Brand asked Sunak how he can have any empathy with people who are in crisis due to the cost of living, given he is more or less a billionaire. And Sunak answered that he had to make all sorts of sacrifices when he was growing up. Paul Brand pushed him and said, 'Well, what sorts of things?'

'There'll be all sorts of things that I would've wanted as a kid that I couldn't have. Famously, Sky TV, so that was something that we never had growing up, actually,' said Sunak.

You can imagine the online hilarity at this, the memes and the jokes. Bear in mind Sunak attended one of the most expensive boarding schools in the country and was living in a dormitory in Winchester College as a youth. He is so out of touch, it's not even funny any more.

But hold on – what NOW?

OMG, the Tory MP/candidate for Montgomeryshire, Craig Williams, has been found to have placed a £100 bet on a July election date just three days before his boss Rishi Sunak announced the election on 22 May, and is now under investigation by the Gambling Commission. Williams is Sunak's closest aide at Number 10 and works as his parliamentary private secretary.

I've no idea if Williams knew but it certainly looks that way to the rest of the population. Williams has apologised for what he called 'an error in judgement' but didn't say whether the bet was placed based on insider information. Honestly, if you had to run the worst election campaign of all time, I think this would be it.

18 JUNE 2024

Not long to go until the general election. Poll after poll is saying how desperately bad the prospects are for the Conservatives.

Our tactical voting website StopTheTories.Vote has now had 2 million page views and that will build as we enter the final two weeks. We know that anyone who uses it is seriously thinking of voting tactically with one purpose alone – to get a Tory out.

I'm struggling with updating this book simply because of work pressures elsewhere but it'll be done. A stupid first world problem. Crack on.

21 JUNE 2024

The Tory campaign has imploded. I feel like I say this every day now, because just when you think it can't get worse, it gets worse. Following the revelation last week that Craig Williams, MP for Montgomeryshire, placed a £100 bet on the date of the election, over the last 24 hours, a second Tory candidate – Laura Saunders – is under investigation by the Gambling Commission for allegedly placing a bet on the election date too. She is the candidate in Bristol North West and has no hope of winning there.

That news seemed strange until, hours later, it was revealed that her husband, Tony Lee, is the Tory director of campaigning. The

Gambling Commission is investigating both of them and the case has been referred to the Met Police. Tony Lee has taken leave of absence. Sunak's Met Police close protection officer also allegedly placed a bet, but – contrary to the dithering Tories – action has been taken by his superiors and he has been immediately arrested and suspended.

The *Financial Times* has done a lot of digging and found that bets of significant sums of money were placed on the election date the day before the announcement. So what has been going on? It's a huge story and is surely the final nail (if one was needed) in the Tories' coffin.

Sunak was on *Question Time* in the leaders' debate last night and said he was very angry about it all but he still refuses to suspend the two candidates.

The Gambling Commission has notified the Conservative party that a number of investigations are being opened in relation to bets on the election. It's hard to escape the conclusion there are so many rotten apples in this party that the whole barrel is now putrified.

25 JUNE 2024

Finally, Sunak has suspended Craig Williams and Laura Saunders, the two Tory candidates caught allegedly placing bets.

Sunak has refused to say whether or not he told Craig Williams the date of the election . . . hmmm.

We are now at five Tories and seven Met Police officers under investigation in this sorry tale.

28 JUNE 2024

Just one week to go before we can say goodbye to the Conservative party for a very long time. Now a Labour candidate, Kevin Craig, has been suspended for betting *against himself* in the election! He was suspended within ten minutes of Starmer being told. This isn't illegal, apparently. How the hell is this not illegal?

Sir Keir Starmer, in fairness, is sounding firm and acting quickly. Starmer: 'I've never placed a political bet, I only bet on the horses. So that's where I stand on this. And I don't think that we should be lured into thinking this is a problem with the rules; it's a problem with politicians. You can see from the reaction of the public that they know straight away that what's been going on in the Tory party, this sort of insider dealing, is wrong.'

Oh – here's another Tory: Philip Davies, husband of Minister for

Common Sense Esther McVey, both GB News presenters. Davies has placed £8,000 on himself to lose in his Shipley constituency. He's a known associate of the gambling industry – he has a second job with a slot machine company and receives a lot of hospitality from the industry (which he has declared). It's likely he'll lose his seat so let's see how much his bet pays out![80]

Who knows who else will become embroiled? What an utterly shambolic state of affairs.

3 JULY 2024

Only one more day. It's the night before the election. The online world is fired up with loathing for the Conservative party. Reform, meanwhile, is getting a lot of support. On the telly, particularly on the BBC, it tends to be the same Tory faces. I can't wait for the time when the faces change.

Stop The Tories has had massive support today, including from Hugh Grant, Billy Bragg, Gary Neville, Mick Hucknall, Mick Lynch and thousands of others. With no money and only hard-working volunteers, we've had almost 5 MILLION page views, which is quite extraordinary. Around 1.75 million postcodes have been typed in; I would assume that those people are active and hungry to vote tactically. That's huge.

Right. Now to bed! Got to pack for London . . . again!

4 JULY 2024

6am: I've woken up early – stupid girl. I've got to be on TV and radio throughout tonight. Heck. Might need Lucozade to keep me awake. I've never tried Red Bull but it might be a first tonight.

It does feel a bit like Christmas, though, with the Tory turkey about to get stuffed! Pass the sherry.

TV is always strange during polling day as the broadcast media is hugely restricted in what it is allowed to say or cover. The newspapers are, however, allowed to say what they like. A strange old mixture.

8pm: Counting down to the exit poll, which will be released at 10.01pm, just one minute after the polls close. It has given a pretty accurate forecast in past elections. I hope to hell it shows a Labour win with the Lib Dems in second place.

Three . . . two . . . one . . .

10.01pm: The exit poll shows a huge landslide to Labour and . . . 131 seats to the Tories. Noooooooooooooooooo, that's far too many. Hoping it's far fewer by morning.

Off to the Channel 4 election night TV studio. I'm sitting with Hugh Fearnley-Whittingstall (good man – Greens), Richard Walker, the MD of Iceland stores who switched his allegiance from Tory to Labour during the election campaign (another good man), and Vince Cable (former Lib Dem Leader and minister in the coalition government with David Cameron). We're gabbling away on our table. Emily Maitlis and Krishnan Guru-Murthy are hosting along with podcast superstars Alastair Campbell and Rory Stewart.

5 JULY 2024
(THROUGH THE NIGHT)

12 midnight: Well, that was funny. I might have spoken my mind a bit and said how so many of us have been fed up with the lies and the corruption: Partygate, the VIP PPE lane and much more. I might also have called out the two disgraced former Chancellors in the studio (Kwasi Kwarteng and Nadhim Zahawi, both of them previously sacked from prominent positions) and Nadine Dorries, a woman who barely turned up in her last year as an MP. And, er, it might have gone a bit viral!

I can't get over the fact that the Westminster Bubble continues this conversation with people who have been utterly disgraced.

I'm hoping that the Lib Dems do better than the exit poll suggests. Not many results through yet.

3am: I'm now at LBC in the Millbank Studios opposite the Houses of Parliament. It's a powerhouse in political broadcasting; lots of different studios for radio stations, Sky, ITV and the BBC share the same building.

I love being part of the LBC family. The election coverage tonight is being hosted by Andrew Marr and Shelagh Fogarty. They are brilliant both separately and together. It's very exciting in this studio – Ian Hislop and I have just hot-seated. At the end of the show, we were asked to sum up the last 14 years in three words. I said, 'Entitlement, privilege, corruption.' I think that just about sums it up.

6am: Off to see my friends from Stop The Tories, many of whom I haven't met in the flesh before, strange though that may seem, as almost all of our work has been done online as volunteers. They're lovely people and passionate about what they do. Josh Russell has been our 'leader' and is exceptional.

Left at 8am, back to my hotel . . . I need sleep.

Later today: The results are in!

Wow. (See Preface, page 2, for all of the numbers.)

Labour has won with a landslide of 412 seats and an enormous majority of 172. The Tories have ended up with 121 seats, more than I'd hoped, but hey, it's still their worst result in history.

The stories of the night are endless.

The big beasts fell like some Roman god of war had ravaged their ranks. The majorities they had held until last night, which in yesteryear would have guaranteed a job for life, have come toppling down. Some survived by a whisker. I have to admit a wry smile when some of my 'favourites' lost out and will be MPs no longer. What a night.

Tactical voting unquestionably had an impact; the media is

talking about exactly that. This was the first time it had been organised and recognised as such through the power of the internet.

The Lib Dems have done brilliantly with 72 seats, up by 61 seats from 2019. I loved Ed Davey's happy antics in the election campaign. It was noticeable that in many of the new Lib Dem seats the Labour vote fell to virtually nothing, which indicates just how many people lent their vote tactically to the Lib Dems in those seats. And elsewhere natural Lib Dem supporters lent their vote to Labour in many Labour wins.

But there is disquieting news too if you look behind the headlines. The overall turnout was the second lowest since 1815 at 59.9 per cent of registered voters. Even worse, an IPPR (Institute for Public Policy Research) report says that of all adults who could have voted (including those who hadn't registered), only 52 per cent did so. The lowest percentage since 1928.

What does that tell us?

That people feel more detached from Westminster than ever.

In addition, a huge number of would-be voters were turned away due to not having the approved voter ID. Current indications report around 400,000 voters may have been affected in this way. What a mess.

Interestingly, the votes for the Tories and Labour combined was the lowest of all time at less than 60 per cent of votes cast. Meaning that other parties are managing to push their agenda through and that the electorate (or those who voted, at least) has had enough of the two-party system.

The Greens did well, winning all four of the seats they had targeted, including my own constituency of Bristol Central. Carla Denyer, the joint leader of the Green party, romped home with a decisive majority.

The SNP, on the other hand, had a disastrous night, perhaps not surprisingly given they have had three leaders in quick succession in recent times. First, Nicola Sturgeon left under the cloud of police investigation into alleged financial irregularities within the SNP, then Hamza Yousaf resigned after scrapping the power-sharing agreement with the Scottish Greens, then he was followed by John Swinney as the new SNP Leader. The SNP lost some good people in the election.

Even Labour who are victorious have had some big losses and also some lucky scrapes.

Sir Keir Starmer, the new prime minister, saw his majority in Holborn and St Pancras cut down significantly from a majority of 22,766 in 2019 to 11,572, after a pro-Palestine supporter stood against him.

Wes Streeting, the new Secretary of State for Health, saw his majority slashed from 9,000 to just 528.

These election surprises have been in areas with a high proportion of Muslim voters due to both the Labour and Conservative stance on the Israel–Gaza situation. Labour has lost five seats where there are large Muslim populations – four to independents and one to the Conservatives.

And let's not forget that more than 4 million people voted for the Reform. They won five seats.

Perhaps the biggest story of all is how voters now see the disproportionate effect of the first past the post system, and how extraordinarily 'unfair' it is.

If a purely proportional system based on the number of votes had been used in the 2024 general election, it would have given the following results:

- Labour 221 seats and no parliamentary majority
- Conservatives 156 seats
- Reform 91
- Liberal Democrats 78
- Greens 45

Very different to what we've ended up with. However, it's important to know that voters might well vote differently if proportional representation had been used.

For now, we have a majority Labour government so let's see how this pans out.

Where do we go from here?

We have to look at our entire political system with fresh eyes. It's rarely been so important.

THE PLAN FOR CHANGE

July 2024. Here we are with a new government and a new hope for our future.

Our collective disgust with the actions of successive Conservative governments over 14 years took the Tory party to its worst election result in history on Thursday 4 July 2024.

Life goes on but the system we have been left with isn't anywhere near good enough.

Trust in politicians has never been as low as in recent years and that has bred in voters a sense of detachment from political debate, which in turn has led to the 'privileged elite' being able to do what they want with less scrutiny. It's also led, unsurprisingly, to a resurgence of right-wing politics.

The low turnout in the general election indicated how politically homeless many feel.

We need people all over the UK to feel reattached. We need all of us, no matter our age or our situation, to feel hope and a sense of justice again.

No more should the purse strings and the law be in the hands of the privileged and greedy few.

With all of that in mind, I've put together my own ten-point Plan for Change.

I think there will be a few things in here that make you smile. And others where you might share my righteous fury. And maybe, some where you hugely disagree with me. All of these reactions are good. Above all, I hope it makes us think about how to make things better for generations to come.

CHANGE NUMBER 1:
NO CONFLICTS OF INTEREST

There must be no conflicts of interest between MPs and public sector contractors – a problem that has mushroomed in recent years. To stop this, changes need to be made:

- All government contracts (for both primary and secondary contractors) need to be transparent and there must be tighter measures in place to crack down on potential corruption.
- 'Significant persons' working within, or owning shares in, any public sector contractor should not be allowed to donate to any political party.
- No public sector contract should be given to any company which is, through any form of company structure, avoiding UK tax. Very specifically, any company which is owned in any form in tax-avoiding tax havens should not be allowed to become a public sector contractor.
- Rachel Reeves, Labour's Chancellor, and the first

woman Chancellor in history, is appointing a Covid corruption commissioner for a set period of time to delve into the obscene contracts freely given to Tory associates, resulting in eye-watering profits, through what became known as the VIP PPE lane.

- I want there to be a permanent and independent corruption commissioner who assumes that role regarding all public sector contracts.

- And all appointments which have been made to public bodies by the last government must be scrutinised, and where they are found to have been biased and/or self-interested, they must be changed. The revolving door of chums and associates must end now.

For many, one of the key issues today is the perceived dishonesty of politicians, specifically those in the previous Conservative government. Partygate, the VIP PPE lane, endless stories of conflicts of interest . . . Then there was Rishi Sunak apologising for his government placing a childcare agency in which his wife Akshata Murthy had invested onto a list of just six agencies where would-be childcare workers could add their names. No conflict of interest, he claimed, when there clearly was. The list really is a long one with party donors, associates, supporters and family often mixed up in government policy and potential contracts.

Since January 2015, £8.4 BILLION of government contracts were given to firms controlled by Tory donors who collectively gave the

Tory party over £53 million in the same time frame.[81] Not illegal. But it is politicians who make the laws and this apparent conflict of interest must stop for any semblance of trust in the system to be reinstated.

In 2023, a *Byline Times* survey conducted with pollsters Omnisis found that the majority of voters (53 per cent) believed that Rishi Sunak's government was 'institutionally corrupt'. Only 15 per cent disagreed. In addition, 57 per cent also thought that 'the level of corruption in government had increased in their lifetime'. Just 7 per cent thought it had decreased.

This was undoubtedly a significant influence on the results at the general election, wrapped up with the extraordinary investigation by the Gambling Commission and the Met Police into multiple Conservative party members, staff and candidates who had placed bets on the date of the general election only a few days before Rishi Sunak's announcement on 22 May. There was a collective sense that 'they haven't changed' and 'how many times does someone have to tell you that they're bad before you believe them?'

These perceptions were supported by the UK falling to its worst level in Transparency International's Global Corruption Perceptions Index. Also, the Council of Europe's Group of States against Corruption (GRECO) stated that the UK was 'not in sufficient compliance' with its recommendations and that the UK had failed to implement measures designed to tackle corruption in government and policing.

Change must happen right now – no excuses.

To counter this, politicians, one and all, must now be whiter than white, and also be seen and verified independently as being exactly that. It isn't enough to say it, or to attempt to give that impression through friendly media. There must be absolutely no conflicts of interest between any public sector contractors and any MPs, Lords or political parties. NONE.

We must also bring an end to the system of so-called 'blind trusts', where senior politicians have put their assets into trusts which they then don't control. These trusts are used to claim there can be no conflict of interest.

But of course they know precisely what went into the trust at the moment it was created. So is this a smoke-and-mirrors system? I believe it is nothing more than that.

Unbelievably, the Code of Conduct for Ministers says with regard to a potential conflict of interest that it is the 'personal responsibility of each minister to decide whether and what action is needed to avoid a conflict or the perception of a conflict'.

Nothing should be off limits. Every scintilla of information regarding shares and profit from any company or asset which could be perceived as a conflict of interest needs to be available to the public to end this issue once and for all.

CHANGE NUMBER 2:
HIGHER STANDARDS OF CONDUCT
IN PUBLIC LIFE

There should be much stronger and more rigorous laws about conduct at Westminster. No ifs, no buts. No more cosy unofficial guidelines or unwritten rules; we need proper laws:

- There should be DBS checks before any candidate can be even chosen to run for office, and we should have similar rules to other areas of public sector employment, such as the police force.
- Lying in Parliament without an immediate apology should lead to an equally immediate ban for a fixed number of days, together with a fine. A suspension should automatically follow if an MP has received two fines. This might then trigger a by-election. I believe only this will stop the appalling false rhetoric we often hear in the House of Commons.
- MPs should be stopped from employing connected parties, such as partners or children, immediately.

(New employment of this kind was banned in 2017 after the MPs expenses scandal, but it was allowed to continue indefinitely if a family member was already on the payroll.)

- There should be random drug and alcohol tests at Westminster. No person should be allowed into the chambers of the Houses of Commons or Lords if they have blood alcohol levels that would make them legally unable to drive. If they are found to be trying to enter either House inebriated or with drugs in their system, then they should be banned for a set number of weeks together with a heavy fine. Two bans and they must step down.

- The prime minister can no longer be in control of the ministerial code. He/she cannot appoint their own ethics adviser.

- Finally, second jobs. If you say you are going to devote your time to your constituents, then that is what should happen. Your time spent as an MP should represent a full-time commitment. A whole review of second jobs and other forms of income should be undertaken.

It's time that we, the taxpayers and electorate, were treated with respect. For the past 14 years (and before that), the opposite has often been true.

There is a great quote from the science fiction writer Frank Herbert that sums up my thoughts on this subject: *'All governments suffer a recurring problem: Power attracts pathological personalities. It is not that power corrupts but that it is magnetic to the corruptible.'*[82]

Trust in politicians has never been so low.

Everything we've seen over recent decades would make you think politics is a little like the Wild West – but with even more sex and boozing. But there are rules that all those in public office are expected to stick to. The problem is that they are quite fuzzy and there has been no Wild West sheriff enforcing them – or when there has, the sheriff has been leaned on so heavily that they've often just put down their weapon (that's probably enough of the cowboy analogy).

It's time now for those in Westminster who get paid by the public to be held to account with rigorously enforced rules and truly tough penalties, including potential imprisonment.

At the moment, instead of hard rules there are 'principles', known as the Nolan principles. They were named after Lord Nolan, the first chair of the Committee on Standards in Public Life, which was set up in 1994 after the John Major government lurched from one sleazy crisis to another. Also known as the 'Seven Principles of Public Life', they boil down to these basic values:

- Selflessness
- Integrity
- Objectivity
- Accountability

- Openness
- Honesty
- Leadership

These are noble ambitions. But as we know, they have become 'word salad' to so many MPs.

Out of these came an 11-point Code of Conduct for Members of Parliament. I won't list all 11, but they include matters such as: members must treat their staff and all those visiting or working with dignity, courtesy and respect; accepting a bribe is against the rules; and they must tell the truth if they have any personal interest in an issue being discussed. They also can't give any 'off the books' paid parliamentary advice to mates.

It does make you wonder about an institution if it needs to put in writing that its members must be polite to people, tell the truth and not take bribes. But there you are.

The enforcer of the code of conduct is the Parliamentary Commissioner for Standards, who reports into a standards committee made up of MPs from across the political parties. This committee decides what penalty is appropriate for any wrongdoing.

In any sense, this shouldn't be run by MPs in future, but it should be an independent body. Self-regulation does not seem to work well enough.

There is also a privileges committee, which deals with any wrongdoing that affects Parliament's ability to do its work – things like lying to the House, leaking stories or financial misconduct. Again, an independent body seems necessary.

Finally, there is the ministerial code, with similar rules around integrity and transparency for those at the top of the tree. For years, there was a precedent and understanding that anyone who broke the code should quit (that all changed under a certain mop-haired PM).

So there are plenty of principles and codes of conduct already in place. But this is not enough, it seems, to keep the worst offenders in check. And in recent years, things have become worse.

In 2020, Home Secretary Priti Patel was found to have broken the code by bullying officials. When PM Johnson refused to sack Patel, his independent adviser on ethics resigned, apparently in disgust. Next to be given the thankless job of Johnson's ethics adviser was Lord Geidt, who quit less than two years later when it emerged Johnson had broken the ministerial code with his repeated lies about Partygate.

Geidt had earlier tried – and failed – to hold Johnson to account over the funding of the infamous 'gold wallpaper' refurb of Johnson's Number 11 flat, to which Tory donor Lord Brownlow had pitched in £50,000. Now, taking the money knowingly would be a breach of the ministerial code. But Johnson persuaded Geidt he hadn't known where the money had come from. Later, it turned out that Johnson hadn't shown Geidt crucial text chats with Brownlow. But Johnson got away with it again.

There was more scandal in 2021 when Owen Paterson, a former Northern Ireland and environment secretary, was investigated for breaking lobbying rules. The standards committee recommended he be suspended for 30 days – long enough to mean a by-election could be called in his constituency.

But in a stunning two fingers to the committee's ruling, Tory MPs then attempted to undermine the process and protect Paterson by voting to create a new committee to investigate such cases instead. They were literally ripping up the rule book. It was only after a public outcry that the government backed down on the plan. Finally, Paterson quit.

Then in May 2022, with the Partygate inquiry ongoing and stories of wine fridges, staff partying until they were sick and a child's swing being broken by boozed-up aides, Johnson came up with a new plan. He simply rewrote the ministerial code. In future, ministers who broke the code would no longer be expected to resign, it said. Instead, they might just have to apologise or be docked pay.

Johnson also blocked his supposedly independent ethics commissioner from launching his own investigations. The foreword to the ministerial code was rewritten, removing all references to honesty, integrity, transparency and accountability. It was a shameful attempt to save his own skin.

Although the rule changes weren't enough to save Johnson, the scandals continued under Truss and Sunak.

Suella Braverman, Nadhim Zahawi, Dominic Raab . . . all have faced allegations of breaching the ministerial code in the last couple of years. And then there are all the cases which haven't even been investigated. A report from the Public Administration and Constitutional Affairs Committee in December 2022 found 40 potential breaches of the ministerial code had not been looked into.

The systems are too easy for people to dodge around and the

penalties aren't strict enough. And clearly there is still the option for the government to just change any rules they don't like.

We need tougher laws and stricter sanctions. We need truly independent bodies free to investigate whatever and whenever they choose. The ministerial code must be rewritten and become law, and those who break it need to be hauled up in court. Then, and only then, will they have to face real consequences for their actions.

CHANGE NUMBER 3: DUTY OF CANDOUR

There should be a 'duty of candour', whereby civil servants and all those who work in the public sector, or as government contractors, have a legal responsibility to tell the truth or face criminal prosecution.

This is not without precedent: NHS staff have had a 'duty of candour' to be open and honest with patients since 2014. Their organisation could, and has been, prosecuted on occasion when this standard of truth has not been met.

The cover-ups that have been involved in the large-scale scandals of modern times have repeatedly left us dumbfounded. To change this desperate state of affairs, some form of criminal prosecution needs to be introduced for individuals who deliberately bury the truth in public office or under government contract.

Let's look at four recent examples where a duty of candour was sorely needed.

Hillsborough

Hillsborough was the worst disaster in British sporting history.

On 15 April 1989, Liverpool was playing Nottingham Forest in the FA Cup semi-final at the Hillsborough Stadium in Sheffield. After calamitous decisions by South Yorkshire Police, a human crush occurred at the Leppings Lane end of the ground.

Ninety-seven people died, 79 of whom were between the ages of just 10 and 29. Three hundred were hospitalised. Due to the trauma of that day, many others are known to have needed psychiatric care afterwards, or they took to alcoholism or drugs, and some tragically took their own lives.

I'm of the generation old enough (I was 28 at the time) to remember watching it live on TV. When it became obvious that something was unfolding, we couldn't believe what was happening – we didn't understand it; it was so horrific it couldn't compute in our brains. There was a high fence to keep fans off the pitch but there were too many people hemmed in. Other areas of the ground seemed empty. The game was started even though it was obvious there was an enormous problem. Then the real crush began – where were all these people coming from? Some managed to scramble over the top of the fence, but many couldn't.

As the reporting began to come out that day and in the weeks that followed, the public was duped. The *Sun* newspaper printed horrendous lies about victims and fans. We were told that the fans were drunk, that it was their fault (it wasn't), that they were stealing from dead bodies (they weren't). It never rang true. The establishment lied, the media lied and there followed more than 20 years of cover-up.

But all the while, the Hillsborough Family Support Group continued their campaign for the truth. And in 2012, 23 years after that terrible day, the report of the Hillsborough Independent Panel was finally published. This finally showed, once and for all, that the Liverpool fans were not responsible in any way for what happened that day. The main cause was 'lack of police control' by the South Yorkshire Police. Crowd safety had been 'compromised at every level'.

I was hosting ITV's *Loose Women* on the day the report came out, and I truly can't remember a time when I had ever been more shocked by the conclusions of a report. I shook with rage for the victims and the families, and the decades during which they had endured wrongful blame, unforgivable humiliation from the establishment, and grief and suffering beyond comprehension.

These are some of the report's findings:

- 164 witness statements had been identified for substantive amendment by South Yorkshire Police.
- 116 of those statements had been altered to remove/ change comments that were unfavourable to South Yorkshire Police.
- South Yorkshire Police had taken blood from the dead victims, including children, to test for alcohol to try to show fans were drunk, and the police ran computer checks on those with a non-zero alcohol level to try to 'impugn their reputation'.

- The local Conservative MP Irvine Patnick had passed on inaccurate and untrue information from the police to the press.

By 2016, new inquests into the deaths of all those killed had concluded that they died due to 'unlawful killing'.

Margaret Aspinall, the chair of the Hillsborough Family Support Group, lost her 18-year-old son James at Hillsborough. I met her when she won a Pride of Britain Award. She's an extraordinary woman and mother.

Result: Ninety-seven people were killed. Millions of words have been written and spoken about that day in 1989 and yet justice remains elusive. Nobody from South Yorkshire Police has been convicted of any offence or lost a day's pay.

The Grenfell fire

The Grenfell Tower fire took place on 14 June 2017.

The 24-floor block of council-owned residential flats, which stood in the heart of London, burned for more than two days. Seventy people including many children died that night; one was a baby just six months old. Two more lives were later lost as a consequence of the fire.

The fire was started by a fault in a fridge-freezer on the fourth floor. It quickly spread via the exterior of the building to other floors, helped along by cladding and an exterior structure that did not comply with regulations.

The Grenfell Action Group of residents (GAG) had been criticising fire safety standards in the building for over a decade before the fire, pointing out that firefighting equipment had not been checked for years, extinguishers were empty, the building only had one entrance and exit, and corridors had been allowed to fill with rubbish. They had been warning of a catastrophe for years. In 2013, two residents, Mariem Elgwahry and Nadia Choucair, were reportedly threatened with legal action by the council after they had campaigned for fire safety. They died in the fire that night.

Result: There has been an ongoing public inquiry into the disaster, with the phase two report due to be published in September 2024. The cladding companies, government and council bodies agreed a civil settlement with 900 people, of a total of £150 million. The burned shell of the building remains until such time that it will be taken down and a memorial will be made to honour the lives lost and the trauma of all of those involved.

But what of criminal investigations? What of someone accepting responsibility for a lack of transparency and action when residents complained about fire safety standards for all of those years?

The infected blood scandal

In the 1970s and 1980s, 30,000 people in the UK were given blood and blood products bought from America that were infected with hepatitis C and/or HIV. This led to more than 3,000 people (some children) dying horrifically.

In May 2024, the definitive *Infected Blood Inquiry Report* was published by Sir Brian Langstaff (whom many of the victims consider a hero). It found that a 'chilling' NHS and government cover-up had taken place and that the catastrophe could 'largely, though not entirely, have been avoided'. Many children with haemophilia were sent for treatment to Treloar's College in Hampshire, a boarding school for children which had a specialist NHS haemophilia centre. The report described the children as 'objects of research'. Of the 122 who were sent there, only 30 are still alive. The others would now have been in their sixties.

The report says: 'By 1986, the government can have been under no illusion about the scale of what had happened to people with haemophilia.'

Yet it took over 30 years from when it was known that blood products could transmit HIV until an inquiry was announced in 2017. Thirty years.

Other countries which had also bought these products held public inquiries in the 1990s. In France, individuals and some politicians were taken to court and found guilty.

Sir Brian Langstaff's report has recommended that ministers and all civil servants should have a 'duty of candour'.

Result: There had been a number of cover-ups within the NHS, by individuals and by government organisations and politicians. Three thousand people died, many needlessly. Nearly 50 years after it began, some victims will receive a financial payment – to call it 'compensation' is insulting.

The Post Office scandal

Between 1999 and 2015, the Post Office falsely accused 900 subpostmasters of theft, fraud and false accounting. They were prosecuted and 236 were sent to prison. In addition, the Post Office demanded thousands of subpostmasters make unexplained accounting discrepancies good under threat of losing their jobs or initiating debt recovery procedures, etc. – these people were not accused of a crime, though many were put under threat of criminal investigation.

When the subpostmasters tried to protest their innocence, they were told they were the 'only one' complaining of the problems with the Horizon system. Over the years, many were left bankrupt and some victims took their own lives.

Fujitsu, the company which had built and maintained the Horizon IT system, was found to have a dedicated department which could go into both sub Post Office and also into Crown Office branch accounts, meaning they had full (and for many years unaudited) access to every aspect of the Horizon IT system. But the subpostmasters didn't know; nobody outside knew. It was something Fujitsu and the Post Office denied.

In 2019, the Horizon Issues Judgement was handed down showing that bugs, errors and defects did exist in the Horizon system; indeed, on many occasions, these had caused financial discrepancies in branch accounts. All of this had been denied by the Post Office.

After the judgement, along with the quashing of some convictions and the Jo Hamilton judgement at the Court of Appeal, a full statutory public inquiry was ordered, which is now, finally, taking place in 2024.

But it was only when Alan Bates, one of the subpostmasters, decided to call a meeting in 2009 that the scale of the problem began to be known. He had also submitted material to *Computer Weekly* magazine, which provided significant support throughout this dreadful ordeal, along with notable journalists such as the incredible Richard Brooks from *Private Eye* as well as investigative journalist Nick Wallis.

The ITV drama *Mr Bates vs The Post Office* told the story to millions of us in very human terms. It was broadcast in January 2024 and had a significant impact on the attention of politicians, many of whom were keen to distance themselves from their predecessors' decisions.

Result: It took over 20 years of misery and cover-ups for some semblance of partial justice to be seen. Thousands of subpostmasters are still awaiting compensation. Some have received theirs. Convictions have been overturned. Since the damning report was published in 2019, Fujitsu, the company which ran the flawed Horizon system, has received a further £3.4 billion of new government contracts. Hardly a punishment.

There have been many other scandals over the years that have shocked us, broken our hearts and made us doubt the nature of the country we live in. They rock the lives of those involved, while the political class so often sit on their hands, talk a lot and then achieve very little.

The Covid inquiry has seen Tory after Tory claiming they have somehow 'lost' the WhatsApp messages they sent and received during that time. Billions of pounds of taxpayers' money was handed to cronies via the VIP PPE lane, while during lockdown, Tory staff danced and drank while others weren't allowed to hold their loved ones as they died. The state of politics over the last years has been a disgrace – I would consider it 'morally criminal' – but the laws aren't there as yet for duty of candour with proper punishment. It's my hope that they will be soon.

Our new prime minister Sir Keir Starmer has said that he wants to see duty of candour legislation across all public services. Rachel Reeves has promised a Covid corruption commissioner. I hope all of these promises are actioned. The sooner the better, as far as I'm concerned.

CHANGE NUMBER 4:
TRUE LEVELLING UP

True levelling up (not the politicians' version) means that for three months every year, Parliament should sit outside of London. It also means understanding how 'the other half' lives.

I believe that in the first year after every general election, all MPs should spend three days each month doing their own version of national service to gain 'real-life' experience of a range of jobs.

'Levelling up' – the Conservatives' much-vaunted attempt to reduce economic imbalance across the UK – has not happened and it's not going to happen unless some real leadership is shown at the top. (In fact, the political phrase 'levelling up' has become so meaningless that Labour are no longer using it.)

In a blatant attempt to capture votes in the 'Red Wall' in 2019, the Tories promised £10 billion would be spent attempting this feat, which of course was nowhere near enough. Then they only spent 10 per cent of that in the last Parliament. They cancelled HS2 and the list of failures goes on. There was no intention whatsoever to level up the country.

In March 2024, the Public Accounts Committee (I enjoy their reports) stated that they 'also found a worrying lack of transparency in DLUHC's [the Department for Levelling Up, Housing and Communities] approach to awarding funds'.

I have lived all over the UK. I grew up in North Wales, and have spent a lot of time in Manchester, Liverpool and around the north west. I've lived in the east of England, the west, London (for five years) and even the Home Counties. For many years, I lived and worked in Leeds where we recorded *Countdown* at Yorkshire Television on Kirkstall Road. I knew Yorkshire well and loved every minute there.

So let's make sure politicians get a similar sense of the variety, beauty and challenges of this country by getting out and working all over it.

The Westminster year looks not unlike a school calendar, with terms and half-term holidays:

Winter term: Parliament sits for a couple of weeks at the beginning of September. Then, after the party conferences, which take place in September and October, the politicians go back to Westminster around mid-October until Christmas holidays in late December (with a little half-term in November).

Spring term: They come back in early January until Easter, with a half-term in February.

Summer term: This runs from April through to July with some mini breaks. Then there's a big summer holiday from the middle of July until they go back in September.

So if you think of it as three terms with some fiddly bits, my proposal is that for one of those terms every single year, the business of Westminster is conducted at least 80 miles from London.

We should have five purpose-built and secure buildings capable of housing the Commons at any time. You choose where they should be. How about five from the following?

Liverpool	Lancaster
Newcastle	Great Yarmouth
Glasgow	Lincoln
Swansea	Hull
Manchester	Leeds
Birmingham	York
Plymouth	Bangor
Exeter	Belfast
Bristol	Nottingham

Wherever WE decide, we invest in those five cities and build.

Then, once a year, all the MPs and their associates have to sit in that city and make their decisions there. That would mean that within a five-year parliamentary term, they will have spent a third of their time outside of London. Not much to ask for, is it?

National Service for MPs

In recent times, our MPs have been so detached from the reality of life for most of Britain that it is now an issue which needs to be urgently addressed.

In the last Parliament (before the general election in July), only 1 in 100 Tory MPs entered Parliament from a working-class job.[83] It's a party dominated by private-school kids, people from finance backgrounds and career politicians, often working as SPADs (special advisers) before being nominated as a candidate in one constituency or another.

Even the percentage of Labour MPs from working-class jobs has halved since the 1980s and in 2019 was down to just 13 per cent of their total MPs.

Here's an idea.

After the Tory party suggested in their dying days that 18-year-olds should do national service, let's take that thought and apply it to MPs of all parties. They could undertake their own form of national service in order to understand how our country actually works at all levels, rather than just parachuting straight into the cosy and subsidised world of Westminster. These people make decisions to spend over £1.2 TRILLION of our money every year, so it makes sense that they understand what actually goes on in the real world.

I'm suggesting that for the first year of every Parliament, every MP other than Cabinet ministers should spend three days every month for twelve months in a selection of roles, acting as an intern for that time.

Suggestions include:

- Hospital porter
- Train trolley attendant
- Shop floor factory
- With the ranks in one of the Armed Forces
- Social care
- Food bank
- Old people's care home
- Teaching assistant
- On the bins
- Roadworks
- Working with the police

And perhaps a few other areas too, to give a spread of experience:

- In the City with a broker
- With a barrister understanding the system
- Data collection

You can probably think of many more.

I can think of no reason why this shouldn't happen, as the political class becomes ever more detached from the reality of the people it claims to 'serve'.

CHANGE NUMBER 5:
ELECTORAL REFORM

Our system of so-called 'democracy' is archaic. I believe we need both proportional representation (PR) and mandatory voting in order to have a fairer society and to give smaller parties and more people a better chance to influence how the country is governed.

Without doubt, our democracy needs upgrading.

We have, effectively, a two-party system. Vote red for Labour, vote blue for Conservative – and it has swung like a rusting pendulum between the two for over a hundred years.

How has that happened? With the use of first past the post (FPTP): a ridiculous system whereby if you want to vote for, say, the Green party in all but a handful of seats, your vote is effectively 'wasted'.

We are now the only country in Western Europe which has no form of proportional representation for our general election. The consequences of our archaic FPTP system are many and serious.

In 1951, after six years of Labour government under Prime Minister Clement Attlee – who introduced the NHS and the welfare state after the horrors of two world wars – a general election was held.

Just 13,718,199 people voted for Winston Churchill and the Conservative party. By contrast, 13,948,883 people voted for Labour, a record number of votes for any political party in history by that time. In other words, they received 230,000 more votes than the Tories. The people wanted Labour but FPTP put the Tories in power with 321 seats against Labour's 295 and the course of welfare reform was paused. By 2024, the manner in which the system is rigged effectively gives the Conservative party a 50-seat advantage over Labour.

So the democratic process continues in fundamentally the same way as it did a hundred years ago.

In 2019, the Tories swept through to achieve a commanding majority under Boris Johnson to 'get Brexit done'. Under the FPTP system, they gained just 29.4 per cent of the total potential vote of the electorate (if everyone registered had voted), 43.6 per cent of the actual vote and 100 per cent of the power.[84]

It was the highest percentage vote for a single party since 1979, when Margaret Thatcher won with 43.9 per cent of the vote. She gained power for more than a decade and started privatisation and the sell-off of more or less all the things we owned and controlled. It ushered in a decade of capitalism and the destruction of a lot of things many of us would now hold dear.

In the 2024 general election, Labour only achieved 33.7 per cent of the votes cast, with less than 10 million people voting for them. And yet it resulted in a colossal majority of 172, meaning that they can push through more or less any policies they wish.

So what's the solution?

Proportional representation

Under PR, neither Boris Johnson's landslide nor Keir Starmer's would have happened. Interestingly, the 2024 election showed a surge of support for smaller parties. Yet that was not reflected in the number of seats gained by them.

PR usually leads to more necessary consensus between political agendas – unlike in recent years, when there has been no compromise. With PR, the pendulum doesn't swing from left to right like some fairground ride. Instead, the whole system of governing is dampened down with fewer explosions.

Not only that, who we vote for changes too. For instance, under PR, many more people, particularly the young, would vote for the Green party. As it is, many would consider that vote might be 'wasted' in most constituencies, under first past the post. The 2024 election saw a high proportion of would-be Green voters choosing to vote tactically for another party in order to unseat a Tory in their constituency. That in itself leads to fewer people engaging with politics in any form, as well as fewer independent candidates and MPs. Imagine a Parliament with people who are passionate about a singular subject, such as Feargal Sharkey beating his drum about water privatisation while holding some form of power and influence from within. Marvellous.

PR would incentivise parties to appeal to all voters and not just to 'swing' voters in marginal constituencies. In that way, it would encourage turnout – although I would prefer mandatory voting (see below).

It is also true that with PR, far-right (or far-left) parties would have representation, mollify some part of their agenda to appeal to more voters and, in that way, gain power. We've witnessed this in France with President Macron calling a snap election and the right-wing influence growing but the party not gaining power under Marine Le Pen.

Many argue that PR produces 'weak government' and too many coalitions. Perhaps both systems have their faults but proportional representation is the only way in which we can stop the nonsense of FPTP in the UK with a natural Conservative bias built into its engine (see page 151).

For now, the phrase 'nothing will change, they're all the same' will probably continue to be heard, and until we have electoral reform, it is hard to argue with the sentiment.

Mandatory voting

Historically, the Conservative party has benefited from low turnouts for elections, which can then, together with first past the post, skew the result in its favour.

A higher percentage of older people vote Conservative. And they are the category of voter with the highest turnout at election time. In the 2019 election, only 54 per cent of people aged 18–34 voted, whereas 77 per cent of those 65-plus ticked a box on their ballot papers.

In the last three general elections, it isn't only age which has skewed the result. Guess who else votes more?

Probably not surprisingly, the rich vote significantly more than the poor. Homeowners vote more than those who rent property, graduates more than those who haven't been through further education, and white people more than ethnic minorities.

There are reasons for this, and the Westminster Bubble which largely speaks to the white middle class is one of those reasons.

There have been seven general elections since 2000 in which only around two-thirds of voters have voted.[85] But it was in the Brexit referendum of 23 June 2016 where the non-turnout changed the course of our history and opened the door to economic chaos and a demotion of our freedoms. That day, just 72.2 per cent of the 46,500,001 registered voters turned out.

The Brexit vote was won by a majority of 1,269,501 votes. To put that in context, the huge number of those who *didn't* vote that day, 12,948,018, was ten times larger than the Vote Leave majority. With mandatory voting, there's an argument that the result would likely have swung to Remain (although not by very much at all).[86]

In the 50 years up until 2000, the turnout at most general elections stood at over 70 per cent. The highest was in 1950, when Clement Attlee's Labour was voted in, and over 83 per cent took part. Since 2000 (other than for the Brexit referendum), we've had two of the lowest turnouts in history.[87]

So in spite of more media coverage and political news channels and stations than ever before, the sense of disillusion with politics seems to have increased.

I'm a great believer that the future belongs to the young and yet they are largely discouraged from being involved. I want that to change. A good democracy should have all voters taking part.

So let's make it right once and for all. Let's have mandatory voting for every national election.

Mandatory voting exists in around 15 per cent of countries in the world, particularly across South America and parts of Africa. It's also notably been the practice since 1924 in Australia, where it is regarded as one of the cornerstones of their democracy. In Europe, it's found in Belgium, Luxembourg, Cyprus, part of Switzerland, Greece and Turkey.[88]

Former US President Barack Obama suggested that the mandatory voting in the United States would have a 'transformative' effect on its political system and its future.

The way in which it is enforced varies: some countries don't have any 'penalties' if the vote isn't cast, others impose a small fine. We can decide on ours, but the principle remains.

Mandatory voting together with proportional representation is the way ahead.

CHANGE NUMBER 6:
REFORM THE HOUSE OF LORDS

The House of Lords should be stripped out and started anew:

- It should be replaced with a fixed number of people, 250 maximum, most of whom are elected with some appointed by independent outside bodies representing, say, the judiciary, police, military and nursing.
- The meaningless and deferential titles of 'Lord' or 'Baroness' should go.
- Each member of this House should have a fixed term of ten years, no more.
- Lords should also be able to vote remotely (as they did during the pandemic), as well as physically at Westminster.

There is undoubtedly a need for a second chamber to process the revision of any bill. But our current totally unelected House of Lords is put together in an archaic and ludicrous manner.

It is also simply too big. With nearly 800 members, it's even bigger than the House of Commons. In fact, it's the second biggest parliamentary chamber in the world (only China's rubber-stamping National People's Congress is larger).

Some of these older (average age 71), predominantly male (71 per cent) peers undoubtedly do a fine job, scrutinising the laws put forward by the House of Commons and asking MPs to 'think again' by tabling amendments to legislation. This is painstaking, important work which is essential to a functioning democracy.

But it is hard to escape the fact that the House of Lords is bloated beyond usefulness. The Conservatives have placed so many new peers in there over the last 14 years, they have the majority and may use that to stop Labour's bills being passed in some tit-for-tat horror which will only damage our country more. What will Labour do? Throw in many more Labour peers like an overflowing bathtub, prioritising party above country? Well, Labour's manifesto set out plans for 'immediate modernisation' of the House of Lords. They have proposed removing hereditary peers and a mandatory retirement age of 80. In the longer term, they have pledged to replace the House of Lords with an alternative second chamber. Good.

There should be 250 maximum in our House of Checks and Balances (not the real name, obvs – I'm sure you can think of better). Other countries manage with similar numbers in their revising chambers – France has 348, Spain has 265, Japan has 245. Even India, with a population of 1.4 billion, currently has only 245 members in its Rajya Sabha.[89]

Not only that, but many of our lords hardly bother to vote at all. In 2022, *Byline Times* found that in the previous six-year period, 142 peers (13.6 per cent) attended the Palace of Westminster on 25 days or fewer, with 58 *never* attending the House during that time.[90]

Jeffrey Archer, the former Conservative MP and convicted criminal, only voted once in the Lords since he finished his jail sentence for perjury in 2003. Mindboggling.

And let's not forget Lord Evgeny Lebedev of Hampton and Siberia – the Russian newspaper baron – whom Boris Johnson ennobled in 2020, against security advice. How many times has he voted in the House of Lords? You guessed it: not once.[91]

Then there's the make-up of the peers in our second chamber. Not a single one of its members has been elected – in fact, we are the only country in Europe to have a fully unelected revising chamber. All our peers have either inherited their titles or they have been appointed by ministers. This means around 70 per cent of the House of Lords votes strictly on party lines. In fact, some 29 per cent of peers were politicians themselves before entering the Lords (many of them MPs) and a further 8 per cent were previously political staff. The Bubble protecting the Bubble.

Although lords are not paid a salary, their generous expenses system means that in one year alone (2022–23), £21.1 million was spent from the public purse on allowances and expenses, which works out at over £27,000 per peer (even if you include the ones who never bother showing up).[92] Even those who rarely attend debates enjoy taxpayer-subsidised food and drink and other benefits of office. Nice work if you can get it.

The whole system is not fit for purpose. It is high time for an elected second chamber, filled with smart, engaged people who care about this country and have earned their position because they are our brightest minds and/or have deeply relevant life experience and a passion to help others, and not themselves.

In addition, the ludicrous dominance of London must end. At the moment, the House of Lords is dominated by peers from London, the south east and the east of England (55 per cent but representing only 35 per cent of the population). Other parts of the UK are woefully underrepresented – the East and West Midlands can claim only 6 per cent of peers between them and yet 16 per cent of the population lives in these areas. You see how it works.

There is no excuse for the archaic system of having to attend in person. Speaking as a provincial woman, I can tell you it's just another way for London to keep its dominance. In a time when many work from home, we should be harnessing twenty-first-century technology. Peers should come from every corner of the country, so all our regions have a proper voice.

For too long, the House of Lords has been run like a cosy club for the privileged few, totally unrepresentative of the population as a whole. Far too many unsuitable people have been parachuted in because they were cronies of whoever happened to be the prime minister at the time or – by complete coincidence, nothing fishy at all – they donated large sums of money to whichever party was in power (turn back to page 180 for more details on this).

I am sick of seeing the same privileged elite in our corridors of power. Let's slim down the House of Lords, vote in new peers (or whatever they will be called) and make sure that we have a properly representative second chamber working for us, and not for them.

CHANGE NUMBER 7: RENATIONALISATION

Renationalise some sectors, especially those which operate as monopolies.

For this, I want to take you back to my time growing up, when most of our industries and utilities were nationalised. They belonged to the people.

It's difficult to explain how life was growing up in 1960s and 70s in terms of what our expectations were. The children of this era (I was born in 1960), even those of us who were poor, as in my family's case, were healthier than generations before, enjoyed a peace and freedom that our parents hadn't, did not have to pay fees if we went to university and could, if necessary, on account of our financial situation, access maintenance grants that would cover our living costs while we were there too. We could expect to marry and be able to have a council house of our own while young, to grow up around our families, have a bit of a holiday somewhere once a year, have kids while we were young and maybe have a car and few worries. If you wanted to buy a modest house somewhere, that was also a reasonable ambition for people in normal jobs. Of course, there was also racism, sexism and a host of other -isms, so this is not a comment on that aspect of society, it's about our reasonable expectation of how life would be.

What I didn't appreciate at the time, and I think many of us didn't, was that the public sector ran more or less everything for us. It creaked and we moaned but no profit motive was involved. It was all nationalised; in other words, we owned it.

Telecoms, electricity generation, gas, oil, our airline British Airways, canals, water utilities, railways, the list goes on. We owned it all.

And then privatisation became the fashion. How did we fall for that free market fallacy? As with all things, when the pendulum of politics swings too far to the right or the left, the counterbalance is almost always a vast swing in the other direction.

Let's go back to the 1970s when strikes were hugely prevalent. There was a declaration of a State of Emergency in 1970 and the three-day working week in 1974, when businesses had to decide which three days they would have electricity. There were strikes everywhere in the Winter of Discontent in 1978/79. Lorry drivers, miners, even some gravediggers went on strike. Inflation briefly leapt up to 24 per cent.

In May 1979, Margaret Thatcher swept to power on a promise to sort out the unions, but Thatcher went much further than many imagined from her initial manifesto. She generated the era of the 'yuppie', the explosion of the idea that you can have it all without social responsibility, that any form of looking after others was to be scoffed at. I remember being in London for work in the 1980s (I lived in Leeds at the time) and trying to use a zebra crossing with an older lady, when a Porsche-driving yuppie shouted, 'Get out of my way, I'm rich!' Yes, that defined Thatcherism for me. House prices jumped and council houses were sold off, all to the cost of the generations to follow.

It was all free markets and income-tax cuts (most beneficial to the better-off) and taking power from local councils, deregulation, and on and on.

I didn't truly understand it at the time. I was just making my way in the world and thinking how lucky I was to have a roof over my head.

Thirty years later, when David Cameron came to power, he and his disgraceful 'free market thinkers' sold the UK down the river for their own continuing privilege and financial gain. The UK was ripe for the picking after the financial crash of 2007/08, and even more so after the Brexit vote.

Even the NHS was put onto the motorway of privatisation in 2012 when David Cameron established NHS Trusts with the mandate to put services and care out to tender. Billions of pounds a year, which would previously have been used within the service, is now paid out as pure profit for private healthcare companies.

Many Tory party donors have also benefited financially from their connections with the Department of Health and Social Care – one of the most notable being Frank Hester, whose company has enjoyed multiple government health-related contracts while he has donated £15 million to the Tory party.

The water companies were privatised in 1989, and since then, they have borrowed (and maintain a debt of) over £85 billion. Quite by coincidence, they have also paid out dividends of around the same amount . . . They haven't invested in infrastructure as they should and now we face record water bills with daily reports of sewage in the rivers, wildlife destroyed and swathes of our coastline often unfit to swim in.

Seventy per cent of water companies in the UK are now privately owned; only three of them are on the stock exchange. The adverts at the time told us that we would all own a piece of the new companies – we would be 'H2Owners' – but what they failed to mention was that before privatisation we already owned our water. Many of us just didn't realise. The Tories – Thatcher and her cronies – were shaking our hand and stealing our watch from our wrist while they smiled.

But one thing at a time.

I want to see the renationalisation of many companies, particularly those which are effectively monopolies.

If you aren't happy with your water company, can you go elsewhere? No, you can't. If you have a problem with the hike in bills, can you do anything about it? No, you can't.

It's time to renationalise many sectors, beginning with water, trains (many have already had to be taken back into government hands after failing as privatised companies) and the National Grid.

I also want no new private contracts for the NHS, and an active reduction of current contracts, with annual targets once waiting lists have reduced to bring it fully back into the public sector.

CHANGE NUMBER 8:
TAX REFORM

For 14 years and many more, the super-rich have made the rules about how much money they don't pay in tax. For the wealthy who don't rely on income from work (unlike most people), schemes to avoid paying tax – legally – proliferate.

Thus, there is now an inbuilt inequality between those who work to earn 'income' and those who (legally) obtain money by other means, usually capital gains.

The tax system needs levelling.

As Benjamin Franklin said back in 1789, *'In this world, nothing is certain except death and taxes.'* Let's take a closer look at the latter.

Before I start, please note that all rates quoted were correct at time of writing. Also, as there are many complex elements to tax, please don't take this piece as a recommendation or tax advice. I have simplified and given examples only. This is written as an observation of the absurdity of the system we currently have, and to show how unfair that system can be.

Taxes – and who pays what and when – are in the power of the government to determine. Are some governments biased towards their own voting base? Or are their decisions made on the basis of what's good for the country? You decide.

In the year leading up to the 2024 election, we heard detailed debate on which taxes would rise or be cut under governments formed of the different parties to the point of dizziness and confusion. The Tories, in their final days, thrashing around in an empty barrel of desperate policies, decided to just lie about the '17 taxes you'll get under Labour'. When Rishi Sunak appeared on the last leaders' debate a week before the election, the Conservative party press office even changed its social media name to 'Tax Check UK' in real time in an appalling attempt to convince online users that Sunak was speaking the truth. It only served to persuade people just how awful the Tories had become, as if they needed further proof.

But who understands the tax system?

Sadly, one of the greatest issues politically is that around half of voters don't understand how the basic banded tax system and thresholds work. So let me briefly explain.

These are the personal income tax bands at the time of writing:

Tax rate band	Income threshold 2023/24	Income tax rate (excl. dividends)
Basic rate	£12,571 to £50,270	20 per cent
Higher rate	£50,271 to £125,140	40 per cent
Additional rate	Over £125,140	45 per cent

The misunderstanding of these rates was shown in polling evidence from WeThink for Tax Policy Associates. The question was asked: if you had a pay rise that increased your total earnings by just £1 from, say, £50,270 to £50,271, and, therefore, put your salary into the higher tax band of 40 per cent, would *all* of your earnings be taxed at that 40 per cent rate? Half of respondents believed that would be the case. Yet that isn't true. Only the amount of earnings in that tax band (i.e. the £1) would be taxed at that rate. The rest would be taxed at the rates in the other bands. That is the essence of tax banding.

Dan Neidle is a special guy. A former leading tax lawyer, he set up Tax Policy Associates, an independent think tank dedicated to improving tax policy and the public understanding of tax. He was a part of the investigative scenario which brought down former Tory Chancellor Nadhim Zahawi. Zahawi was eventually sacked for a 'serious breach of the ministerial code' by not telling officials he was being investigated by HMRC when he was appointed Chancellor by Johnson. He'd also failed to declare that he'd paid a penalty for tax avoidance to HMRC. In total, his bill was estimated at £3.7 million plus a 30 per cent penalty, plus interest charges, taking the total to around £5 million.

Tax Policy Associates has also found that in the tax years from 2018 to 2022, 420,000 HMRC late filing penalties (40 per cent of these penalties) were charged to people who didn't even earn enough to be required to pay tax. They each received a penalty of £100 (a total of £42 million), which in most cases is more than half of their weekly income. To fine people so much for filing their tax return late when they didn't even owe tax in the first place is an utter disgrace.

By 2023, the UK had its highest tax burden in 70 years. Sunak and the Tories had been raising the amount paid in income taxes by applying a freeze on the tax thresholds. How did that affect people? Well, wage inflation meant more people have been earning more money, and because of that they had been entering higher tax bands whether they liked it or not.

The Office for Budget Responsibility (OBR – the official financial watchdog that gives independent and authoritative analysis of the UK's public finances) predicted that the last Tory policies including freezing of tax bands, if continued through the next Parliament, would mean: 'Between 2022–23 and 2028–29 . . . nearly 4 million additional individuals will be expected to pay income tax, 3 million more will have moved to the higher rate, and 400,000 more onto the additional rate.'

Contrast that with the super-rich – the people who have tax lawyers and advisers on speed dial. This is where capital gains tax comes into play. Headline tax rates on capital gains have fundamentally remained unchanged at 20 per cent during Sunak's time as Chancellor and then prime minister.

So let's take the example of Rishi Sunak, the unelected Conservative prime minister for 20 months, a man who barely knew how to use a debit card in a petrol station. He shared the basics of his tax return in February 2024.

He paid a total of £508,308 in tax in the financial year 2022–23 on 'earnings and gains' of £2.23 million. However, Sunak only paid an effective overall tax rate of 23 per cent in the UK – much lower than the top rate of income tax, which is 45 per cent.

If all of the £2.23 million had been charged with 'income tax' rates, he would have paid around twice the amount in tax – not £508,308, but around £1,036,313.

Why was it lower for him?

Well, he did pay a high rate of income tax: £163,364 in tax on a total 'income' of £432,884. But he also paid only £359,240 in capital gains tax on around £1.8 million of capital gains from a US-based investment fund.

The rate of capital gains tax is fundamentally 20 per cent (up to 24 per cent for property), much lower than that of income tax, which is what halved his overall bill.

The Trades Union Congress (TUC) tweeted after Sunak's tax return release: 'It really is a mystery why Rishi Sunak raised income tax but not capital gains tax.'[93]

The system needs redress. The large gap between income tax and capital gains tax encourages significant tax avoidance.

The London School of Economics produces many papers on this matter. Professors Arun Advani and Andy Summers's work is fascinating (well, it is to a nerd like me). In one paper, they propose an alternative minimum tax rate. This would impose a minimum average tax rate which would limit the extent to which any individual can lower their overall tax bill. An alternative minimum tax set at 35 per cent (the same average rate as someone earning £100,000) on total remuneration including any capital gains could raise up to £11 billion.

Let's look at other ways in which the rich can legally avoid tax, when others can't. The non-dom tax status claimed by many super-rich will hopefully be coming to an end imminently, but it's worth looking at it here. A non-dom is a UK resident who only pays tax to HMRC on the money they earn in the UK. They do not have to pay tax to HMRC on money which is made elsewhere in the world. For wealthy individuals, this gives them the opportunity of significant, legal tax savings.

Sunak's wife, Akshata Murthy, claimed (legal) non-dom tax status, meaning she did not pay UK tax on the dividends paid on her shares in Infosys (the firm established by her father in India). By claiming this tax status, she avoided paying an estimated £20 million in tax over the period of time her husband Sunak was an MP. Once her tax position (although legal) was discovered by the press, in April 2022, Mrs Sunak dropped her non-dom tax status.

Another example of legal tax avoidance for the super-rich is the special deal struck between 'private equity' managers and HMRC. There are only around 2,000 'private equity' managers in the UK, yet 255 of them 'earned' a mind-boggling £2.7 BILLION between them in 2021–22 tax year.

Did they pay the higher rate of income tax on that amount? No, they didn't. Why not?

Well, in 1987, their industry lobbied the Thatcher government, who agreed that they shouldn't pay income tax of around 45 per cent like everyone else, but they should only pay 28 per cent in what's known as 'carried interest'.[94] Why?

Because governments decide. Had they been taxed at the same rate as the majority, it would have raised from just these 2,000 individuals alone a further £600 million in tax in one year. Almost the equivalent of the reduction in the GP surgeries' budget over the last five years. These uber-wealthy private equity managers have saved literal fortunes in tax at the expense of others.

And then we come to what's known as 'offshore' tax havens. But for now, I think that's enough numbers.

Yes, even I think that's enough! I don't want your eyes to glaze over.

The point is that there is no equality in any sense unless what we pay into the system is changed. It needs radical change.

The system also needs to give more help to those who haven't been taught to understand it.

CHANGE NUMBER 9:
SCRUTINISE THE THINK TANKS

There should be full scrutiny of the work of the shadowy think tanks.

- They should not retain their charitable status without transparency about their funding.
- And their political persuasion must be taken into account in regard to political bias in broadcasting.

Tufton Street is a five-minute amble away from the Houses of Parliament. A great number of right-wing think tanks have taken up residence in that street and the surrounding area. It's a political network. Remarkably, most of these political organisations are registered charities.

You might not know much about them because they like to operate in the shadows, but they have affected your lives radically in the last 14 years.

Remember the mini-budget that crashed the British economy

and hiked mortgage rates in September 2022? Well, its contents were dreamed up by the people who work in 55 Tufton Street and other buildings nearby. On its launch, the Centre for Policy Studies (CPS) bragged that it was 'great to see so many CPS policies included in today's announcement by the Chancellor'. The head of policy at the Institute of Economic Affairs (IEA) was equally delighted.

Many of these free market, free speech, so-called think tanks receive some of their funds from secret donors. Many think tank executives or members also bankroll the Conservative party. These cheerleaders for the catastrophic mini-budget have given the Tory party £35 million in recent years.

We need far higher scrutiny of their often opaque funding if think tanks are to maintain charitable status, together with tougher rules and transparency when their representatives appear in the media. The scale of their influence has been a sinister blight on this country for too long.

Led By Donkeys, Democracy for Sale (follow them both online) and the excellent investigative journalist Peter Geoghegan trawled through Electoral Commission data and found the following:

- Lord Michael Spencer, chairman of the CPS, has donated more than £7 million to the Tories.
- CPS board member Lord Anthony Bamford (now resigned from the Lords) and his family have given around £9 million to the Tories.

- Lord Michael Hintze served as a trustee of the IEA for 17 years. During that time, he gave £4.3 million to the Conservative party and its MPs.
- Neil Record is the IEA's 'Life Vice President'. Since being involved with this think tank, he's given £475,000 to the Tories. He's not a Lord – yet.
- Graham Edwards has donated £3.5 million to the Conservatives since he was appointed to the CPS board.
- Lord Jamie Borwick is another IEA adviser. He's given more than £275,000 to the Conservatives.
- Ben Elliot is another board member at the Centre for Policy Studies. While he was Tory party chairman, he helped to raise over £70 million for the Conservative party.

These aren't independent think tanks, not by any stretch of the imagination.

Former Tufton Street staff members became SPADs (special advisers) and worked throughout Westminster from 2010 onwards. They seem to have become a critical part of the Tory party (some now support Reform) and many have been put into the House of Lords to drive through legislation that the rest of us have to follow.

They are unaccountable. Their additional funding is often shrouded in secrecy. OpenDemocracy has an index of transparency known as 'Who Funds You?' In January 2024, all the right-leaning think tanks at 55 Tufton Street had the lowest rating of an 'E', with the exception of the TaxPayers' Alliance, Centre for Policy Studies and the Institute of Economic Affairs, which have the second-lowest rating, 'D'.

Their representatives have appeared many times on television as 'independent' commentators, particularly on the BBC, and yet they aren't independent at all.

They are established as charities and the Charity Commission seems happy to flex their rules to accommodate them. Indeed, the last chair of the Charity Commission defended them. The Good Law Project is actively seeking legal clarification on their activity right now.

I believe it's time these bodies were made accountable.

Their prominence has coincided with an appalling time for most in the UK. Their funding should be transparent, they should not hold charitable status and they should not be treated as independent thinkers in terms of broadcasting rules.

CHANGE NUMBER 10:
BAN OLD ETONIANS FROM CABINET

To rectify the government of the masses by the 'elite', a ban on anyone from Eton College holding a position in Cabinet before 2050.

One of the things which angers me most is the arrogance of many recent politicians: how they have treated voters like chattels and hide from us what they don't want us to see. It's been breathtaking to witness.

Think Partygate, or contracts with party donors, or a little further back and Labour's attempt to exempt MPs from the Freedom of Information Act, and you'll instantly see what I mean. This is largely down to the Conservative party but MPs from other parties have also sometimes acted in just as arrogant a manner.

What we have had is an establishment system set up for the already privileged.

We have had 57 prime ministers in this country since 1721. Twenty of them attended Eton College, including five of the fifteen PMs since 1955.[95]

Read that again, please. A third of our prime ministers since 1955 went to the same school.

By 2021, the dominance of boys from Eton College had reached a peak, with more influence over the public life of this country than even a hundred years before. Let me give you just a few examples of the ultra-exclusive school's alumni (the list is long):

- Boris Johnson, the former prime minister
- Justin Welby, Archbishop of Canterbury
- General Mark Carleton, Chief of the General Staff (military)
- Lord Leggatt, Justice of the Supreme Court
- The future king, Prince William
- The Duke of Sussex
- Charles Moore, former editor of the *Daily Telegraph*, who was made a lord by Boris Johnson
- Oliver Letwin, Chancellor of the Duchy of Lancaster in David Cameron's government
- Nicholas Coleridge, former editorial director of Condé Nast
- William Shawcross, given job of chair of Charity Commission by David Cameron (old Etonian) then the top job as Commissioner of Public Appointments by Boris Johnson (old Etonian)

This is a tiny part of a list which includes members of the Cabinet, the Commons, the Lords, the Church, the press, the military and the Royals – and all from a school which only takes in about 230 boys a year. For example, of the 644 members of the House of Lords whose schooling is on record, 65 went to Eton.[96] If that isn't privilege gifted by birth, then describe to me what is.

This is the system that you and I were born into, under which we allow a minority 'elite' to represent us and govern our lives on a day-to-day basis, making decisions for millions of people whose lives they cannot even begin to comprehend.

Many of the more elite private schools breed entitlement. Generally, those who attend are already living a life of privilege within a micro community of power, money and, for some, tax avoidance. Let's look at the rogue's gallery of people who ruled us when the Tories were last in power:

First, David Cameron – Eton – became prime minister and brought in austerity, something he would never have experienced in his life. It was the start of our rapid decline.

George Osborne became his Chancellor. He was educated at St Paul's School and given £15 million by his parents. Nice.

Jacob Rees-Mogg – need I say more – and obviously Eton.

Kwasi Kwarteng, Liz Truss's Chancellor: Eton.

Boris Johnson: Eton.

Rishi Sunak: Winchester College (former pupils include two prime ministers, four archbishops and endless Cabinet ministers.)

Let's look at the relationship between top private schools and the country's top MPs more widely. To give you the context, around 7 per cent of students attend private schools nationally. Over the last couple of decades, the percentage of Cabinet MPs who went to fee-paying schools in each government went like this:[97]

- Pre-2010 Labour governments: around 32 per cent
- 2010 Tory/Lib Dem coalition: 62 per cent
- 2015 Conservatives, under David Cameron: 50 per cent
- 2016 Theresa May's government: down to 30 per cent
- 2019 Boris Johnson: back up to 64 per cent
- 2022 Liz Truss: even higher, at 68 per cent
- 2022 Rishi Sunak: 65 per cent
- 2024 Sir Keir Starmer's Labour: less than 10 per cent

It isn't just about money, it really isn't. It's about their contacts, their feelings of superiority – there's not a cell of 'imposter syndrome' in their bones – and, above all, their sense of sharing the goods between a small, impenetrable circle. Now think about how that impacts on their ideology and decision-making.

In many of these Cabinets, two-thirds of the MPs or more had no experience whatsoever of our state system of education, let alone experience of homelessness, of being on benefits, of not knowing how you're going to pay your bills.

The influence of certain private schools for the overly privileged in positions of government and society should come to an end if we want a proper system of democracy. For that, we have to crack the nut. Remember also that Eton only takes boys, so as a woman who went to a comp and was on free school meals, I think it's time for enormous change.

This will predictably be described as the 'politics of envy' by those in power.

I don't care what they call it. We are a quarter of the way through the twenty-first century, yet the positions of privilege for the few have only increased. It's time to address the inequality and if that takes particular actions – just as the Tories cut back on education, cut back on schools spending, cut back on our NHS provision – then bugger them, it needs redress.

Full disclosure: I sent my own kids to private school (including a school for Special Education Needs for my son) and through that I've learned even more about the privilege and opportunities afforded to children in the private-school sector. I am not against private schools per se, but I am alarmed by the huge amount of influence a tiny proportion of these schools have on this country. It's always the same cry of: 'We can rule over you but don't you dare suggest that we should change the system in any way. It's rigged to our benefit and that is how it's going to stay.'

Let's ban all Old Etonians from positions of governmental power for the next 25 years . . . or more!

AFTERWORD

Here we are with a new Labour government. Fourteen years of Tories over and done with. Now we have to pick up the pieces and hopefully rebuild.

I've found the last (nearly) two years to be shattering at times. Threats, legal letters, harassment, sacking – all added to the anger I've felt almost every day, anger about the injustice, corruption and misery which the previous government caused.

But for all of that, I know how lucky I am to have a roof over my head that nobody can take away, food in the fridge, kids who are safe and a bunch of people who'd fight for me until the world ran out.

I remember the times when life was very different to that. Those times, no matter how long ago they may have been, never leave you.

And I know the anguish and pain that worry brings.

I hope that all of us together have managed to take the first step towards a kinder and more competent government than the last one we had to endure.

When we vote, we effectively catch a bus in the direction we want to travel. The bus might not have all the fancy bits we want inside it, it might take a little longer to get to our destination and it might stop at places we'd rather it didn't, but it must keep us safe and give us confidence. That is the primary role of a government.

This new government will not be perfect, and we will have to hold it to account, and we will have to shout loudly where and when we need to. But I truly hope the crazy, delusional days of the Tories are over.

Meanwhile, we will have another general election in less than five years. It's likely that it will be conducted with the first past the post system once more.

It'll be Labour versus, perhaps, some sort of Tory/right-wing Reform merger. If so, I pray that by that time Labour will have brought more trust into politics and that voters feel less detached from Westminster than we do today. If not, I hate to think of the possible consequences.

For now, let's take the win against the Tories and smile.

I want to end this brief period of time together by telling you how much love I've felt from new friends in this political adventure, online, in person and from strangers in the street. You're so very special. Thank you, every single one of you, for your support; you completely understood that we needed to do this together.

There are many more adventures to come, campaigns to join, voices to bring together. I know I'll see many of you there.

Until then, from this old bird with an iPhone, I wish you peace and every happiness in the world.

With love, Carol xxx

REFERENCES

1. Tom Wall, 'Babies are dying because of NHS failings, poverty and inequality, charities warn', *Observer*, 14 May 2023
2. Scott Compton, 'Why are 300,000 families in full-time work still in poverty?', Action for Children, 22 February 2024
3. Sammy Gecsoyler, '"Rat bites and chronic asthma": schools on the frontline of UK housing crisis', *Guardian*, 17 April 2024
4. Anna Highfield, 'Schools crisis: Sunak halved budget for rebuilding programme', *Architects' Journal*, 4 September 2023
5. Hannah Rose Woods, 'Universities are in crisis', *New Statesman*, 8 April 2024
6. 'Student loan statistics', House of Commons Library, 10 July 2024
7. Michael Race, 'Eleven million Britons struggling to pay bills', BBC News, 17 May 2023
8. 'Worries about the rising costs of living, Great Britain: April to May 2022', Office for National Statistics, 10 June 2022
9. 'New data shows food insecurity major challenge to levelling up agenda', The Food Foundation, 7 February 2022
10. Michael Savage, 'Alarm at growing number of working people in UK "struggling to make ends meet"', *Observer*, 21 April 2024
11. Viktor Berg, 'Care home fees and costs: How much do you pay?', carehome.co.uk, 4 July 2024

12. David Batty, 'England's worsening care shortages leave older people struggling – Age UK', *Guardian*, 17 February 2023

13. Dame Laura Cox, DBE, 'The Bullying and Harassment of House of Commons Staff', Independent Inquiry Report, UK Parliament, 15 October 2018; 'The Observer view on the toxic workplace that is Westminster', *Observer*, 13 November 2022

14. Rowena Mason and Aubrey Allegretti, 'MPs bullying and humiliating staff, Speaker's inquiry told', *Guardian*, 2 November 2022

15. Sam Bright, '"VIP" Firms Referred by Tory MPs and Peers for PPE Deals See Profits Soar', *Byline Times*, 29 November 2022

16. Anna Bawden, 'UK government wasted nearly £10bn on unused Covid PPE, figures show', *Guardian*, 25 January 2024

17. Rowena Mason, 'PPE bought via "VIP lane" was on average 80% more expensive, documents reveal', *Guardian*, 10 December 2023

18. David Conn, Russell Scott and David Pegg, 'Firm with mystery investors wins £200m of PPE contracts via "high-priority lane"', *Guardian*, 21 December 2020

19. David Conn, 'Revealed: Tory peer Michelle Mone secretly received £29m from "VIP lane" PPE firm', *Guardian*, 23 November 2022

20. David Conn, 'Michelle Mone: leading entrepreneur or lucky baroness?', *Guardian*, 25 January 2024; 'Michelle Mone's lingerie firm publishes £388,000 losses', *Business Matters*, 14 October 2015

21. Laura Benjamin, '"Lay off Penny", says Rod', *Daily Mail*, 30 March 2024

22. Wilma Riley, 'Accountant claims Michelle Mone made life hell for Ultimo workers who got on the wrong side of her', *Daily Record*, 15 February 2014

23. Deadline News Journalist, 'Mone mocked after making triple boast about world-class skills in one tweet', Deadline, 5 March 2018

24. Jemima Kelly, 'The baroness, the ICO fiasco, and enter Steve Wozniak', *Financial Times*, 3 September 2018

25. Hamish Morrison, 'Michelle Mone claimed ALBERT EINSTEIN lived in her Glasgow home', *The National*, 3 February 2023

26. David Conn, 'Tory peer Michelle Mone settles libel claim "for more than £50k"', *Guardian*, 8 August 2022

27. Euan McColm, 'Scots Tory cringe over Michelle Mone', *Scotsman*, 16 August 2015

28. Aisha Majid, 'UK newsbrand trust rankings: The Sun is least-trusted and BBC and FT lead the way', Press Gazette, 31 May 2023

29. David Conn, 'Revealed: Tory peer Michelle Mone secretly received £29m from "VIP lane" PPE firm', *Guardian*, 23 November 2022

30. 'Jeremy Clarkson and The Sun', *Sun*, 23 December 2022

31. Mark Sweney, 'Panel approving Richard Sharp as BBC chair included Tory party donor', *Guardian*, 24 January 2023

32. Harriet Sherwood, 'Sexism, vandalism and bullying: inside the Boris Johnson-era Bullingdon Club', *Guardian*, 7 July 2019

33. 'State or private school? The education backgrounds of the newest cabinet', Sky News, 9 July 2024

34. Simon Walters, 'Nadhim Zahawi: New chancellor's finances secretly investigated by National Crime Agency', *Independent*, 6 July 2022

35. Nafeez Ahmed, 'GB News "Founder" in Business with Two Top Priti Patel Appointees', *Byline Times*, 10 February 2021

36. Content Team, '3.5 million women have considered quitting jobs due to lack of menopause support', Work in Mind, November 2023

37. Alexandra Topping, 'Carol Vorderman "disgusted" by ministers' attitude to menopause', *Guardian*, 23 March 2023

38. 'BBC Chair made "significant errors of judgement" over PM loan involvement, MPs say', Digital, Culture, Media and Sports Committee, UK Parliament, 12 February 2023

39. Professor John Curtice, 'What difference will the new constituency boundaries make?', Politics and Society, UK in a Changing Europe, 16 January 2024

40. Benjamin Lynch, 'Small area of Yorkshire that's the most dangerous place to live in the UK', YorkshireLive, 28 February 2023

41. Leila Nathoo and Sam Francis, 'Why did Boris Johnson resign?', BBC News, 9 June 2023

42. George Grylls, 'Military morale at five-year low over poor pay and housing, *The Times*, 2 June 2023

43. 'Food bank use is a choice, suggests minister', BBC News, 4 July 2023

44. 'MP Johnny Mercer quits £85k job to fulfil minister's role', BBC News, 31 July 2019

45. Johnny Mercer, 'Plymouth MP Johnny Mercer's "brutal week" – in his own words', PlymouthLive, 13 July 2023

46. Tom Bryant, 'EXCLUSIVE: Carol Vorderman snubs bizarre GB News offer following BBC exit', *Mirror*, 6 December 2023

47. Joshua Nevett, 'Watchdog criticises decision to pay Johnson's £265,000 Partygate bill', BBC News, 19 September 2023

48. Anushka Asthana and Jack Abbey, 'Covid Inquiry: Government set to spend £55m on lawyers with £14m already spent, ITV News reveals', ITV News, 16 June 2023

49. Aletha Adu, 'Homelessness among armed forces veterans in England rises by 14%', *Guardian*, 26 December 2023

50. Fred Thomas, https://x.com/FredThomasUK/status/1740027154577158621, X, 27 December 2023

51. EJ Ward, '"You can hold me to it!": Minister pledges to end homelessness among armed forces veterans this year', LBC, 22 February 2023

52. Mikey Smith, 'EXCLUSIVE: Rishi Sunak's warm-up man Johnny Mercer pocketed £13,500 for being sacked twice', *Mirror*, 1 October 2023

53. Mikey Smith, 'Tory minister Johnny Mercer told to stop spending taxpayers' cash on vanity photos', *Mirror*, 11 November 2023

54. 'Tory MP Johnny Mercer told to repay £930 in expenses', BBC News, 24 January 2019

55. 'Post Office Horizon scandal: Why hundreds were wrongly prosecuted', BBC News, 24 May 2024

56. Carol Vorderman and LED BY DONKEYS, https://www. instagram.com/carolvorders/reel/C2hgAs0ok1A/, Instagram, 25 January 2024

57. David Conn, 'Michael Gove failed to register hospitality with donor whose firm he referred for PPE contracts', *Guardian*, 20 February 2024

58. Laycie Beck, 'Lee Anderson spoon feeds fellow Nottinghamshire MP baked beans on new GB News Show', NottinghamshireLive, 23 June 2024

59. 'Child poverty levels in the UK worst among world's richest nations, UNICEF report finds', Reuters, 7 December 2023

60. Richard Partington, 'The Conservatives' economic record since 2010 in 10 charts', *Guardian*, 2 March 2024

61. John-Paul Ford Rojas, 'Britain's tax burden to be highest since WW2 as households face £44bn stealth tax hit', This is Money, 23 November 2023

62. Theo Harris, 'Draining Every Last Drop of Oil and Gas Won't Ease the Cost of Living Crisis', New Economic Foundation, 6 September 2023

63. William Eichler, 'Dismay as HS2 funds rerouted to fix potholes in London', LocalGov, 21 December 2023

64. Adam Forrest, 'Cost of Boris Johnson's booze-fuelled Brexit bash revealed', *Independent*, 29 January 2024

65. Phillip Inman and Larry Elliot, 'Head of OBR says lack of budget details led to "work of fiction" forecasts last year', *Guardian*, 23 January 2024

66. Poppy Wood, 'MP Michelle Donelan faces calls to resign for using taxpayer cash in libel case', *i* newspaper, 6 March 2024; *Guardian* Editorial, 'The Guardian view on Michelle Donelan: exposed as an online bully, she should now resign', *Guardian*, 8 March 2024

67. 'REVEALED: Minister's partner's firm awarded lucrative Covid contracts', Good Law Project, 4 November 2021

68. Rowena Mason, 'Frank Hester: computer programmer who made fortune from public sector contracts', *Guardian*, 11 March 2024

69. Rowena Mason, Matthew Weaver and Henry Dyer, 'Biggest Tory donor said looking at Diane Abbott makes you "want to hate all black women"', *Guardian*, 11 March 2024

70. 'Sunak took £16,000 helicopter ride from firm who won huge Government contracts', Good Law Project, 15 December 2023

71. 'Revealed: 31,000 sewage discharges into bathing areas last year', Liberal Democrats Official Party Website, 2 April 2024; 'Sewage was spilled into rivers and sea "safe for bathing" 86 times a day last year', Sky News, 1 April 2024

72. Russell Scott, https://x.com/RussellScott1/status/1780686322908487787, X, 17 April 2024

73. Laurence Darmiento, Melody Petersen and Jack Flemming, 'A Pasadena startup got billions selling COVID tests. Then came questions', *Los Angeles Times*, 28 July 2021; Comptroller and Auditor General, 'Test and trace in England – progress update', Department of Health & Social Care, National Audit Office, 25 June 2021

74. Robert Watts, 'Rishi Sunak and Akshata Murty net worth – Sunday Times Rich List 2024', *Sunday Times*, 5 July 2024

75. Adam Bienkov, 'Rishi Sunak Takes Staged Election Questions from Conservative Councillors Posing as Ordinary Voters', *Byline Times*, 23 May 2024

76. Nick Sommerlad, 'EXCLUSIVE: Four Tory MPs who made £5.4million selling taxpayer-funded second homes won't say if they paid tax', *Mirror*, 13 May 2024

77. Henry Zeffman and Becky Morton, 'Starmer accuses Sunak of lying about Labour tax plans', BBC News, 5 June 2024

78. Henry Zeffman and Becky Morton, 'Top official's letter casts doubt on Tory tax claim', 5 June 2024

79. Eleanor Lawson, 'Ex-Tory MP not standing due to "party bullying"', BBC News, 7 June 2024

80. Alisha Rahaman Sarkar, 'Sir Philip Davies latest Tory caught up in gambling row "after betting £8,000 against himself"', *Independent*, 27 June 2024; Rowena Mason and Rob Davies, 'Tory MP Philip Davies takes £500-an-hour job at slot machine company', *Guardian*, 8 May 2024

81. Michael Goodier and Carmen Aguilar García, 'Companies linked to Tory donors given £8.4bn in public contracts since 2016', *Guardian*, 27 June 2024

82. Frank Herbert, *Chapterhouse: Dune*, Gollancz, 1985

83. Michael Savage, 'Just one in 100 Tory MPs came from a working-class job, new study shows', *Guardian*, 24 June 2022

84. Elise Uberoi, Carl Baker, Richard Cracknell, Grahame Allen, Nerys Roberts, Cassie Barton, Georgina Sturge, Shadi Danechi, Rachael Harker, Paul Bolton, Rod McInnes, Chris Watson, Noel Dempsey, Lukas Audickas, 'General Election 2019: results and analysis', Second Edition, House of Commons Library, 28 January 2020

85. Elise Uberoi, 'Turnout at elections', House of Commons Library, 10 January 2023

86. Various authors, 'What if everyone had voted in the EU referendum?', Politics and Society, UK in a Changing Europe, 28 July 2016

87. D. Clark, 'Voter turnout in general elections and in the Brexit referendum in the United Kingdom from 1918 to 2024', Statista, 5 July 2024

88. 'Compulsory voting around the world', The Electoral Commission, June 2006

89. Replace the House of Lords campaign, Electoral Reform Society, no date

90. John Lubbock, 'The Absent Lords: 13% of Peers Rarely or Never Attend', *Byline Times*, 9 March 2022

91. Peter Walker, 'Evgeny Lebedev's 1% attendance makes him among least active in House of Lords', *Guardian*, 19 December 2022

92. House of Lords: Costs, https://www.parallelparliament.co.uk/question/HL10170/house-of-lords-costs, Parallel Parliament, 13 September 2023

93. Trades Union Congress, x.com/The_TUC/status/1755994687482007726, X, 9 February 2024

94. Dan Neidle, 'Carried interest – the £600m loophole that doesn't actually exist', Tax Policy Associates, 10 March 2023

95. List of prime ministers of the United Kingdom by education, Wikipedia, no date

96. Iain Overton, 'Etonocracy: How One Public School Came to Dominate Public Life', *Byline Times*, 20 August 2021

97. 'Majority of Rishi Sunak's new cabinet went to private school', ITV News, 26 October 2022; Sutton Trust Cabinet Analysis 2022 (Rishi Sunak), The Sutton Trust, 26 October 2022

GOOD ORGANISATIONS AND PEOPLE TO FOLLOW

There are many good journalists and organisations in this wonderful country of ours, you probably know the news outlets you enjoy. This list isn't intended to cover the usual suspects, although there's definitely a few in there. Ha.

The list is really that of the journalists, commentators, activists, social media accounts and organisations I have particularly followed and enjoyed in the last couple of years. We may not always agree on all things, but they are passionate, and I hope you'll find following them online gives you a little boost. Some of them you may already know, others maybe not.

As with everything in this book, the purpose is for us to understand more about our political world – it is, after all, the world which governs most of the decisions in our lives.

For anyone not on the list, by all means berate me – believe me there are hundreds of people who are great on social media – I just can't list everyone or it would end up like the Yellow Pages! (Yes, I'm old enough to still refer to that.)

Organisations:

Best For Britain

Website: https://www.bestforbritain.org/

X: @BestForBritain

Byline Times

Website: https://bylinetimes.com/

X: @BylineTimes

Bylines Network

Website: https://bylinesnetwork.co.uk/

X: @BylinesNetwork

Comment Is Freed

Website: https://samf.substack.com/

Democracy For Sale

Website: www.democracyforsale.uk

Every Doctor

Website: https://everydoctor.org.uk/join/

X: @EveryDoctorUK

Fighting Dirty

Website: https://Fightingdirty.Org/

X: @FightDirtyOrg

Full Fact
Website: https://fullfact.org/
X: @Fullfact

Good Law Project
Website: https://goodlawproject.org/
X: @GoodLawProject

Have I Got News For You
X: @haveigotnews

LBC
Website: https://www.lbc.co.uk/
X: @LBC

Led By Donkeys
Website: https://www.ledbydonkeys.org/
X: @ByDonkeys

Liberty
Website: https://www.libertyhumanrights.org.uk/
X: @libertyhq

National Trust
Website: https://www.nationaltrust.org.uk/
X: @nationaltrust

Neighbourhood Watch
Website: https://www.ourwatch.org.uk/
X: @N_Watch

Open and Candid
Website: https://www.openandcandid.com/
X: @OpenCandid

Open Democracy
Website: https://www.opendemocracy.net/en/
X: @openDemocracy

Politics Joe
X: @PoliticsJOE_UK

Private Eye
Website: https://www.private-eye.co.uk/
X: @PrivateEyeNews

Resolution Foundation
Website: https://www.resolutionfoundation.org/
X: @resfoundation

Spotlight On Corruption
Website: https://www.spotlightcorruption.org/
X: @EndcorruptionUK

Stop Funding Hate
Website: https://stopfundinghate.info/
@StopFundingHate

Tax Policy Associates
Website: https://taxpolicy.org.uk/

The London Economic
Website: https://www.thelondoneconomic.com/
X: @LondonEconomic

The Movement Forward / StopTheTories.Vote
Website: https://themovementforward.com/
X: @MVTFWD

The New European
Website: https://www.theneweuropean.co.uk/
X: @TheNewEuropean

The Organized Crime and Corruption Reporting Project
Website: https://www.occrp.org/en
X: @OCCRP

Transparency International UK
Website: https://www.transparency.org.uk/
X: @TransparencyUK

We Own It
Website: https://weownit.org.uk/ X: @We_OwnIt

An A–Z of good people to follow, from journalists, to commentators, to bloggers and activists:

Adam Bienkov @AdamBienkov

Adil Ray OBE @adilray

Alan Rusbridger @arusbridger

Alastair Campbell @campbellclaret

Anushka Asthana @AnushkaAsthana

Armando Iannucci @Aiannucci

Ava Evans @AvaSantina

Beth Rigby @BethRigby

Brian Moore @brianmoore666

Carole Cadwalladr @carolecadwalla

Chris Packham @ChrisGPackham

Cold War Steve @coldwarsteve

Dale Vince @DaleVince

Damian Hastie @DamianHastie

Dan Neidle @DanNeidle

David Conn @david_conn

David Powell @EuropeanPowell

Dr Julia Patterson @JujuliaGrace

Dr Rachel Clarke @doctor_oxford

Elaine Wilcox @elaineWITV

Emily Maitlis @maitlis

Farrukh Younus @implausibleblog

Feargal Sharkey @Feargal_Sharkey

Femi Oluwole @Femi_Sorry

Gabriel Pogrund @Gabriel_Pogrund

Gary Neville @GNev2

George Greenwood @GeorgeGreenwood

George Monbiot @GeorgeMonbiot

Gina Miller @thatginamiller

Hardeep Matharu @Hardeep_Matharu

Harry Yorke @HarryYorke1

Hugh Grant @HackedOffHugh

James Ball @jamesrbuk

James O'Brien @mrjamesob

Jemima Kelly @jemimajoanna

Jemma Forte @jemmaforte

John Cleese @JohnCleese

John Stevens @johnestevens

Jolyon Maugham @JolyonMaugham

Jolyon Rubinstein @JolyonRubs

Jon Sopel @jonsopel

Jonathan Pie @JonathanPieNews

Josh Parry @joshparry

Josh Russell @JoshFwd

Joshua Rozenberg @JoshuaRozenberg

Keiran Pedley @keiranpedley

Larry & Paul @larryandpaul

Leigh Jones @leighsus

Lewis Goodall @lewis_goodall

Marina Purkiss @MarinaPurkiss

Mario Nawfal @MarioNawfal

Martin Lewis @MartinSLewis

Mike Galsworthy @mikegalsworthy

Natasha Devon @_NatashaDevon

Niall Paterson @skynewsniall

Oliver Bullough @OliverBullough

Otto English @Otto_English

Paul Brand @PaulBrandITV

Peter Geoghegan @PeterKGeoghegan

Peter Jukes @peterjukes

Peter Stefanovic @PeterStefanovi2

Pippa Crerar @PippaCrerar

Poppy Wood @poppyeh

Prem Sikka @premnsikka

Professor Alice Roberts @theAliceRoberts

Richard Brookes @RTWbart

Rory Stewart @RoryStewartUK

Russ Jones @RussInCheshire

Russell Scott @RussellScott1

Sam Bright @WritesBright

Sam Coates @SamCoateSky

Sean Adams @seaninsound

Shelagh Fogarty @ShelaghFogarty

Sophy Ridge @SophyRidgeSky

Stefan Simanowitz @StefSimanowitz

Susanna Reid @susannareid100

Tan Smith @supertanakiii

Tom Burgis @tomburgis

Victoria Derbyshire @vicderbyshire

Vivek Trivedi @VivekNTrivedi

Will Hayward @WillHayCardiff

ACKNOWLEDGEMENTS

My thank yous are many.

I've completed this book, which I hope you've enjoyed, in a very short few months. Consequently, there have been many days at home when I haven't been around for normal cheeky conversation – some might say that's a blessing!

So thank you firstly to my son Cameron whose patience puts him into the category of a sci-fi saint; and my daughter Katie who is always totally supportive of everything her daft mother sets out to do. Thank you both.

Love you so much.

I've never written a book like this before – yes, I've written maths books and detox books and sudoku books and many others – but politics?

The last two years have been an exciting and unexpected 'ride' and I've been honestly overwhelmed by the support of so many, not just for me but also for each other, for all of those fighting the good fight.

So, to my publisher Headline, and especially Yvonne Jacob whose beaming smile never falters and whose leadership is inspiring, she has willed me on in the most charming manner: thank you.

To Lindsay Davies, my editor, who is the most organised person in the world and whose sense of what this book set out to be guided me throughout. Thank you, missus.

Thanks as ever to my lovely agent Josh Byrne and the legendary Gordon Wise, both of Curtis Brown . . . I'm so lucky to know you. Thank you for your guidance and resolute support.

Thank you to Neil Reading and Aimée and Millie Stimpson for all your creativity and encouragement. Heck.

To my best friend Jules whom I've missed during the many months of 'lock up' when 'the book' became the priority in my life. To my many friends whom I've missed terribly – don't think you've escaped me though, I'll be back annoying you very soon!

To my 'rock', my PA (and so much more) Karen Cleverley, whom I couldn't survive without.

To my family, my sister Trixie and my brother Anton and my cousins Sian and Kate and many more besides who've put up with my absence from normal family gigs while I've been 'otherwise engaged' over the last year or so. Love you.

To the new people I've met through this political adventure, many of whom are mentioned in the Good Organisations and People to Follow list. You are many and you are wonderful.

To Josh Russell, Sean Adams and James Southern of StopThe-Tories.Vote and The Movement Forward. You're amazing, your passion is exceptional. Thank you. 'Stop The Tories' was our first adventure, I'm sure we will have many more.

To the ace women Marina Purkiss and Jemma Forte of the Trawl podcast who make me laugh uncontrollably, and whose use of the word 'bellend' is superlative.

To Tan and the gang who I hope go on from strength to strength. You have made a huge difference, I hope you know that.

To all the incredible and brave investigative journalists, some of whom are mentioned in these pages, many more in the Good Organisations and People to Follow list. You are quite extraordinary human beings, fearless, with the potential to lose so much and yet you keep going because of your belief in finding the truth and holding those in power to account. Thank God for you all.

To Carole Cadwalladr who is a powerhouse, a one-off, a unique human being. Thank you for your friendship.

To *Byline Times* and Peter Jukes and the team who publish without fear or favour. More power to you.

To Deborah Ross who cracks me up laughing – NCVD is in the diary and you're not getting home before midnight next time, no matter how much you moan about it being past your bedtime!

To the Good Law Project who have, and are, and will be, making such a difference to this country. You're extraordinary and I hope we can carry on working together into the future.

To my friends at ITV and BBC Wales who supported me in the background through a few little bumps in the road, you know who you are, and you're my cyntafs.

To LBC, to Tom and Caroline, Ellie, Connor and all the friends I've made there and the smiles which greet me every Sunday in the office and in the studio. What a powerhouse of a station. Thank you for your faith and unwavering support.

To my friend, the incredible newspaper editor Alison Phillips, what a woman. Thank you.

To those in political parties who have taken into account the heartfelt messages of many of us in the hope that true change can come. I wish you well.

To all those who have trolled me – you give me the oxygen to continue, bless you, if only you knew that your words have the opposite effect to the one you intend. I actually enjoy a little spat! I hope you find peace one day.

But mostly to every single person on social media who has liked or commented or supported each other in this fight. And to everyone who comes up and says hello in the street, on the train, in a café, wherever.

Together we can change things, together we really can make it better. We've proven that to be the case already. Getting rid of the last government was Step One. We have many more challenges ahead but if you believe that we can do it, then we will do it – together.

Thank you.

Time for a little rest for a day or so and then – build me up, buttercup – we'll be back fighting.

Love ya x